RENNIE

COLLECTION
AT WING SANG

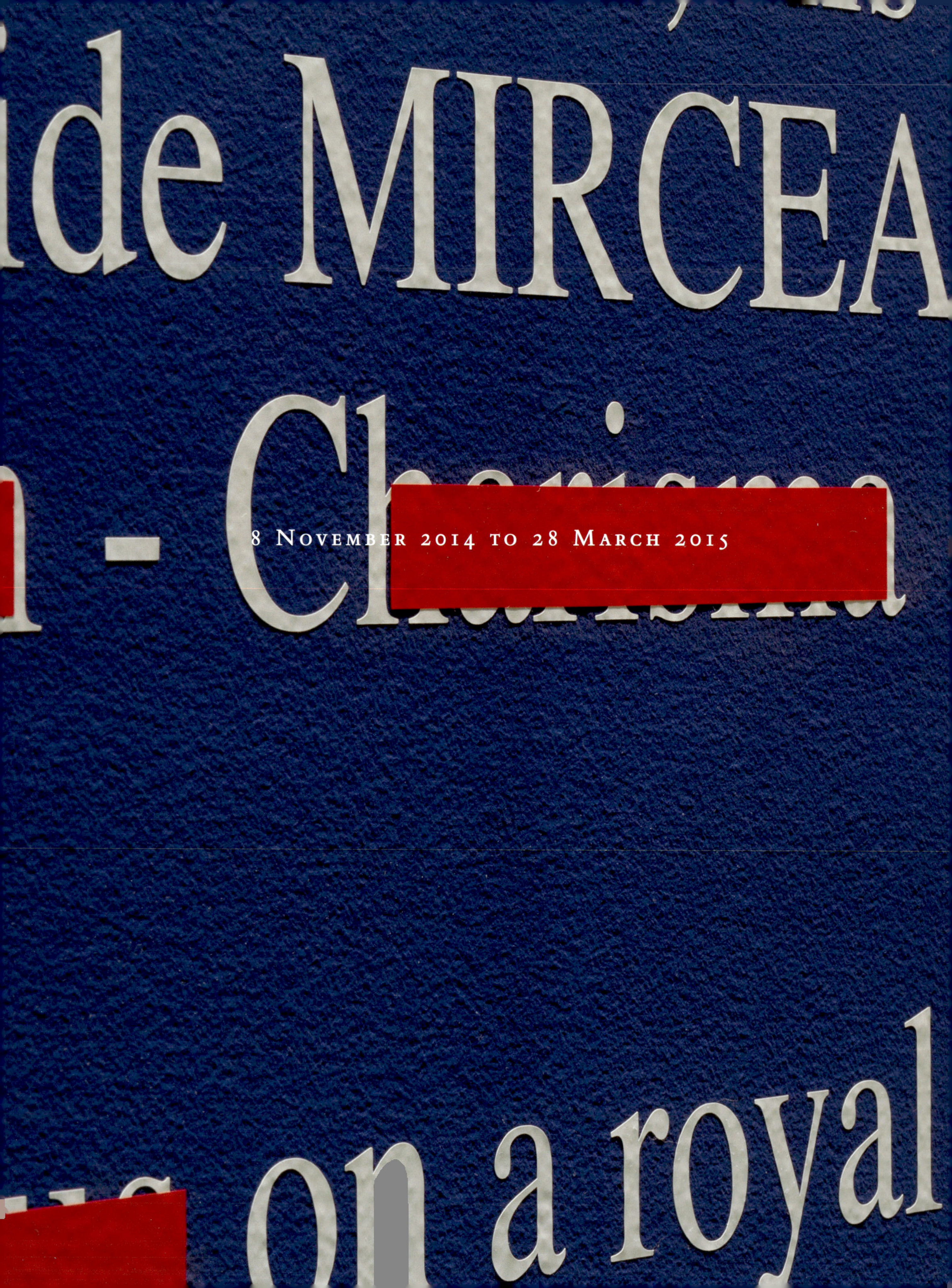

8 November 2014 to 28 March 2015

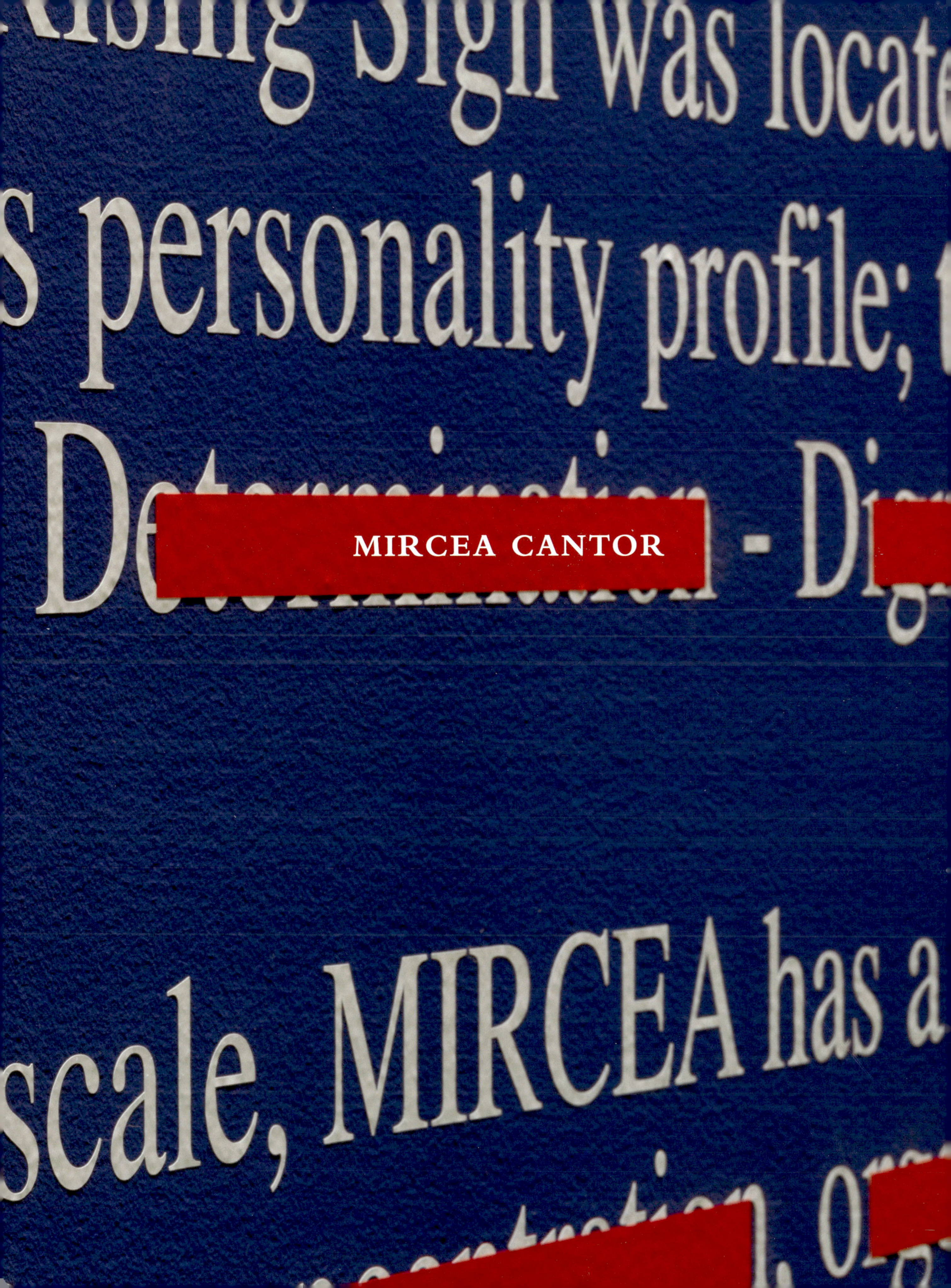
Sign was
personality profile;
MIRCEA CANTOR
scale, MIRCEA has a

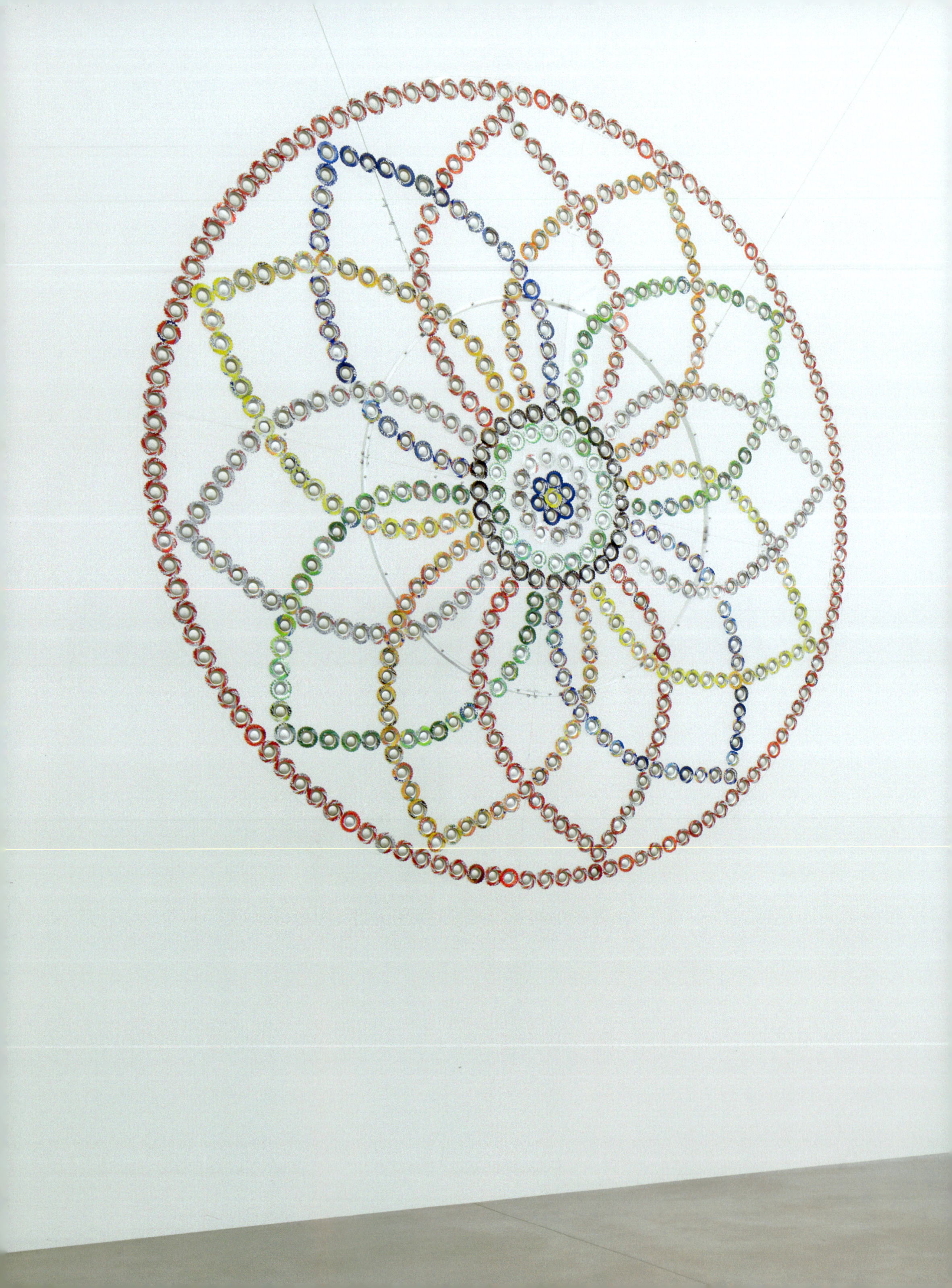

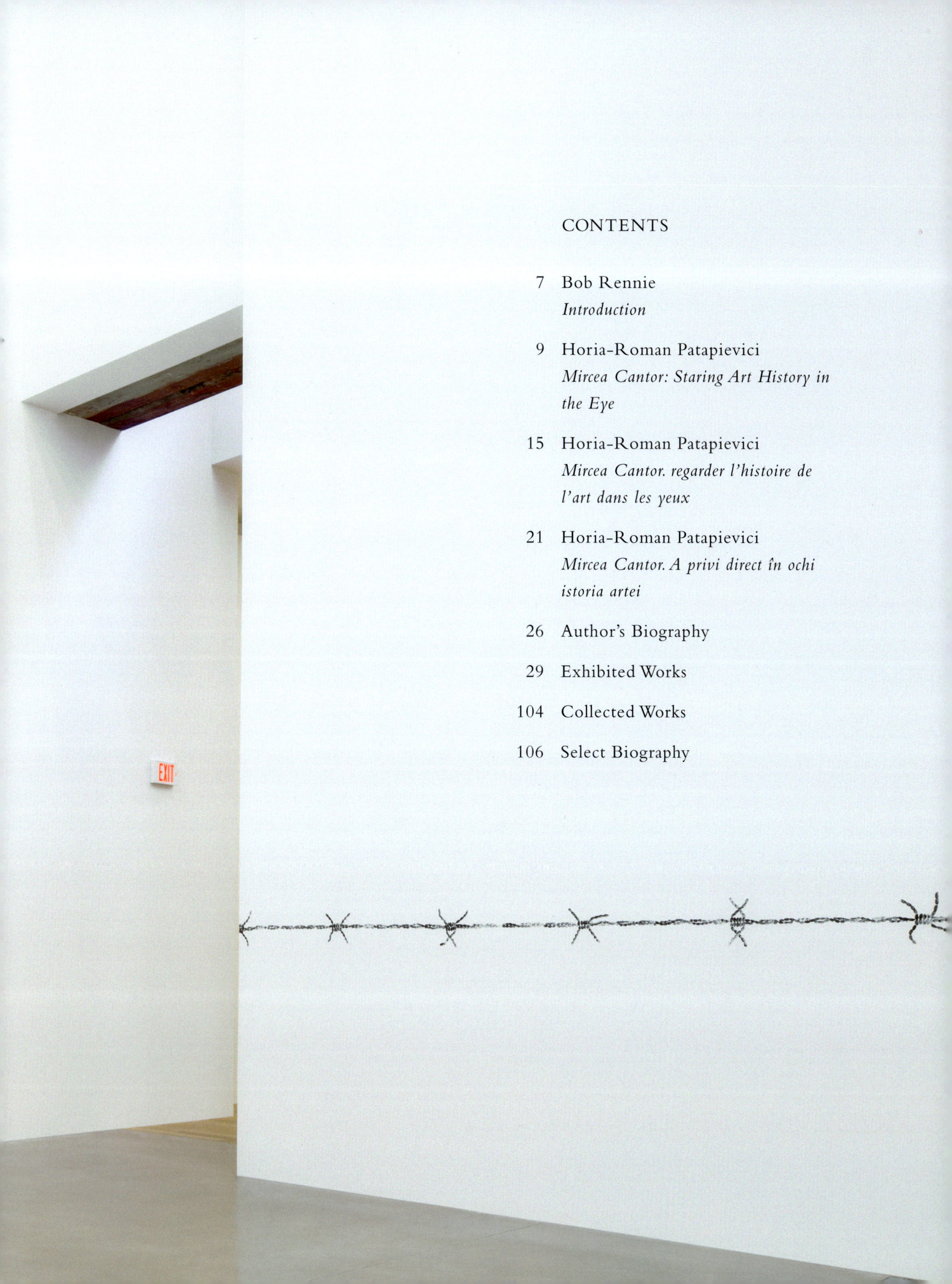

CONTENTS

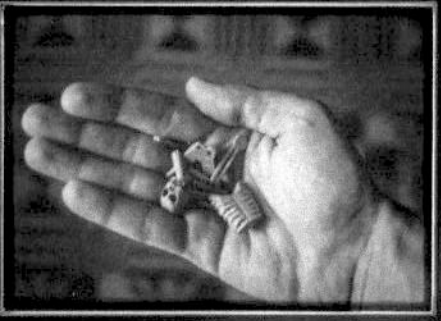

$0 - \infty$, 2004

INTRODUCTION

Bob Rennie

Mircea Cantor is a friend and an artist. We were Mircea's first gallery sale. It was at Yvon Lambert, Paris, in 2002. Carey Fouks and I arrived unannounced in the late afternoon, and the finishing touches, the last strips of red tape that would redact Mircea's "natal chart", were being put on *A fost odata . . . (Once upon a time . . .)* (2002). That simple message of how we edit ourselves – or is it nobody knows me better than I do – would come to occupy an entire wall in my teenage son's bedroom. We eventually also acquired the wedding singer film *The right man at the right place* (2002) from the same show, along with *Double Heads Matches* (2003) and *Deeparture* (2005), a mesmerizing dance where the viewers can place their own life's dance into the film. Who is the wolf? Who is the deer? Who is frightened? Having fun with the film . . . who is the art dealer? Who is the collector? Who is the artist? Look at the protesters in *The Landscape is Changing* (2003) holding up simple mirrors. Pause while you look at the puzzle and the puzzle pieces that are not allowed to fit right now. Mircea's messages are consistent. He takes us to really tough places and lets us deal with those tough places at our own pace.

No work comes into the Rennie Collection that doesn't hold a conversation with other works in the collection. *Rosace* (2007), a spiritual form made of crushed waste, along with *Don't Judge, Filter, Shoot* (2012), are pretty simple. We stop, then we listen. I cannot wait for the day when we install these works next to Yoko Ono's *Mend Piece* (1966/2015) and Mona Hatoum's *Hotspot* (2006). It's pretty simple. Today when one of us has a problem, we all have a problem. I can only hope that my ramble evokes the sensitive heart of Mircea's practice. Whether the collector is the wolf or the deer probably changes day to day depending who is asked. However, one thing I do know is that the collector is merely the custodian. What an amazing journey to have Mircea trust us with the works on the following pages. Thank you, Mircea. To be continued. . . .

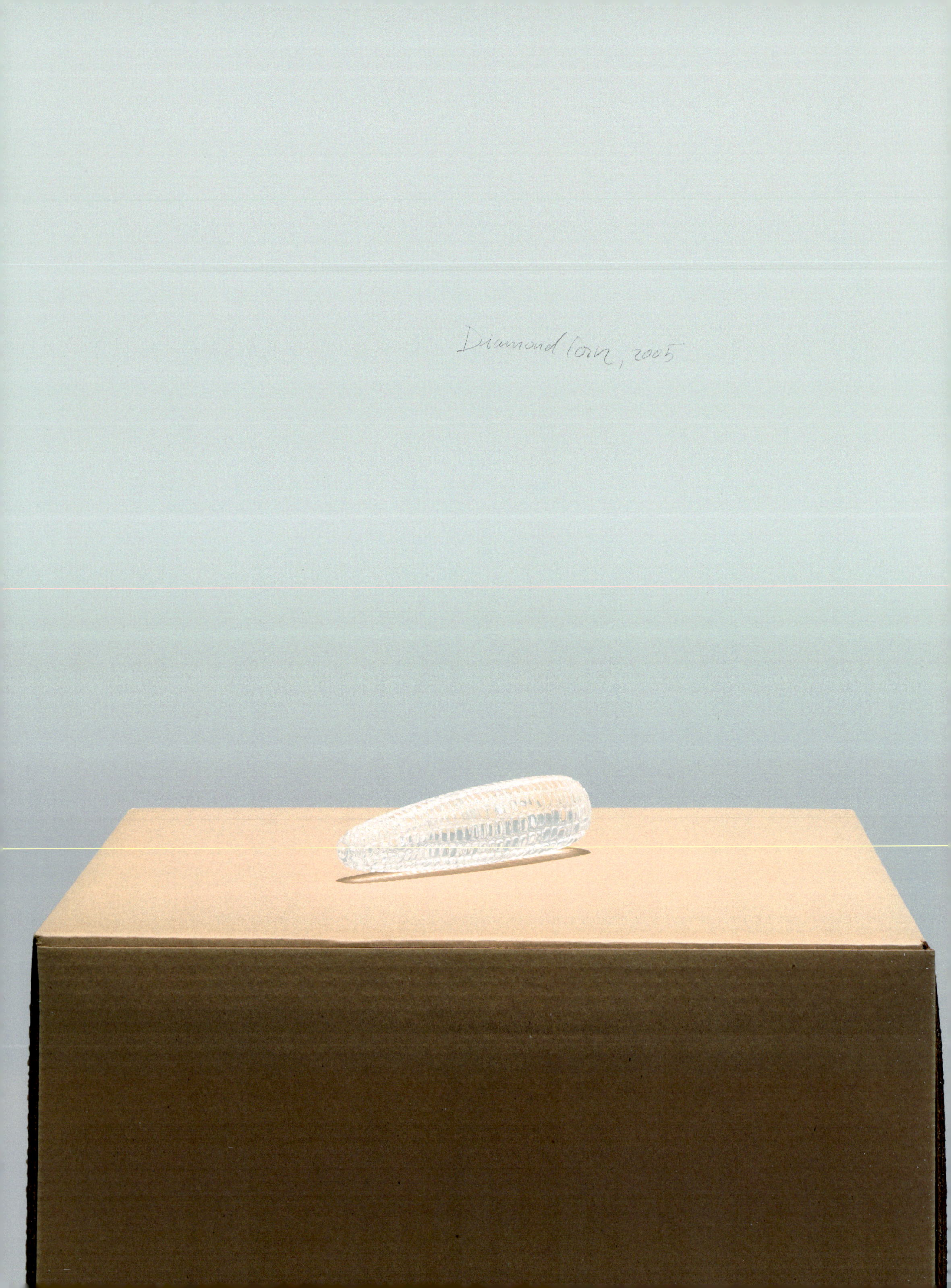
Diamond Corn, 2005

MIRCEA CANTOR: STARING ART HISTORY IN THE EYE

Horia-Roman Patapievici

On discovering an artist, one is keen on figuring out his secret. What one discovers, on figuring it out, is what exactly makes the artist in question an artist in the first place. On discovering a *major* artist, however, what one is keen on is figuring out a way to enter the world he has created. One is not simply satisfied with seeing that world with one's eyes: one yearns to inhabit it as well – one yearns to become a denizen of the world the artist has summoned into being. Whence? From life's potential of being perfect, paradise-like, complete, eternal, all-embracing.

Mircea Cantor is by turns an artist *and* a major artist.

When Cantor is an artist, the keen viewer seeks to comprehend the *punch-line* of his work and the sequence followed by the artist in coming to it. The pursuit is fully rewarding: Cantor the artist is bristling with ingenuity and gimmicks.

When Cantor is a major artist, the keen viewer instinctively shifts his or her attention from the artist's skill to the eerie and contagious awareness of life's perfection inspired by the work. "Inspired" is actually inaccurate: *incorporated* is more to the point, as in amber incorporating in its translucent mass the insect going 200 million years back. The keen viewer yearns to become that insect, to merge entirely with its past life: to become substantively contemporaneous with the perfection of that life turned into eternity. On seeing *Tracking Happiness* (2009) or *Sic transit gloria mundi* (2012), one immediately senses the extraordinary quality of those works, nonetheless perceiving, at the same time, that their beauty is not traditional – it is new, sovereign, enigmatic and triumphant. These works function akin to a vehicle conveying to us, like a drug, the promise of a perfection of life that, though not of this world, is all the same at hand, just as in the perpetually deferred promise "Behold, I come quickly" (*Revelation 22:7*, King James Version) or in the never fully elucidated statement "For the Kingdom of God is already among you" (Luke 17:21).

Beauty is said to be nothing other than the promise of happiness (Stendhal). The beauty of Cantor's best work is, in its turn, a promise of happiness, albeit one that, though built upon the materiality of sensations, is exclusively promised to the mind, to metaphysics, to the religious feeling. On one level of beauty we have works such as *Deeparture* (2005), *The leash of the dog*

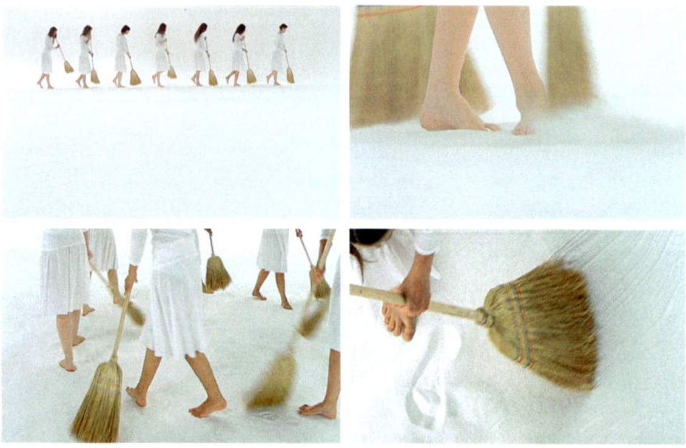

that was longer than its life (2008) or *Zoooooooom* (2007/2009), which are visual reflections on the unfathomable mystery of life, on the competition between life and death or on the geometric order of higher existence. On a second level of beauty we have works such as *I decided not to save the world* (2011), *Wind Orchestra* (2012) or *Vertical Attempt* (2009), representing, in my opinion, the most profound and unsettling visual comments on the famous B 52 fragment left from Heraclitus:

αἰὼν παῖς ἐστι παίζων, πεττεύων• παιδὸς ἡ βασιληίη.[1]

This fragment has been alternately translated as either "Eternity is a child playing, playing checkers; the kingdom belongs to a child", or "Time is a game played beautifully by children" or "Lifetime is a child at play, moving pieces in a game. Kingship belongs to the child." Cantor attains in these works not only depth, but also a sort of *material* perfection of intellectual depth, transfiguring beauty itself: the cold and sovereign beauty enigmatically connected to the fact that our life is not truly our own, save in the instant we are happy or unhappy, and our being happy or unhappy is of no consequence to anyone – neither to the god, nor to God, nor to the playing child. We are perfect, yet our perfection is of a kind that has already sentenced us all to death – that's what Cantor tells us with the beauty of his works.

We enter the retrospective Cantor curated in Bucharest – *Q.E.D.*[2] – through the work *More cheeks than slaps* (2011), telling us the story of the world from two perspectives: the moral one – in the world, there are more cheeks to slap than hands willing to slap them (our deposits of humility and submission are greater than our neighbour's desire to harm us) – and the hermeneutic one – in decoding the message one has to include both the mechanism of inversion (one has to look into the mirror in order to understand the signs) and the recipient's presence. One can only read the message in the mirror where, simultaneously, one can see oneself; for one can only understand when one is in the foreground; and as long as the flesh of *one's own* body does not stand in the way of the light, the light of the world fails to illuminate anything. This technique and its associated metaphysical meaning are characteristic of Cantor and occur simultaneously in his art.

Mircea Cantor
Tracking Happiness, 2009
production still
Super 16 mm film transferred on HDCAM
Sound: Adrian Gagiu
11 minutes
Courtesy the artist; Galerie Yvon Lambert, Paris; and Dvir Gallery, Tel Aviv

Radu Petrescu, a Romanian author who practised his art starting from a literal metaphysics of literature, claimed that Homer was watching the world he described from its own height. When describing it, he placed himself *exactly* level with the things he was facing, *accurately* adjusting his height to theirs. Thus, by watching objects from the height they reached, Homer was placing himself not only opposite them, but also within the horizon from which they themselves would have regarded the world, had they been endowed with sight. In other words, Homer did see them the way they were – that is, the way they would have seen themselves, had they been watching themselves, as making up exactly the world where they would occupy their same exact places, exactly as they were. Radu Petrescu claimed that the enduring attraction people have felt for Homer over the centuries is entirely due to the fact that, through his art, people who can no longer look the world squarely in the face have the opportunity to see what a world watched from its *exact* height looks like.

As regards the attempt to reject the symbolical (as a form of looking at the world from above), contemporary art walks in Homer's tracks: its quest consists in identifying with utmost accuracy the location allowing the art recipient to see the world closest to its natural height. Among contemporary artists, through some of his most enigmatic, most beautiful and most accurately exquisite works (note Cantor's accuracy, it is truly remarkable!), Mircea Cantor appears to have best followed Homer's scent – at least the Homer that Radu Petrescu had in mind.

Rarely have I experienced with more intensity the feeling that I can see the world's enigma from the exact height it occupies naturally, than on watching some of Mircea Cantor's works. Never is this artist's force more visible, in all its liberty and sovereignty, than when he 'copies' a model from the past. In 1998, Mircea Cantor photographed his girlfriend in the exact position Gustave Courbet's model sat for the painting *L'Origine du monde* (1866). In Cluj, where Cantor displayed the work in front of his professors, they were scandalized by the technique. It is a tremendously powerful photograph: strangely enough, comparable in force to the original painting. Yet somehow more unsettling than the painting. Why? In 2009, Cantor reiterated the technique: he photographed three women in a montage reproducing the attitudes and setting of the characters in William Blake's 1796 engraving *Europe Supported by Africa and America*. When compared to the photographic

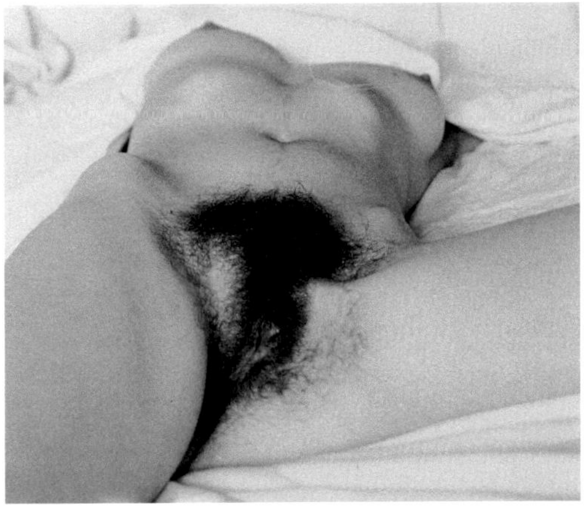

Mircea Cantor
L'origine du monde – after Courbet, 1998
black-and-white gelatin print
$11\frac{13}{16} \times 14\frac{3}{16}$ inches
(30 × 36 cm)
Courtesy of the artist

accuracy of the replica, amazing in itself, the original appears washed out and, what's more, out of focus. Cantor creates, through his replicas, a hyperreality effect, on the one hand, and, on the other, a 'reality-shift' effect. His replica is more real than the object from which it set out; and that's exactly why his replica tends to abolish its object. Both Blake and Courbet are abolished in Cantor's replicas.

Cantor's technique, however, does not fall under the heading of the (already traditional) multiplication of artistic forms, starting from a particular artefact in art history. There is something *else* he does: he dislodges the notion of the original's reality, shifting it elsewhere. Where? Courbet's reality was located in the area of naturalistic reproduction, Blake's in the symbolical scheme; Cantor's replica shifts reality from the naturalistic and the symbolical into the literal. The literal is, by and large, the technique by means of which the moderns represent objects when they want to reproduce them *from their exact* natural height. Through his replicas, Cantor carries out an interpretation of artistic originals from the perspective of seeing the world's literalness. Through his images, Cantor restores literality to the world.

Therefore, in its triumph, Cantor's talent yields works whose beauty resides in their capacity of transporting the viewer into the world's literality – and it is there, in the world of its literality, since the letter is God's since the world's first morning, that the splendour, the miracle and the paradise are to be found.

1 Quoted by Hippolytus, *Refutation of all heresies*, IX, 9, 4 (printed in the Diels-Kranz edition as "fragment B 52").

2 MNAC [National Museum of Contemporary Art], 10 April 2013–10 April 2014.

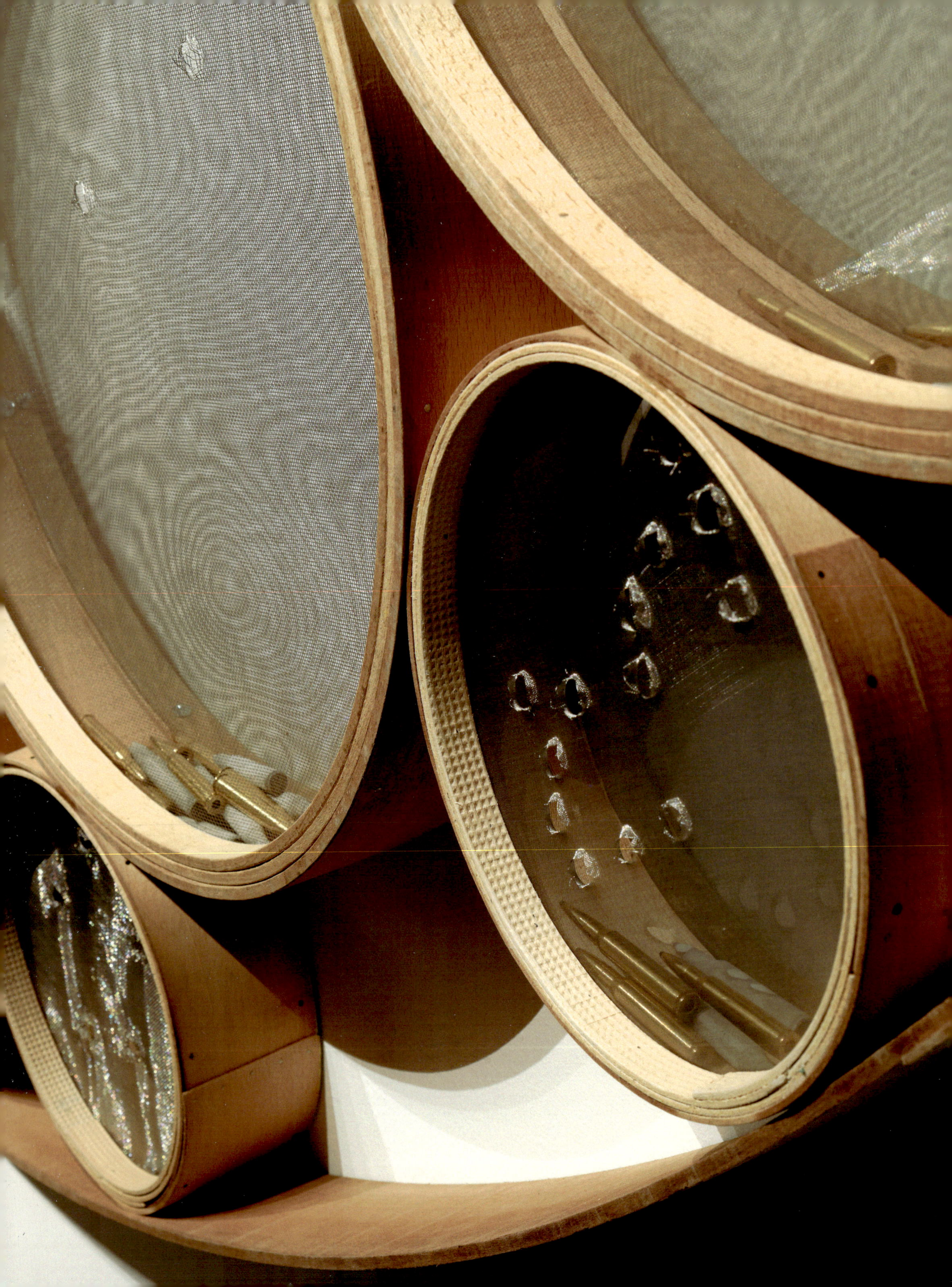

MIRCEA CANTOR. REGARDER L'HISTOIRE DE L'ART DANS LES YEUX

Horia-Roman Patapievici

Quand on découvre un artiste, on cherche à percer son secret ; en arrivant au but, ce que l'on découvre, c'est pourquoi l'artiste est *un* artiste. Quand on découvre un *grand* artiste, ce que l'on cherche à savoir est comment entrer dans le monde qu'il a créé ; et l'on ne se contente pas à voir ce monde de ses yeux, on voudrait y habiter, aussi – devenir un habitant du monde que l'artiste a fait venir au monde. D'où ? De la possibilité de la vie d'être parfaite, paradisiaque, complète, éternelle, sans aucun reste.

Mircea Cantor est parfois un artiste, mais parfois il est un grand artiste.

Quant Cantor est un artiste, celui qui regarde attentivement cherche à comprendre le *hic* de son œuvre, ainsi que la façon dont l'artiste l'a réalisé. Il ne sera pas déçu : l'artiste Cantor est plein d'ingéniosités et autres trucs.

Quand Cantor est un grand artiste, celui qui regarde attentivement déplace instinctivement son attention du savoir-faire de l'artiste vers un étrange et contagieux sentiment de perfection de la vie, que l'œuvre lui inspire. En fait, « inspire » est inexact : que l'œuvre *incorpore*, tel l'ambre qui incorpore, dans son or, l'insecte d'il y a deux cent millions d'années. Celui qui regarde attentivement voudrait devenir cette insecte, s'unir à sa vie passée : il veut devenir, substantiellement, contemporain de la perfection de cette vie muée en éternité. Quand on voit *Tracking happiness* (2009) ou *Sic transit gloria mundi* (2012), l'on sent tout de suite la qualité extraordinaire des œuvres, mais l'on perçoit, en même temps, aussi le fait que leur beauté n'en est pas une traditionnelle, sinon nouvelle, souveraine, énigmatique et triomphale : elle fonctionne comme un véhicule à l'aide duquel on nous transmet, semblable à une drogue, la promesse d'une perfection de la vie qui, tout en n'étant pas d'ici, serait pourtant à la portée de tous. Comme dans la promesse toujours ajournée « Et voici. Je viens bientôt » (*Apocalypse*, 22, 7), ou dans l'affirmation jamais complètement élucidée « le Règne de Dieu est parmi vous » ou « au milieu de vous » (*Luc*, 17, 21).

On avait dit que la beauté est une promesse de bonheur (Stendhal). La beauté des meilleures œuvres de Cantor est elle aussi une promesse de bonheur, mais une promesse qui, quoique fondée sur la matérialité des sensations, n'est faite qu'à l'esprit, à la métaphysique, au sentiment religieux. A un premier niveau de beauté, il s'agit d'œuvres comme *Deeparture* (2005), *The leash of the dog that was longer than its life* (2008) ou bien *Zooooom* (2007/2009), qui sont autant de réflexions visuelles sur le mystère insondable de la vie, sur la concurrence entre la vie et la mort ou sur l'ordre géométrique des existences supérieures.

A un deuxième niveau de beauté, nous avons à faire à des œuvres comme « I decided not to save the world » (2011), *Wind Orchestra* (2012) ou *Vertical Attempt* (2009), qui représentent, à mon avis, les plus profondes et troublantes commentaires visuels au fameux fragment B 52 qui nous reste des textes de Héraclite :

αἰὼν παῖς ἐστι παίζων, πεττεύων• παιδὸς ἡ βασιληίη. [1]

Ce fragment a été traduit soit comme « C'est un enfant qui s'amuse à jouer aux dames : souveraineté d'un enfant (Léon Robin) », soit par « L'Éternel est un enfant qui joue à la *pettie* ; la royauté est à un enfant », soit par « La vie est un enfant qui joue, qui déplace les pièces sur l'échiquier : royauté d'un enfant. » (Giorgio Colli). Cantor touche dans ces œuvres-ci non seulement à la profondeur, mais aussi à une sorte de perfection *matérielle* de la profondeur intellectuelle, qui transfigure jusqu'à la beauté : cette beauté souveraine et froide, mystérieusement liée au fait que notre vie ne nous appartient que dans la respiration qui nous est coupée lorsque nous sommes heureux ou malheureux, et de cette chose, que nous sommes tels, à personne n'importe – ni aux dieux, ni à Dieu, ni à l'enfant qui joue. Nous sommes parfaits, mais c'est une perfection qui nous a déjà condamnés, tous, à mort – c'est ce que Cantor nous dit par la beauté de ses œuvres.

Dans l'exposition rétrospective que Cantor a organisée à Bucarest sous le titre *Q.E.D.*,[2] on entrait à travers l'œuvre *More cheeks than slaps* (2011), qui nous raconte l'histoire du monde depuis deux perspectives : la perspective morale – il y a au monde plusieurs joues à gifler que de gifles à donner (notre réserve d'humilité et de servitude est plus grande que le désir de nos semblables de nous faire mal), respectivement la perspective herméneutique – dans le déchiffrement du message il faut inclure aussi bien le mécanisme de l'inversion (on doit regarder dans un miroir afin de reconnaître les signes), que la présence du récepteur : on peut lire le message seulement dans un miroir ou l'on est simultanément reflété, car on ne peut pas comprendre sans être soi-même au premier

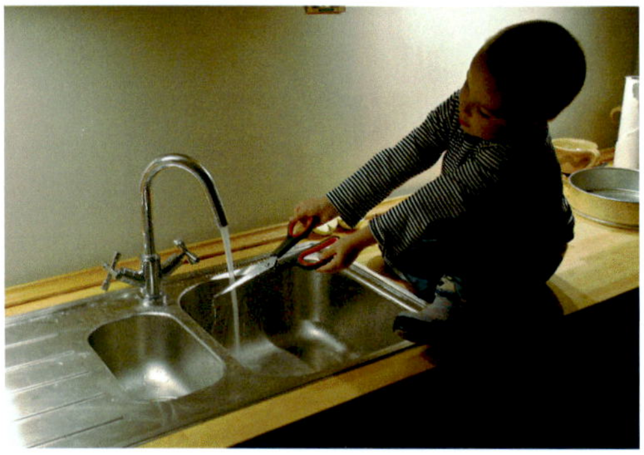

Mircea Cantor
Vertical Attempt, 2009
DVD, colour, 1 sec loop
Edition of 6
Courtesy the artist

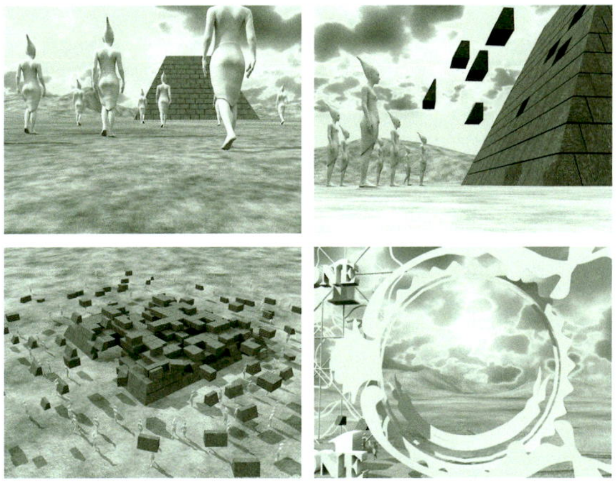

Mircea Cantor
Zoooooom, 2006–2009
animation film, 02:47
Courtesy of the artist

plan ; et si la chair de ton corps à toi n'est pas posée à contre-jour, le jour du monde n'éclaire rien. Ce procédé *technique* et ce sens *métaphysique* sont typiques pour Cantor et sont simultanément présentes dans son art.

Radu Petrescu, un écrivain roumain qui fonde son œuvre sur une métaphysique littérale de la littérature, prétendait qu'Homère regardait le monde qu'il décrivait précisément de la hauteur de ce dernier. Quand il le décrivait, il se mettait exactement en face des choses dont il était question, se situant à leur précise hauteur. Ainsi, les regardant de la hauteur à laquelle elles se trouvaient, Homer se situait soi-même non seulement devant les choses du monde, mais à l'intérieur de l'horizon dans lequel ces choses auraient pu regarder à leur tour le monde. Autrement dit, Homère voyait les choses du monde telles qu'elles étaient – c'est-à-dire telles qu'elles, les choses, se seraient vues elles-mêmes, si elles avaient pu se regarder, comme composantes du monde où elles se trouvaient précisément, telles qu'elles s'y trouvaient. Radu Petrescu soutenait que l'attraction éternelle que le monde, le long des siècles, a eue envers Homère provient justement du fait que, à travers son art, les gens qui ne savent plus comment regarder le monde dans les yeux ont la possibilité de voir un monde regardé précisément de son hauteur.

Pour ce qui est de la tentative de refuser le symbolique (comme façon de regarder le monde du haut vers le bas), l'art contemporain est sur les traces d'Homère : sa recherche consiste en l'identification la plus correcte de l'endroit depuis lequel le récepteur de l'art peut voir le monde le plus proche de la hauteur naturelle de ce dernier. Parmi les artistes contemporains, par certaines de ses œuvres les plus énigmatiques, les plus belles et les plus précisément réalisées (attention à la précision de Cantor, elle est remarquable !), Mircea Cantor semble suivre le mieux Homère, du moins – le Homère dont parlait Radu Petrescu.

J'ai rarement éprouvé ce sentiment, aussi fort, de pouvoir regarder l'énigme du monde précisément depuis la hauteur à laquelle elle se situe, comme lorsque j'ai regardé certaines des œuvres de Mircea Cantor. La force de cet artiste n'est jamais aussi visible, dans la plénitude de sa liberté et de sa souveraineté, que lorsqu'il « copie » un modèle du passé. En 1998, Mircea Cantor a photographié son amie exactement dans la position que Gustave Courbet avait imposée à son modèle pour en faire le tableau *L'Origine du monde* (1866). A Cluj, où Cantor avait présenté ce travail à ses professeurs, cela a fait scandale. C'est une photographie particulièrement forte : étrangement, sa force est comparable à celle du tableau. Mais, en un certain sens, elle est plus inquiétante que le tableau. Pourquoi ? En 2009, Cantor a repris le procédé : il a photographié trois femmes, dans un montage qui reproduisait l'attitude et le décor de la gravure *Europe supported by Africa and America*, composée par William Blake en 1796. Face à la précision photographique extraordinaire de la réplique, l'original semble effacé et, qui plus est, il manque de clarté. Cantor créé par ses répliques un effet de hyperréalité, d'une part, et d'autre – de « déplacement » de la réalité. Sa réplique est plus réelle que l'objet duquel elle est partie ; et, justement à cause de cela, sa réplique tend à abolir son objet. Blake et Courbet sont abolis dans les répliques de Cantor.

Mais le procédé de Cantor ne s'inscrit pas dans la (déjà traditionnelle) multiplication des formes artistiques partant d'un artefact consacré par l'histoire de l'art. Il fait autre chose, *aussi* : il disloque la notion de réalité de l'original, la déplaçant vers un ailleurs. Vers où ? La réalité de Courbet se situait dans la reproduction naturaliste ; celle de Blake – dans le schéma symbolique. La réplique de Cantor déplace la réalité du naturalisme et du symbolique dans le littéral. Or, le littéral est le procédé par lequel les modernes représentent les objets lorsqu'ils veulent les reproduire *précisément à* leur hauteur naturelle. Par ses répliques, Cantor réalise une interprétation des originaux artistiques en essayant de voir le monde dans sa littéralité. Par ses images, Cantor redonne au monde sa littéralité.

Et c'est pourquoi, lorsqu'il triomphe, le talent de Cantor produit des œuvres dont la beauté provient de leur capacité d'emmener celui qui les regarde à l'intérieur de la littéralité du monde. Là-bas, dans le monde de sa littéralité, car la lettre appartient à Dieu dès le premier matin du monde, se trouvent la splendeur, le miracle et le paradis – dont l'art de Cantor en témoigne.

1 Cité par Hippolyte, *Réfutation des toutes les hérésies*, IX, 9, 4 (repris dans l'édition Diels-Kranz comme « le fragment B 52 »).

2 MNAC [Musée National d'Art Contemporain], 10 avril 2013–10 avril 2014.

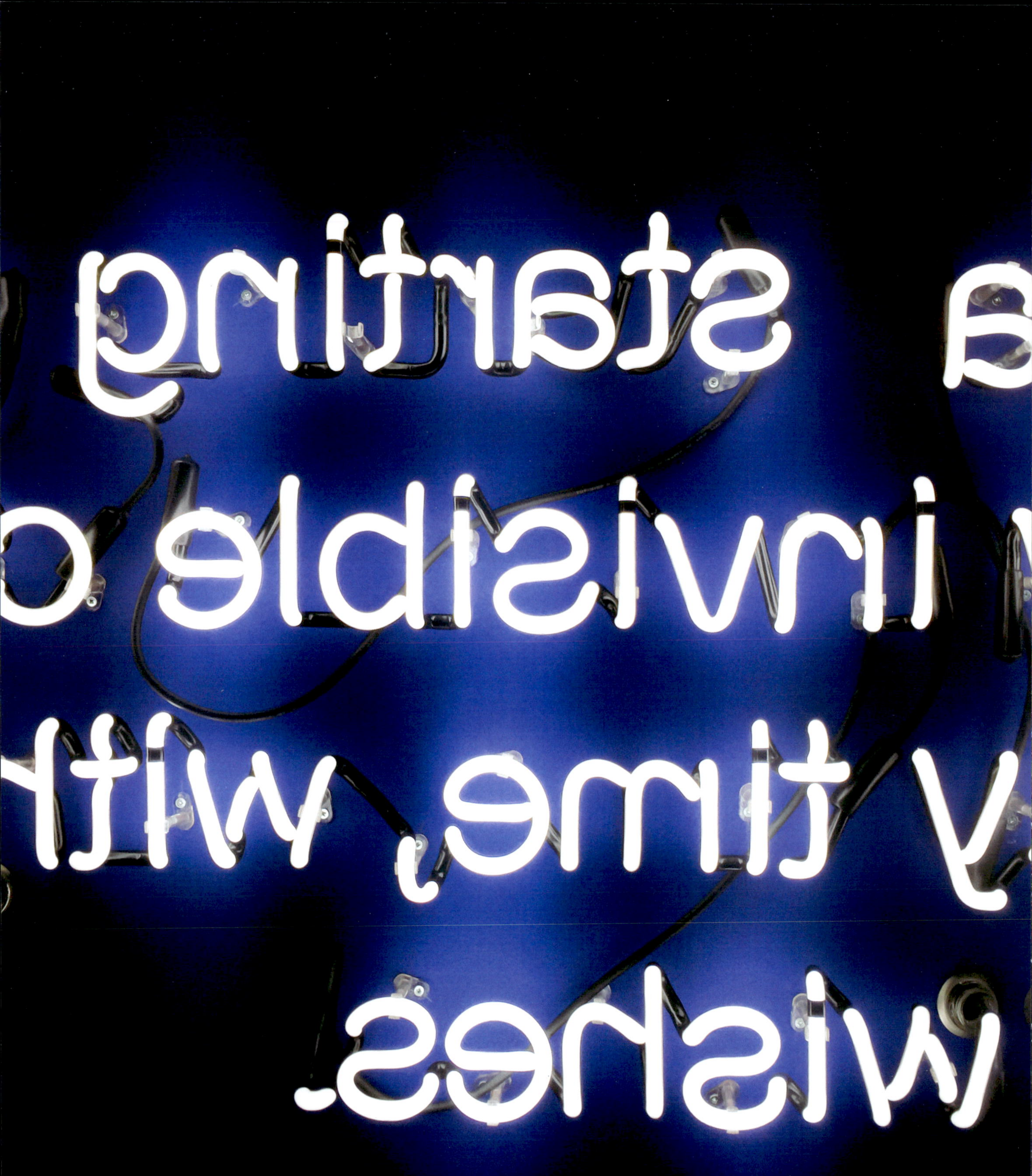
starting
invisible
time,
wishes.

MIRCEA CANTOR. A PRIVI DIRECT ÎN OCHI ISTORIA ARTEI

Horia-Roman Patapievici

Cînd descoperi un artist, cauți să-i afli secretul; ce descoperi, cînd l-ai aflat, este de ce artistul e *un* artist. Cînd descoperi un *mare* artist, ceea ce cauți să afli este cum se poate ajunge în lumea creată de el; și nu te mulțumești numai să o vezi cu ochii lui: vrei să și locuiești în ea – vrei să devii locuitorul lumii pe care artistul a scos-o la iveală. De unde? Din posibilitatea vieții de a fi perfectă, paradiziacă, completă, eternă, fără rest.

Mircea Cantor e uneori artist, alteori e un mare artist.

Cînd Cantor e artist, privitorul atent caută să înțeleagă *poanta* lucrării și felul în care artistul a realizat-o. Nu va fi dezamăgit: artistul Cantor e plin de ingeniozități și trucuri.

Cînd Cantor este un mare artist, privitorul atent își mută instinctiv atenția de la meșteșugul artistului la un straniu și contagios sentiment de perfecțiune a vieții, pe care lucrarea i-o inspiră. De fapt, e inexact spus "inspiră": o încoporează, așa cum chihlimbarul încorporează în ambra sa galbenă gîza de acum două sute de milioane de ani. Privitorul atent vrea să devină acea gîză, să se facă una cu viața ei trecută: vrea să devină în chip substanțial contemporan cu perfecțiunea acelei vieți devenită eternitate. Cînd vezi *Tracking Hapiness* (2009) sau *Sic transit gloria mundi* (2012) simți imediat calitatea extraordinară a lucrărilor, dar percepi, în același timp, și că frumusețea lor nu e cea tradițională, e una nouă, suverană, enigmatică și triumfătoare: funcționează ca un vehicul prin care ni se transmite, ca un drog, promisiunea unei perfecțiuni a vieții care deși nu e de aici, e totuși la îndemînă, exact ca în promisiunea mereu amînată "Iată, Eu vin curînd" (*Apocalipsa* 22, 7) și în afirmația niciodată pe de-a-ntregul elucidată "Împărăția e printre voi" (*Luca* 17, 21).

S-a spus că frumusețea e o promisiune de fericire (Stendhal). Frumusețea celor mai bune lucrări ale lui Cantor este și ea o promisiune de fericire, dar e una care deși e construită pe materialitatea senzațiilor nu e promisă decît minții, metafizicii, sentimentului religios. La un prim nivel de frumusețe, avem lucrări precum *Deeparture* (2005), *The leash of the dog that was longer than its life* (2008) ori *Zooooooom* (2007/2009), care sunt reflecții vizuale asupra misterului insondabil al vieții, al concurenței dintre viață și moarte ori asupra ordinii geometrice a existențelor superioare.

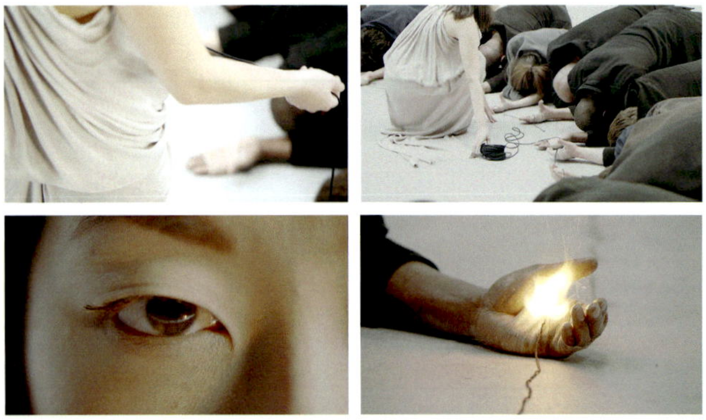

La un al doilea nivel de frumusețe, avem lucrări precum *I decided not to save the world* (2011), *Wind Orchestra* (2012) ori *Vertical Attempt* (2009) care reprezintă, după părerea mea, cele mai profunde și mai tulburătoare comentarii vizuale la faimosul fragment B 52 rămas de la Heraclit:

αἰὼν παῖς ἐστι παίζων, πεττεύων• παιδὸς ἡ βασιληίη.[1]

Acest fragment a fost tradus cînd "Eternity is a child playing, playing checkers; the kingdom belongs to a child", cînd "Time is a game played beautifully by children" ori "Lifetime is a child at play, moving pieces in a game. Kingship belongs to the child." Cantor atinge în aceste lucrări nu doar profunzimea, ci un soi de perfecțiune *materială* a profunzimii intelectuale, care transfigurează și frumusețea: acea frumusețe suverană și rece care e în chip enigmatic legată de faptul că viața noastră nu devine a noastră decît în respirația care ni se taie atunci cînd suntem fericiți ori nefericiți, iar de acest lucru, că suntem cum suntem, nu îi pasă nimănui – nici Zeului, nici Dumnezeului, nici copilului care se joacă. Suntem perfecți, dar e o perfecțiune care ne-a condamnat deja pe toți la moarte – asta ne spune Cantor cu frumusețea lucrărilor sale.

În expoziția retrospectivă pe care Cantor a organizat-o la București sub titlul Q.E.D.[2] se intra prin lucrarea *More cheeks than slaps* (2011), care ne spune povestea lumii din două perspective: perspectiva morală – pe lume sunt mai multe obrazuri de lovit decît palme dispuse să lovească (rezerva noastră de umilință și servitute e mai mare decît dorința semenilor noștri de a ne face rău); și perspectiva hermeneutică – în descifrarea mesajului trebuie incluse atît mecanismul inversiunii (trebuie să te uiți în oglindă ca să înțelegi semnele), cît și prezența receptorului: poți citi mesajul numai în acea oglindă în care, simultan, te vezi și pe tine; căci nu poți înțelege decît cu tine în prim plan; iar dacă nu e carnea trupului *tău* în calea luminii, lumina lumii nu luminează nimic. Acest procedeu *tehnic* și acest înțeles *metafizic* sunt tipice pentru Cantor și sunt simultan prezente în arta lui.

Radu Petrescu, un autor român care și-a scris literatura pornind de la o metafizică literală a literaturii, pretindea că Homer privea lumea pe care o descria exact de la înălțimea ei. Cînd o descria, se punea *exact* în dreptul lucrurilor aflate în fața sa, situîndu-se *exact* la înălțimea lor. Astfel,

Mircea Cantor
Sic Transit Gloria Mundi, 2012
production still
HD film, colour, sound: semantron of Putna Monastery
04:06
Courtesy of the artist; Galerie Yvon Lambert, Paris; Dvir Gallery, Tel Aviv; and Magazzino, Roma

privindu-le de la înălțimea la care se găsesc, Homer se situa el însuși nu doar în dreptul lor, ci în orizontul în care chiar ele, dacă ar fi putut vedea, ar fi privit lumea. Homer, altfel spus, le vedea așa cum sunt – adică așa cum s-ar fi văzut ele însele, dacă s-ar fi putut privi pe ele, ca alcătuind exact lumea în care ele s-ar afla exact acolo unde sunt, în felul în care sunt. Radu Petrescu susținea că atracția nepieritoare pe care lumea, de-a lungul secolelor, a avut-o față de Homer provine tocmai din faptul că, prin arta acestuia, oamenii care nu mai știu să privească lumea exact în față au posibilitatea să vadă cum arată o lume văzută *exact* de la înălțimea ei.

În privința încercării de a refuza simbolicul (ca formă de a privi lumea de sus în jos) ori metaforizarea (ca formă de a privi lumea de jos în sus), arta contemporană e pe urmele lui Homer: căutarea ei constă în a identifica cît mai corect locul din care receptorul artei poate vedea lumea cît mai aproape de înălțimea ei naturală. Între artiștii contemporani, prin cîteva dintre lucrările sale cele mai enigmatice, mai frumoase și mai precis realizate (atenție la *precizia* lui Cantor, e remarcabilă!), Mircea Cantor pare a-i fi luat cel mai bine urma lui Homer – cel puțin a acelui Homer de care vorbea Radu Petrescu.

Rareori am avut mai puternic sentimentul că pot vedea enigma lumii exact de la înălțimea la care ea, în mod natural, se situează, ca atunci cînd am privit unele din lucrările lui Mircea Cantor. Forța acestui artist nu e niciodată mai vizibilă, în toată libertatea și suveranitatea ei, ca atunci cînd "copiază" un model din trecut. În 1998, Mircea Cantor și-a fotografiat prietena exact în poziția în care a pus-o Gustave Courbet să îi pozeze pe femeia care a devenit subiectul tabloului *L'Origine du monde* (1866). La Cluj, unde Cantor și-a prezentat lucrarea profesorilor săi, procedeul a scandalizat. E o fotografie de mare forță: în mod straniu, de o forță comparabilă cu a tabloului. Dar, cumva, mai neliniștitoare decît tabloul. De ce? În 2009, Cantor a reluat procedeul: a fotografiat trei femei, într-un montaj care reproducea atitudinea și decorul personajelor din gravura *Europe Supported by Africa and America*, compusă de William Blake în 1796. Față de precizia fotografică a replicii, care e uluitoare, originalul pare șters și, mai mult, lipsit de claritate. Cantor creează prin replicile sale un efect de hiperrealitate, pe de o parte, și de "mutare" a realității, pe de alta. Replica lui este mai reală decît obiectul de la care a plecat; tocmai de aceea replica lui tinde să-și abolească obiectul. și Blake, și Courbet sunt aboliți în replicile lui Cantor.

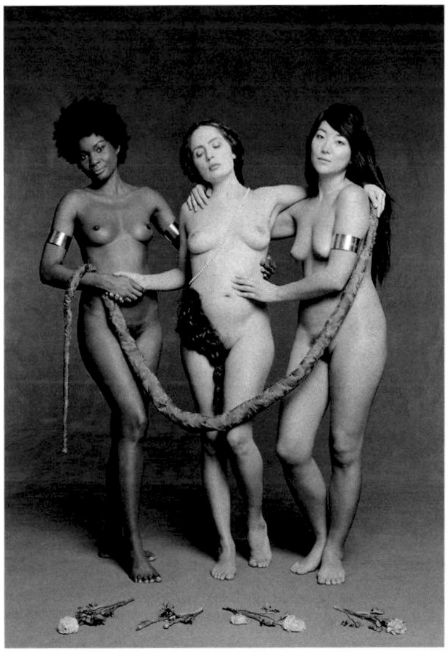

Mircea Cantor
Europe Supported by Africa and Asia, 2009
lambda print
82 11/16 × 59 1/16 inches
(210 × 150 cm)
Courtesy of the artist

Dar procedeul lui Cantor nu se înseriază în deja tradiționala multiplicare a formelor artistice pornind de la un artefact anume din istoria artei. El face și altceva: dislocă noțiunea de realitate a originalului, mutînd-o în altă parte. Unde? Realitatea lui Courbet se situa în reproducerea naturalistă; a lui Blake se situa în schema simbolică; replica lui Cantor mută realitatea din naturalism și simbolic în literal. Or, literalul este procedeul prin care modernii reprezintă obiectele atunci cînd vor să le reproducă *exact de la* înălțimea lor naturală. Prin replicile sale, Cantor realizează o interpretare a originalelor artistice din perspectiva încercării de a vedea lumea în literalitatea ei. Prin imaginile sale, Cantor îi redă lumii literalitatea.

De aceea, cînd triumfă, talentul lui Cantor produce lucrări a căror frumusețe provine din capacitatea de a-l duce pe privitor în interiorul literalității lumii – iar acolo, în lumea literalității ei, pentru că litera este a lui Dumnezeu din prima dimineață a lumii, se află splendoarea, miracolul și paradisul.

1 Citat de Hippolytus, *Refutatio omnium haeresium*, IX, 9, 4 (cules în ediția Diels-Kranz ca "fragmentul B 52").

2 MNAC, 10 aprilie 2013 – 10 aprilie 2014.

AUTHOR'S BIOGRAPHY

Horia-Roman Patapievici is a Romanian physicist, researcher and writer whose most recent works include *Partea nevăzută decide totul* [The Unseen Determines Everything] (2015) and *O idee care ne sucește mințile* [An Idea that Drains Our Minds] (2014), published with prolific Romanian philosophers Andrei Pleșu and Gabriel Liiceanu. He has served as President of the Romanian Cultural Institute (2005–12) and of the European Union National Institutes for Culture (2010–11), promoting the democratization of Romanian culture and ideas. He founded and ran the Romanian magazine *Idei in dialog* [Ideas in Dialogue] (2004–9) and was the creator of two successful public television shows centred around cultural dialogue for Romania's Cultural Channel, called in English *Free Ideas* (2002–5) and *Back to the Argument* (2005–12). He was named an Officer of the Order of Arts and Letters by the French government.

BIOGRAPHIE D'AUTEUR

Horia-Roman Patapievici est un physicien, chercheur et écrivain roumain dont les travaux les plus récents incluent : *Partea nevăzută decide totul* [L'Invisible détermine tout] (2015) et *O idee care ne sucește mințile* [Une idée qui draine nos esprits] (2014), publiés avec les prolifiques philosophes roumains Andrei Pleșu et Gabriel Liiceanu. Il a été Président de l'Institut Culturel Roumain (2005–12) et du réseau des Instituts culturels nationaux de l'Union européenne (2010–11), en promouvant la démocratisation de la culture roumaine et ses idées. Il a fondé et dirigé le magazine roumain *Idei in dialog* [Idées en dialogue] (2004–9) et a été le fondateur de deux émissions de télévision publique à succès autour du dialogue culturel pour la chaîne culturelle de Roumanie appelés en français *Les Idées Libres* (2002–5) et *Retour à l'Argument* (2005–12). Il a été nommé Officier de l'Ordre des Arts et des Lettres par le gouvernement français.

BIOGRAFIA AUTORULUI

Horia-Roman Patapievici este fizician, cercetător privat în istoria ideilor și scriitor. S-a impus în cultura română de după revoluția din 1989 (sub comunism nu a publicat nimic) prin radicalitatea morală a stilului său, prin stringența logică a discursului intelectual și prin anvergura enciclopedică a referințelor. Cărțile sale s-au vândut în zeci de mii de exemplare, si Între cărțile sale recente: *Partea nevăzută decide totul* (2015) și volumul, publicat împreună cu Andrei Pleșu și Gabriel Liiceanu, *O idee care ne sucește mințile* (2014). Ca președinte al *Institutului Cultural Român* (2005–2012) și al rețelei institutelor naționale de cultură din Uniunea Europeană (*EUNIC* 2010–2011) a contribuit semnificativ, pe plan extern, la sincronizarea instituțională a mișcării culturale românești contemporane cu piețele culturale occidentale și, pe plan intern, la promovarea unor politici culturale bazate pe idea de cultură vie și de democratizare a artelor, împotriva ideii, curentă în *establishment*-ul politic și academic românesc, de „cultură română oficială & națională". A fondat și condus revista *Idei în Dialog* (2004–2009) și a creat pentru televiziunea publică din România (canalul cultural) dialogurile culturale de mare succes *Idei în libertate* (2002–2005) și *Înapoi la argument* (2005–2012). Deține *Ordinul Artelor și Literelor* în grad de Ofițer, acordat de Republica Franceză.

EXHIBITED WORKS

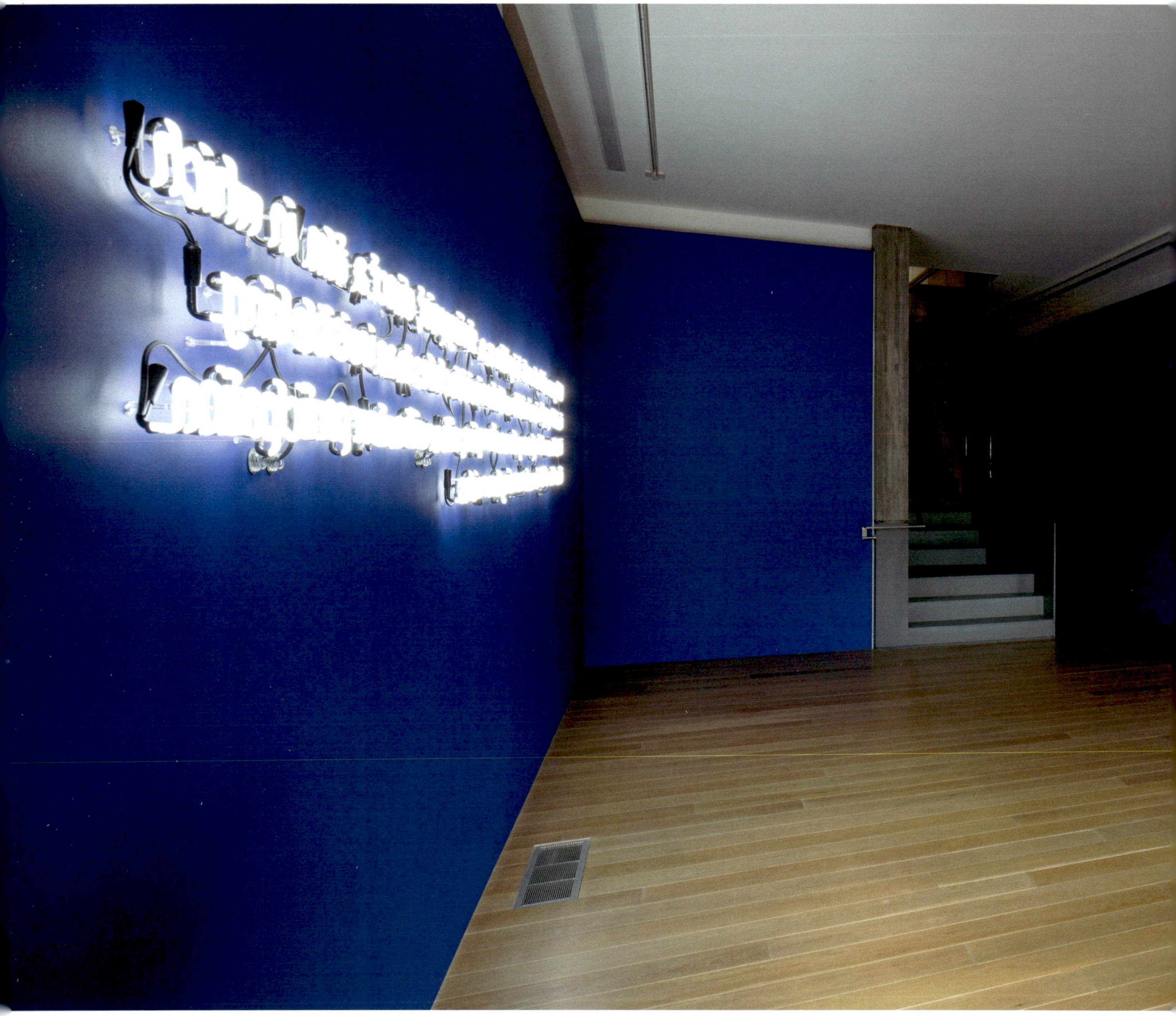

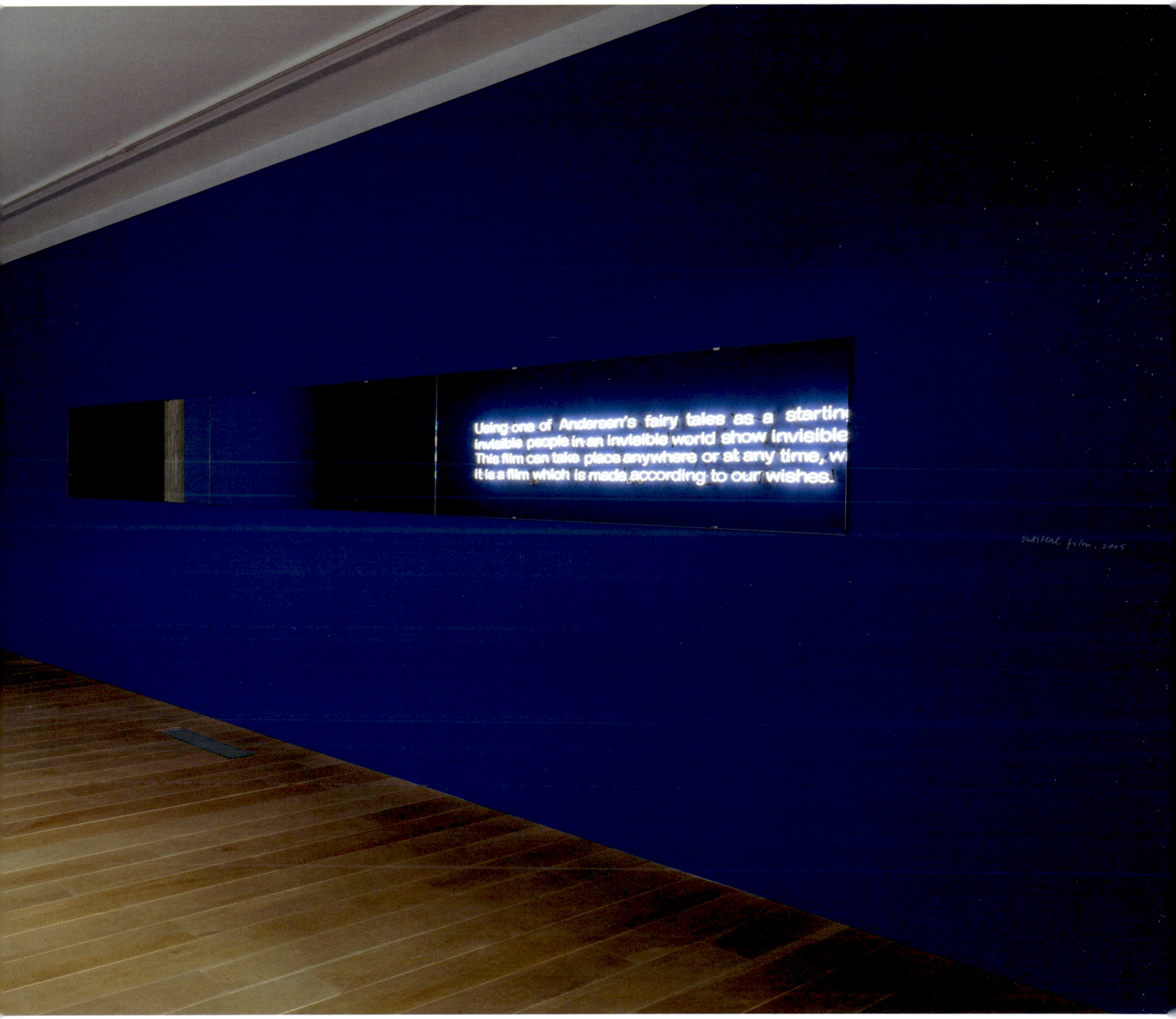
Using one of Andersen's fairy tales as a
invisible people in an invisible world show invisible
This film can take place anywhere or at any time,
it is a film which is made according to our wishes.
Untitled film, 2005

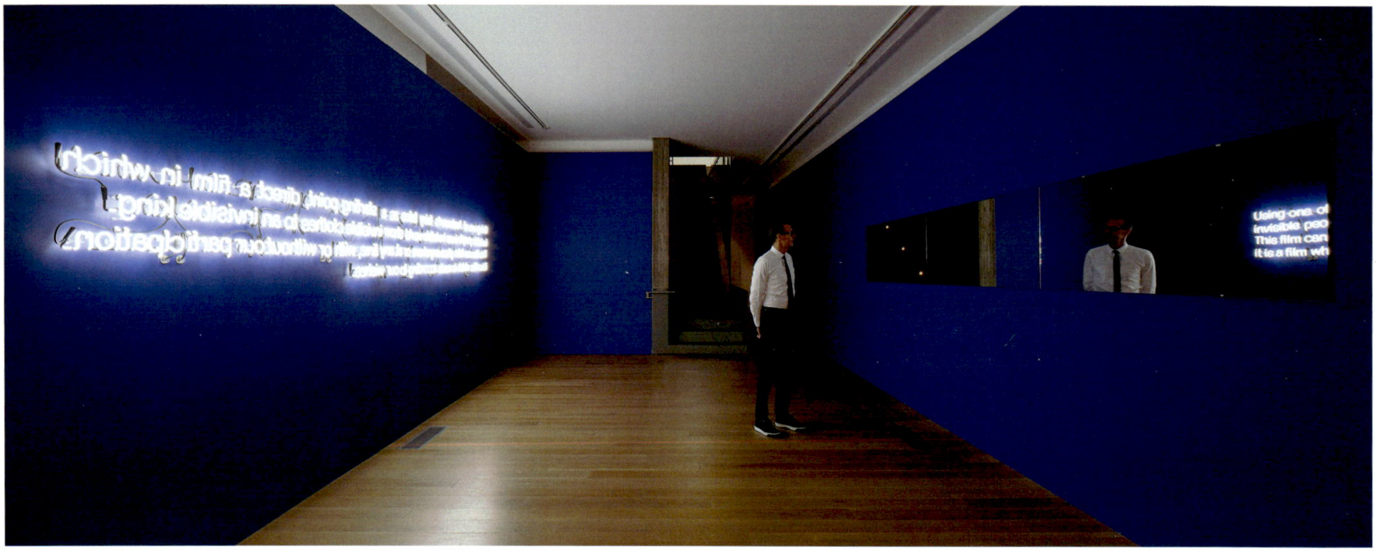

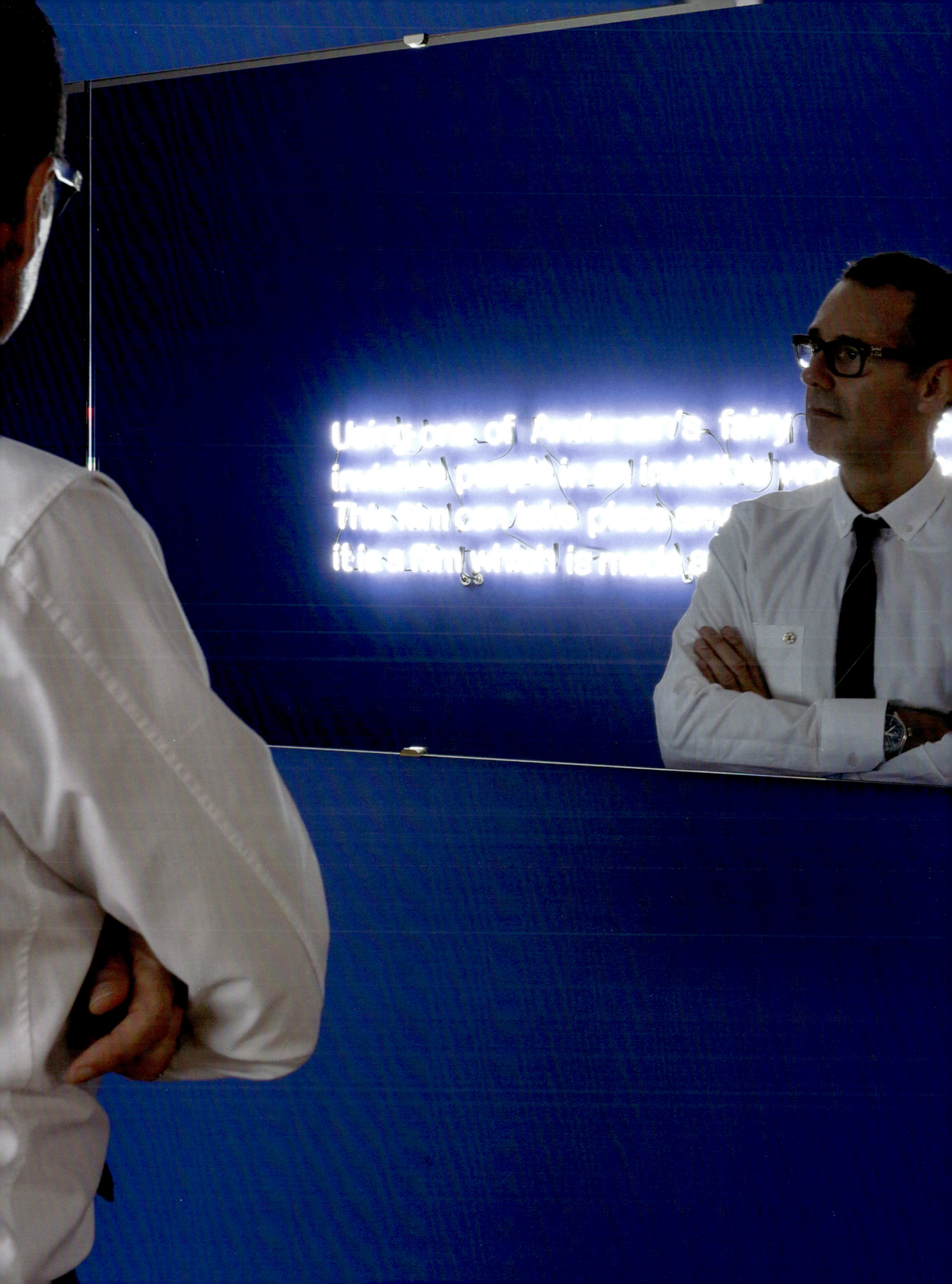
Using one of Andersen's fairy

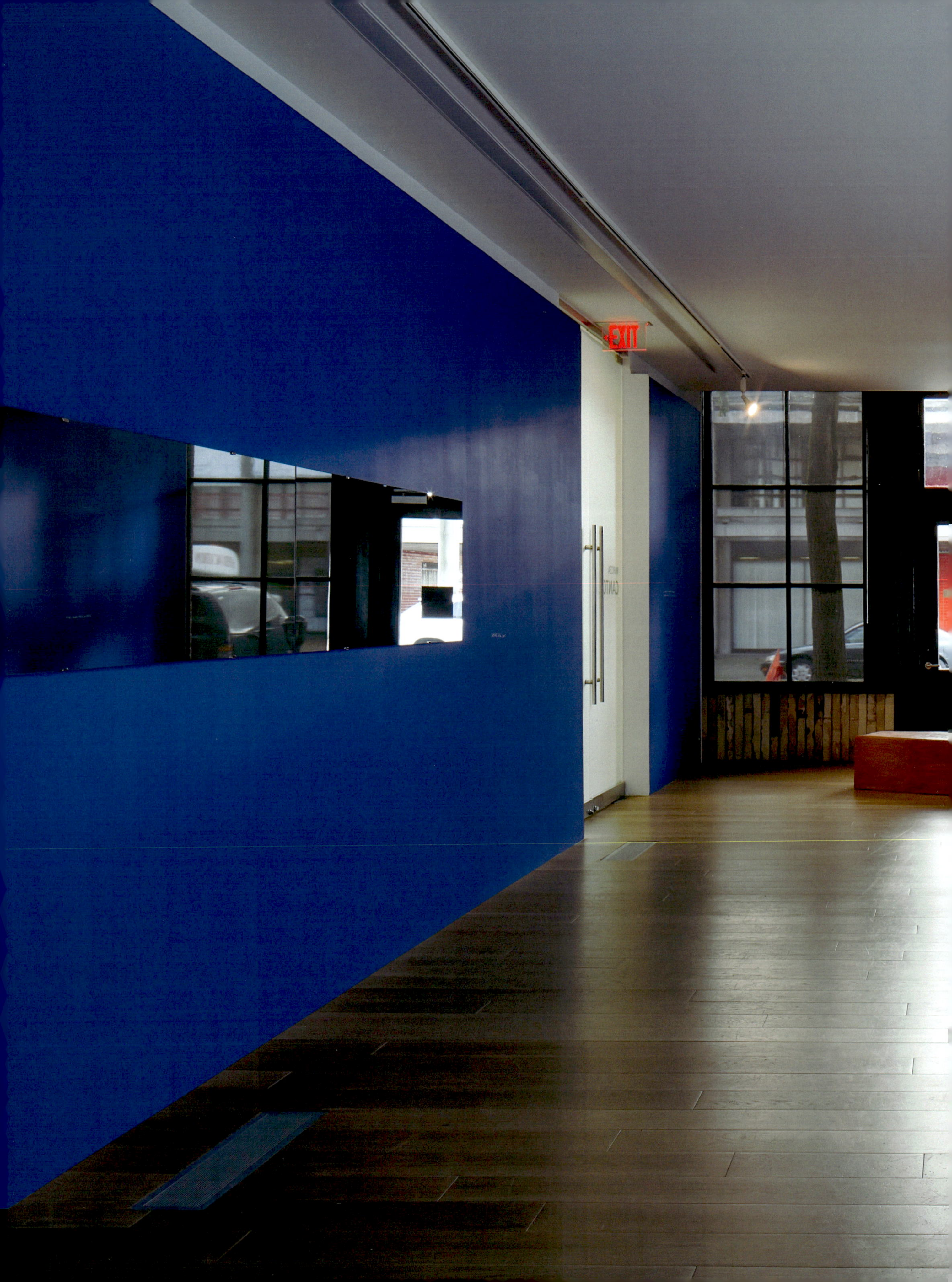
EXIT

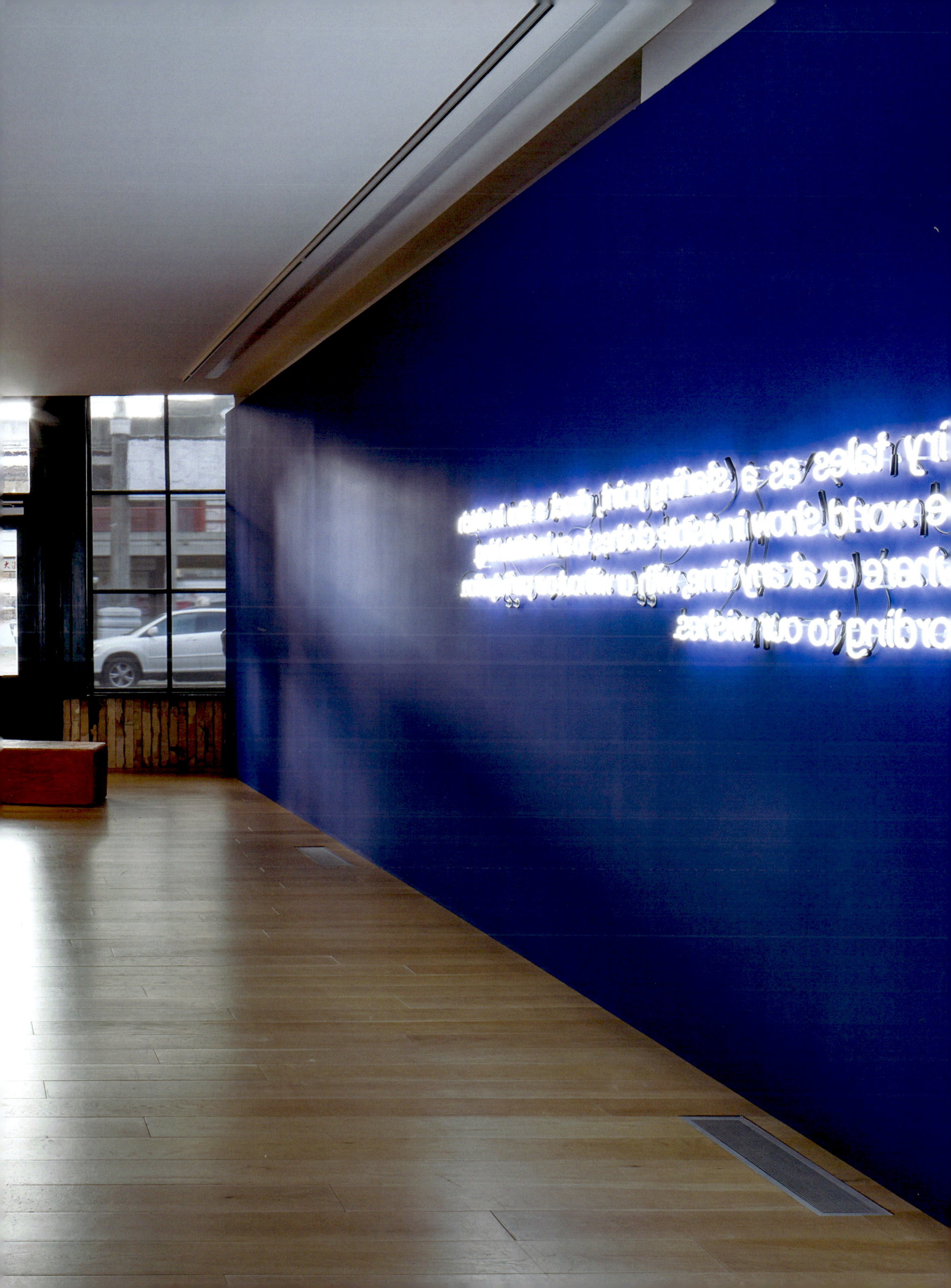

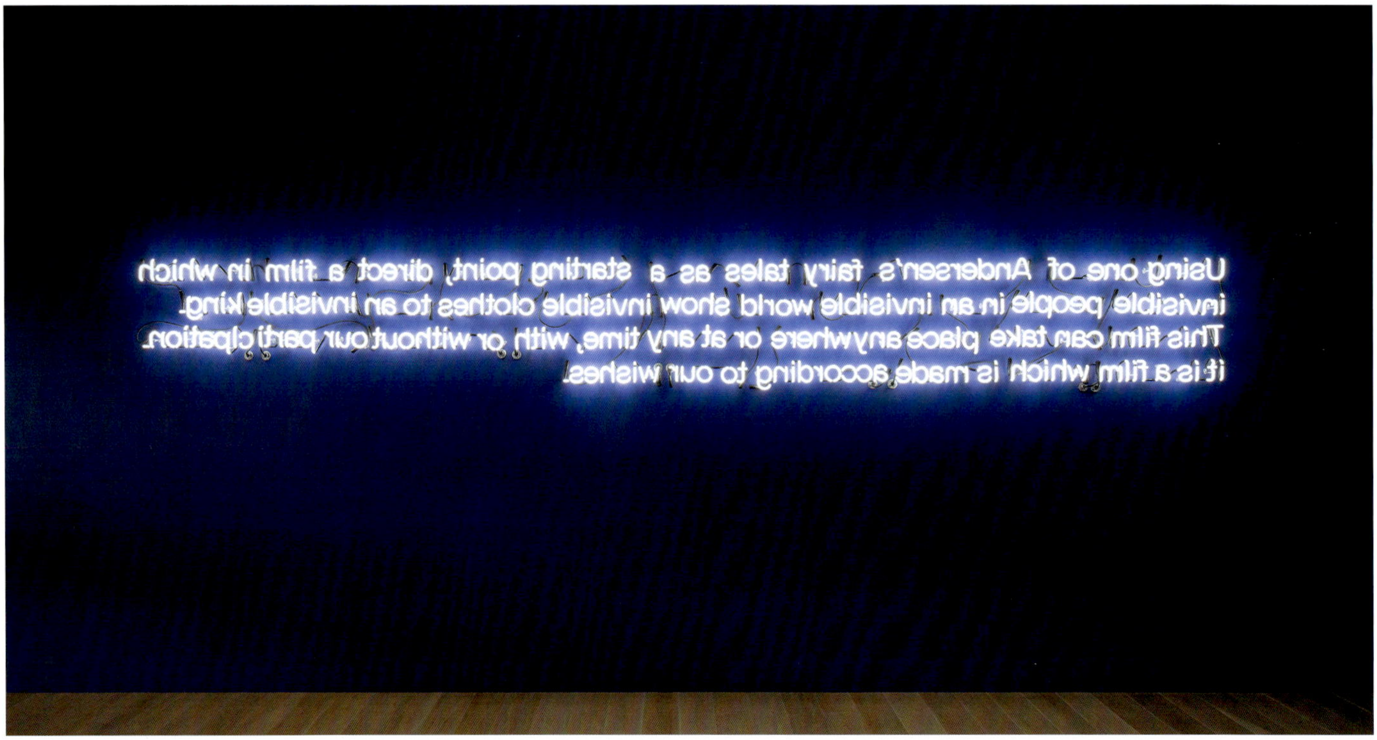
Using one of Andersen's fairy tales as a starting point, direct a film in which
invisible people in an invisible world show invisible clothes to an invisible king.
This film can take place anywhere or at any time, with or without our participation.
It is a film which is made according to our wishes.

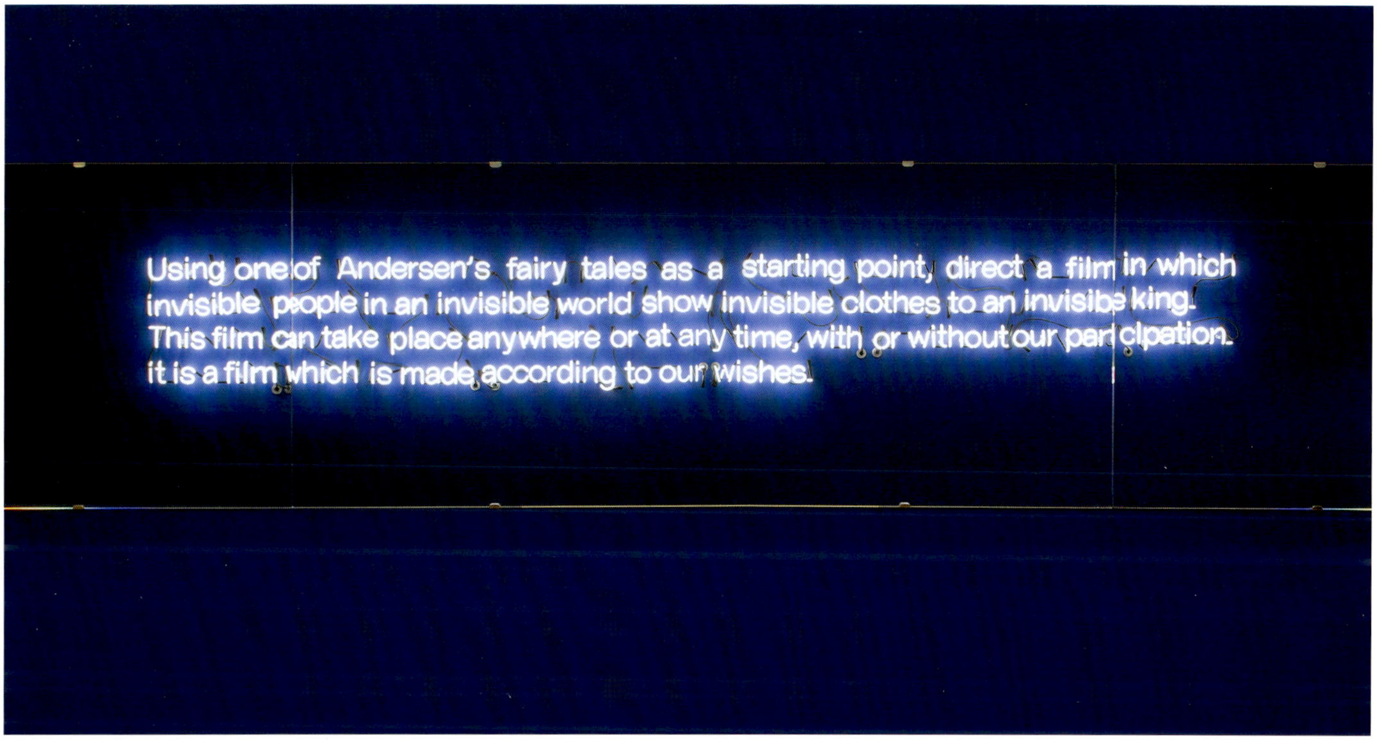
Using one of Andersen's fairy tales as a starting point, direct a film in which
invisible people in an invisible world show invisible clothes to an invisibe king.
This film can take place anywhere or at any time, with or without our participation.
it is a film which is made according to our wishes.

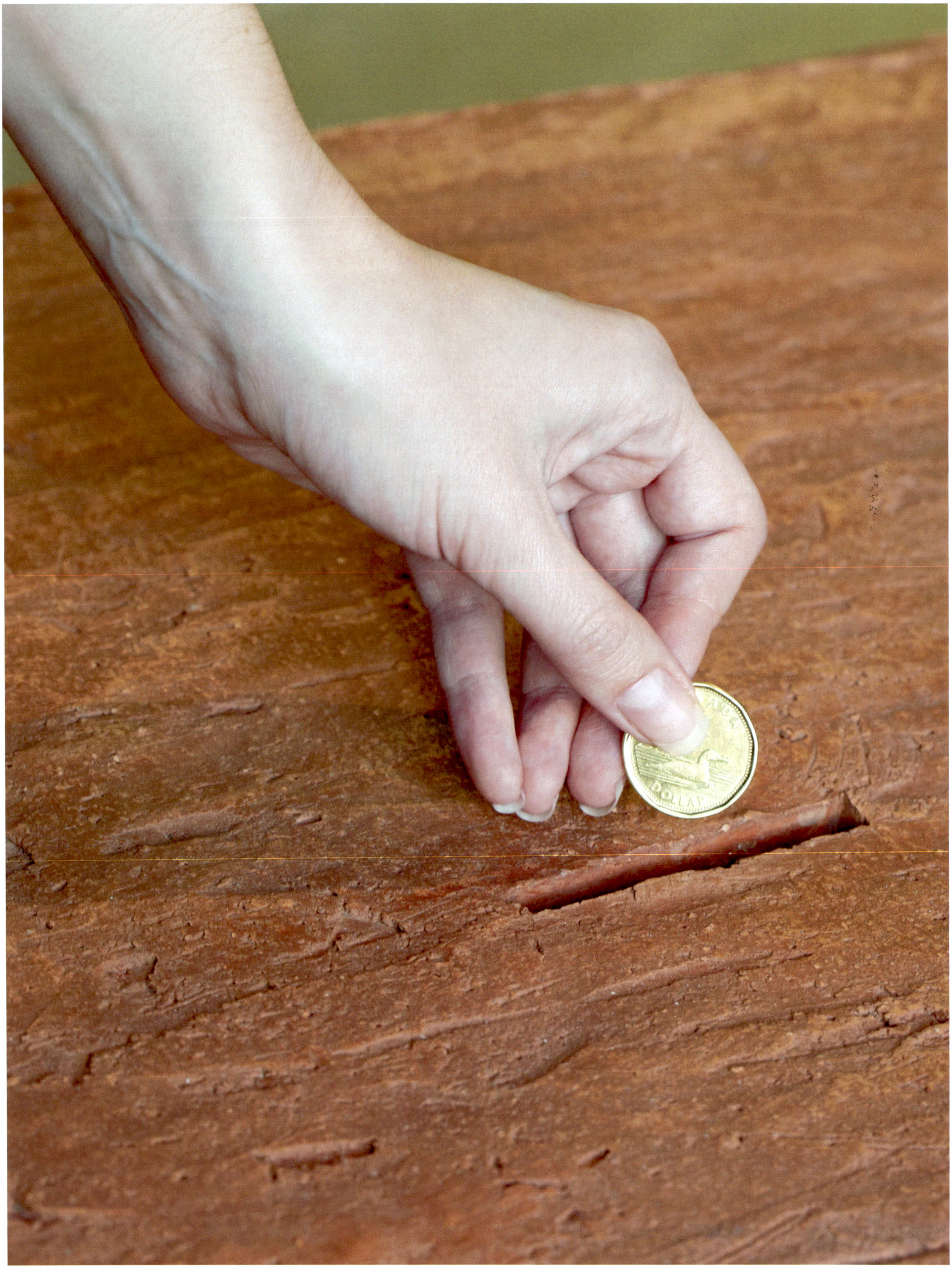

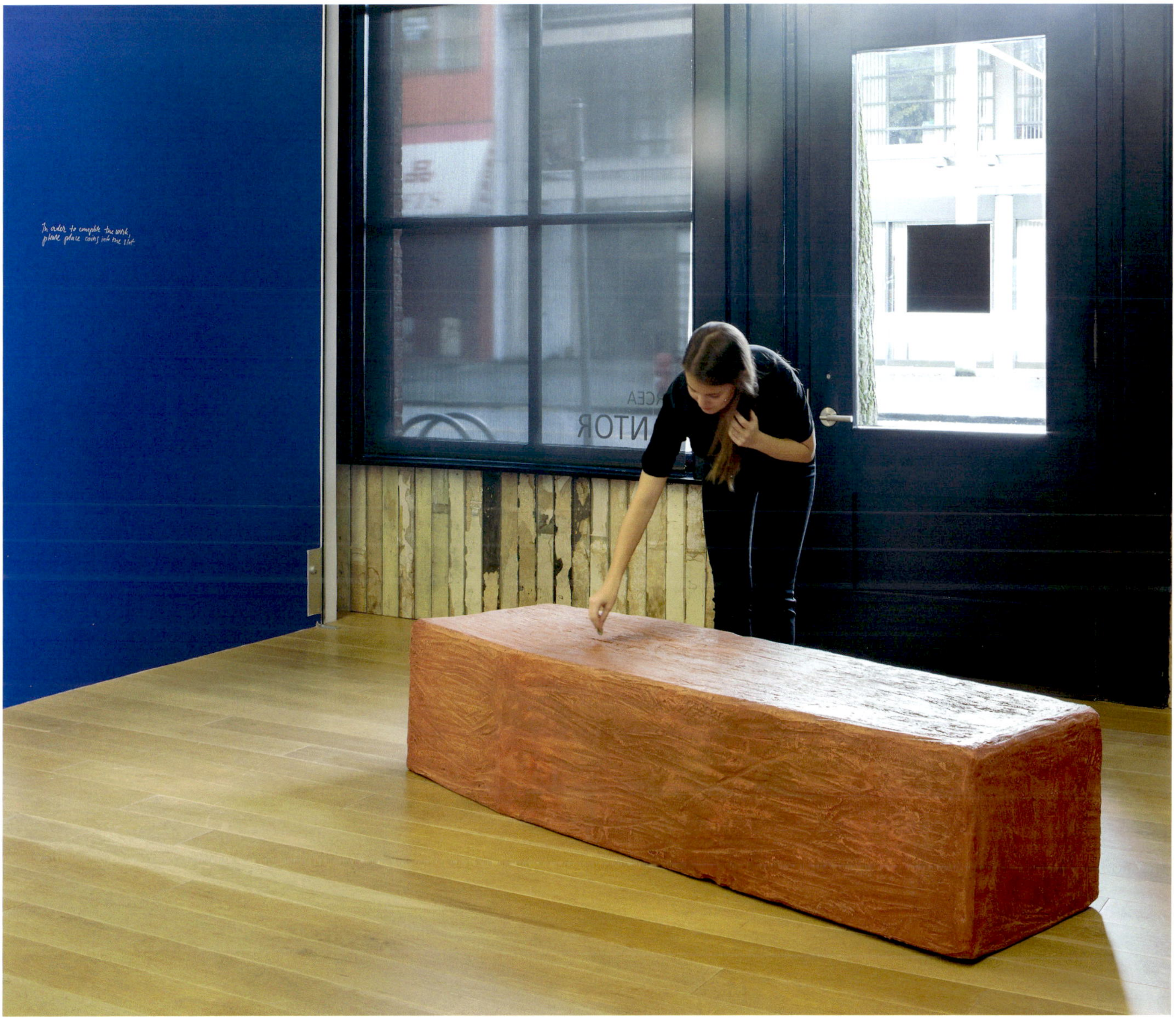
In order to complete the work,
please place coins into the slot

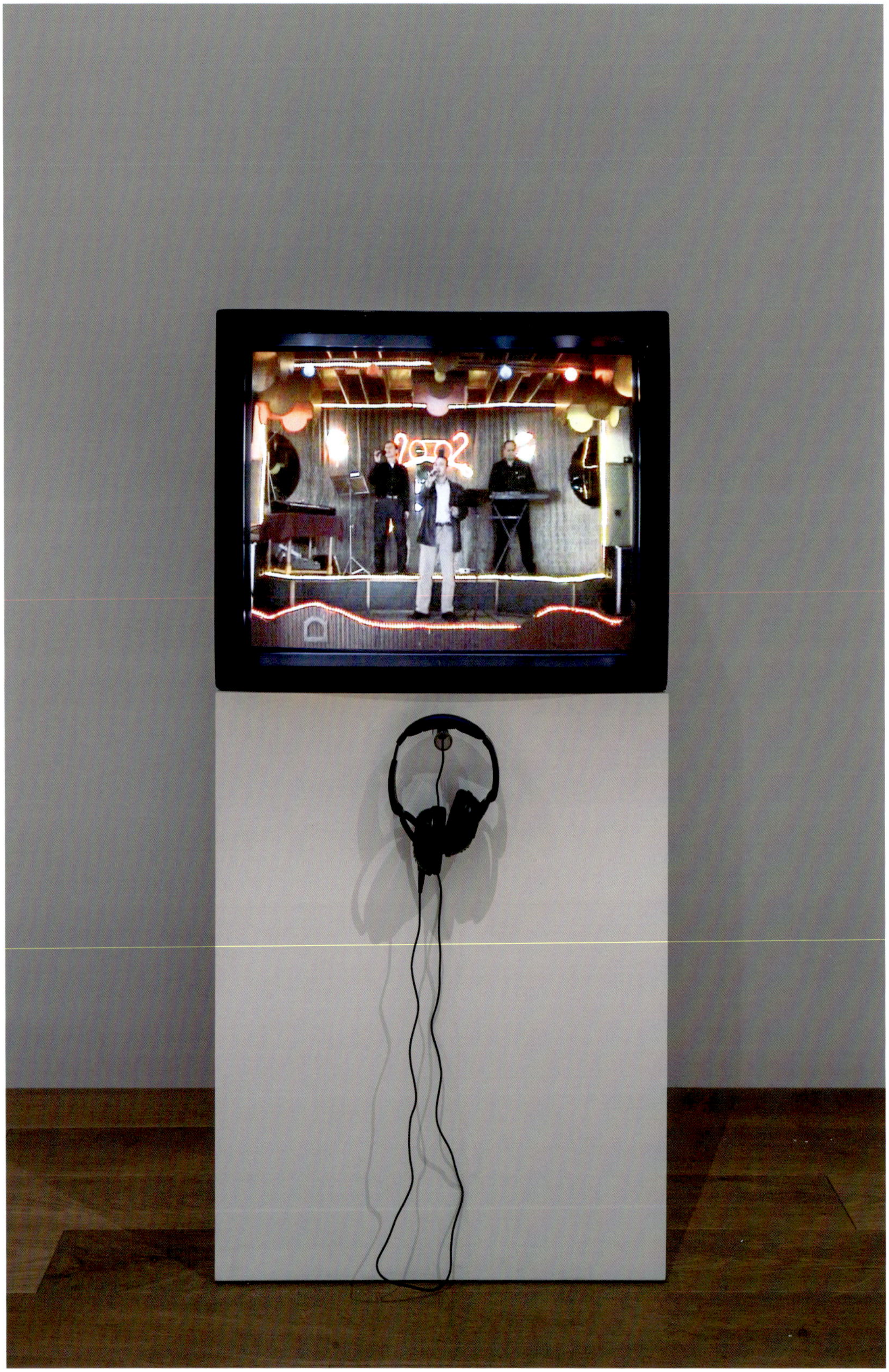

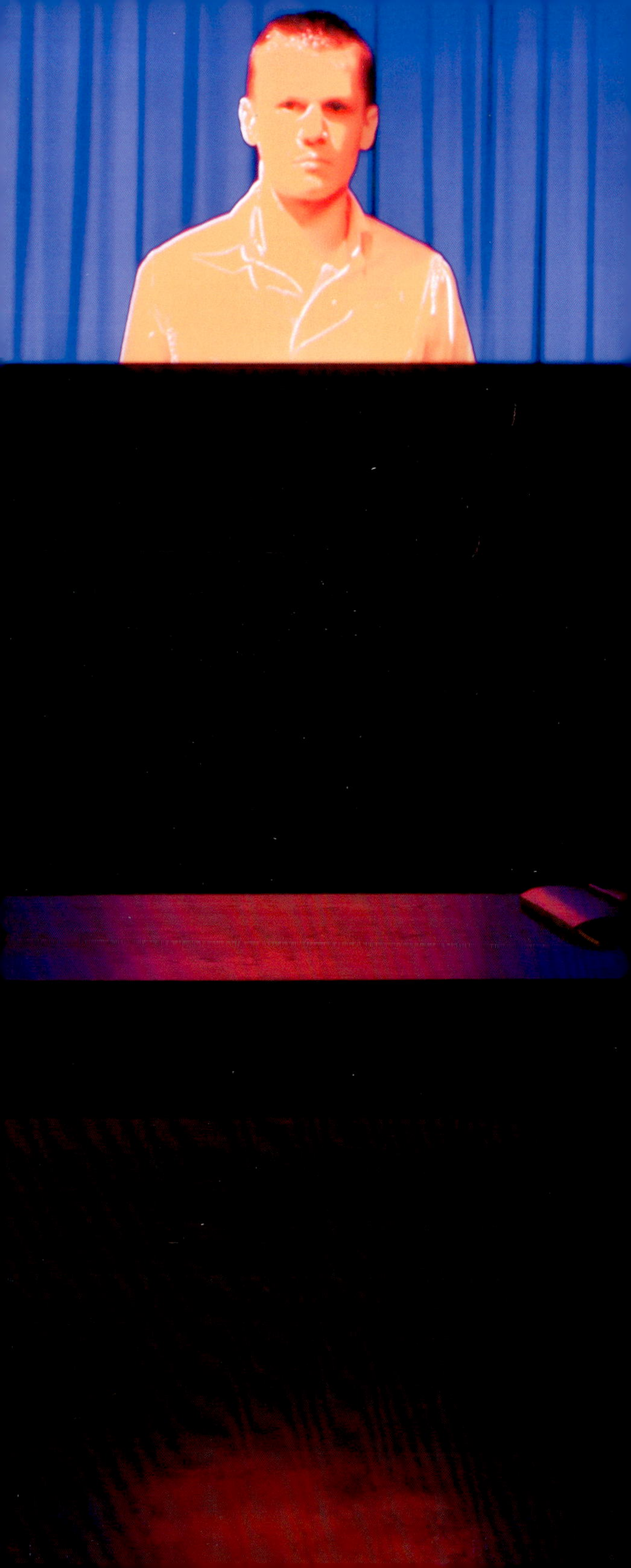

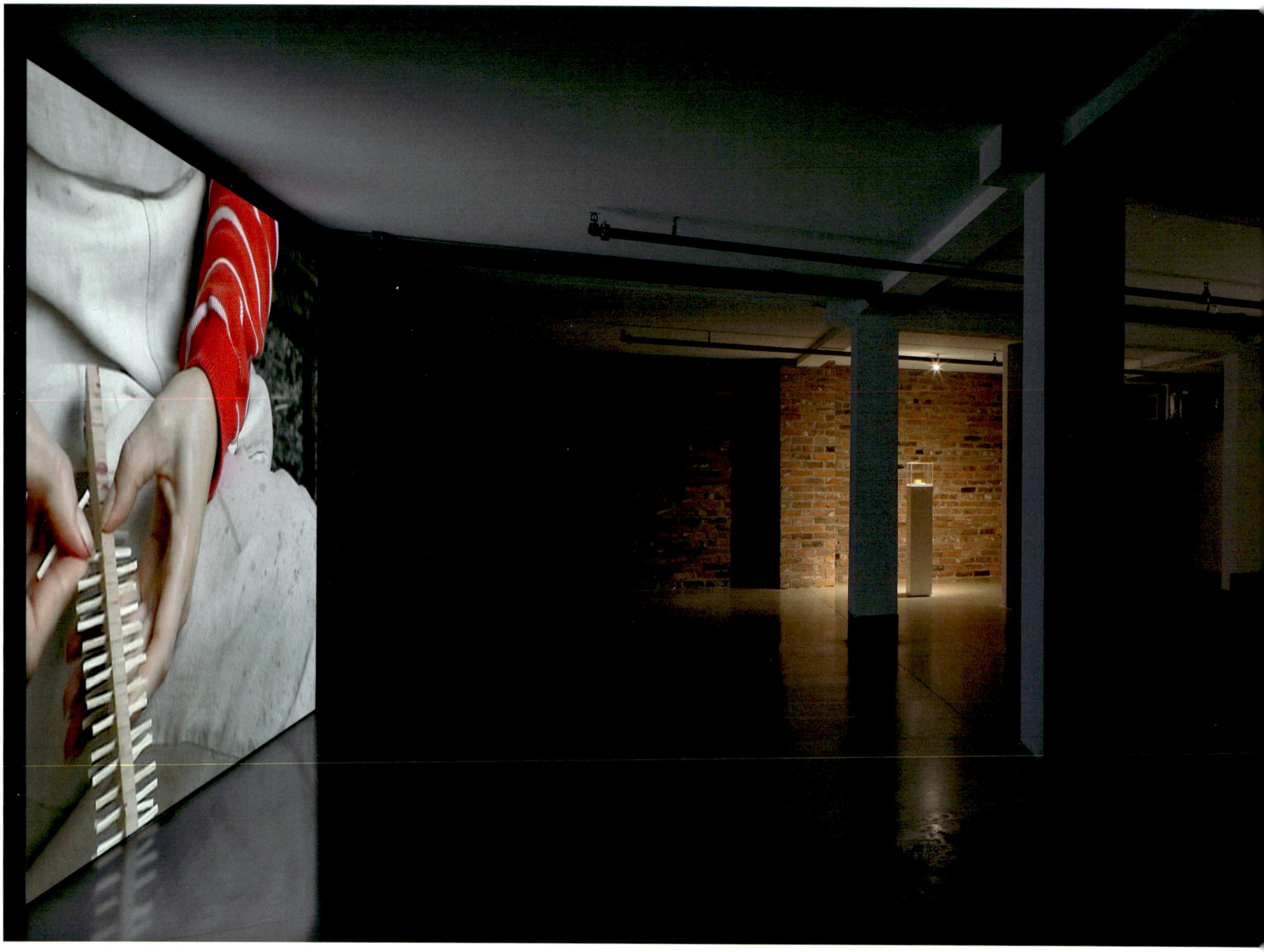

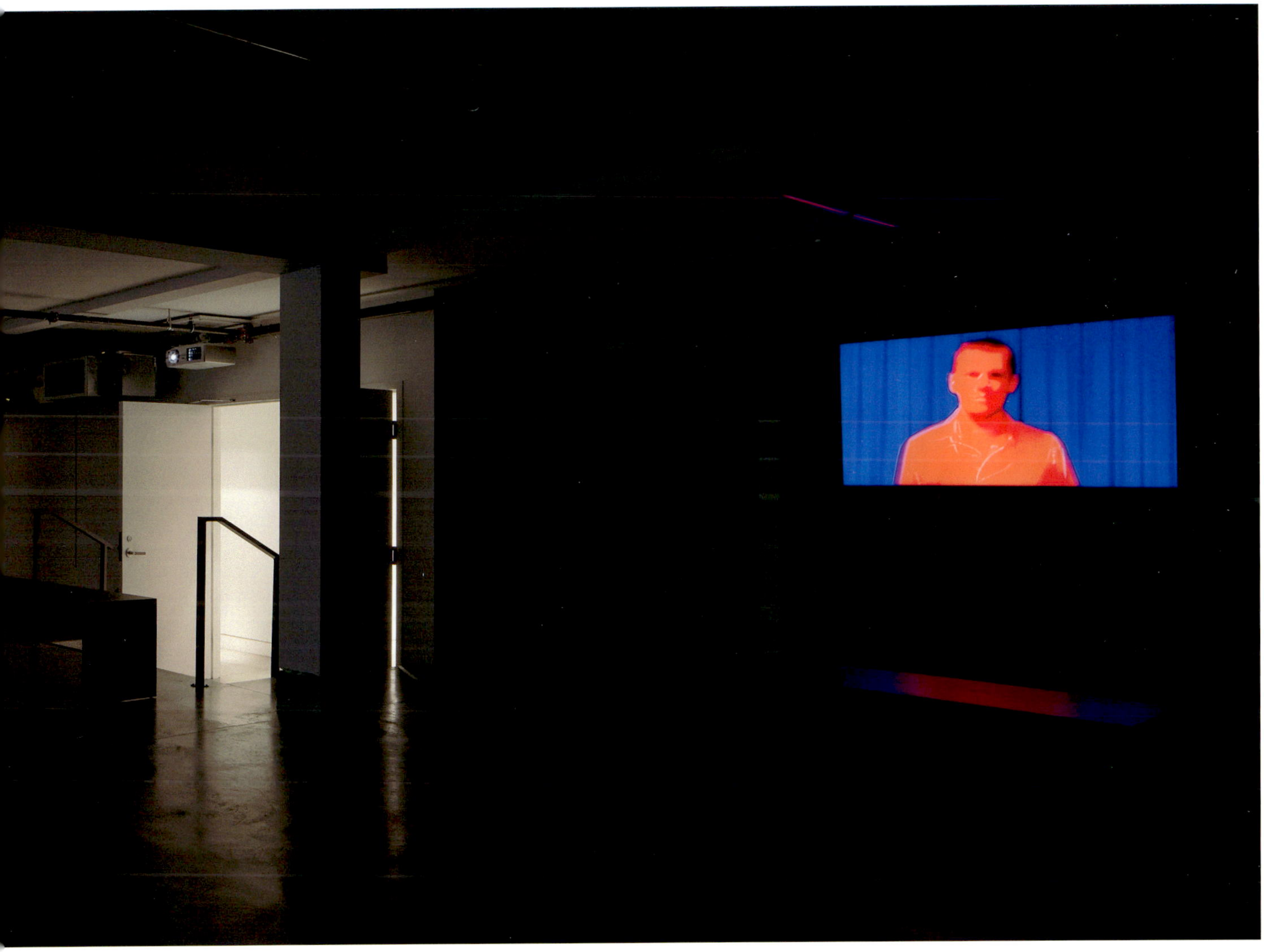

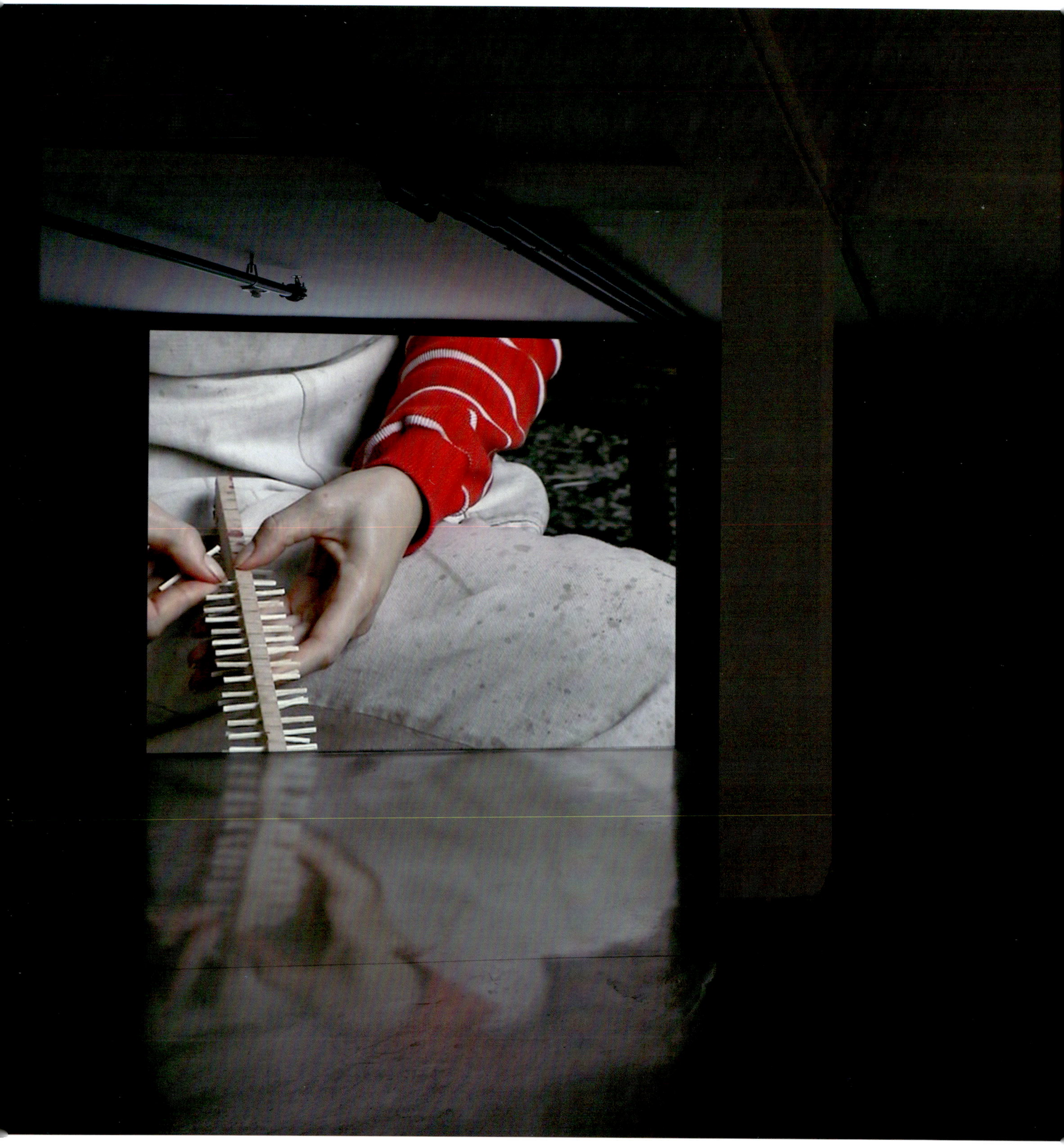

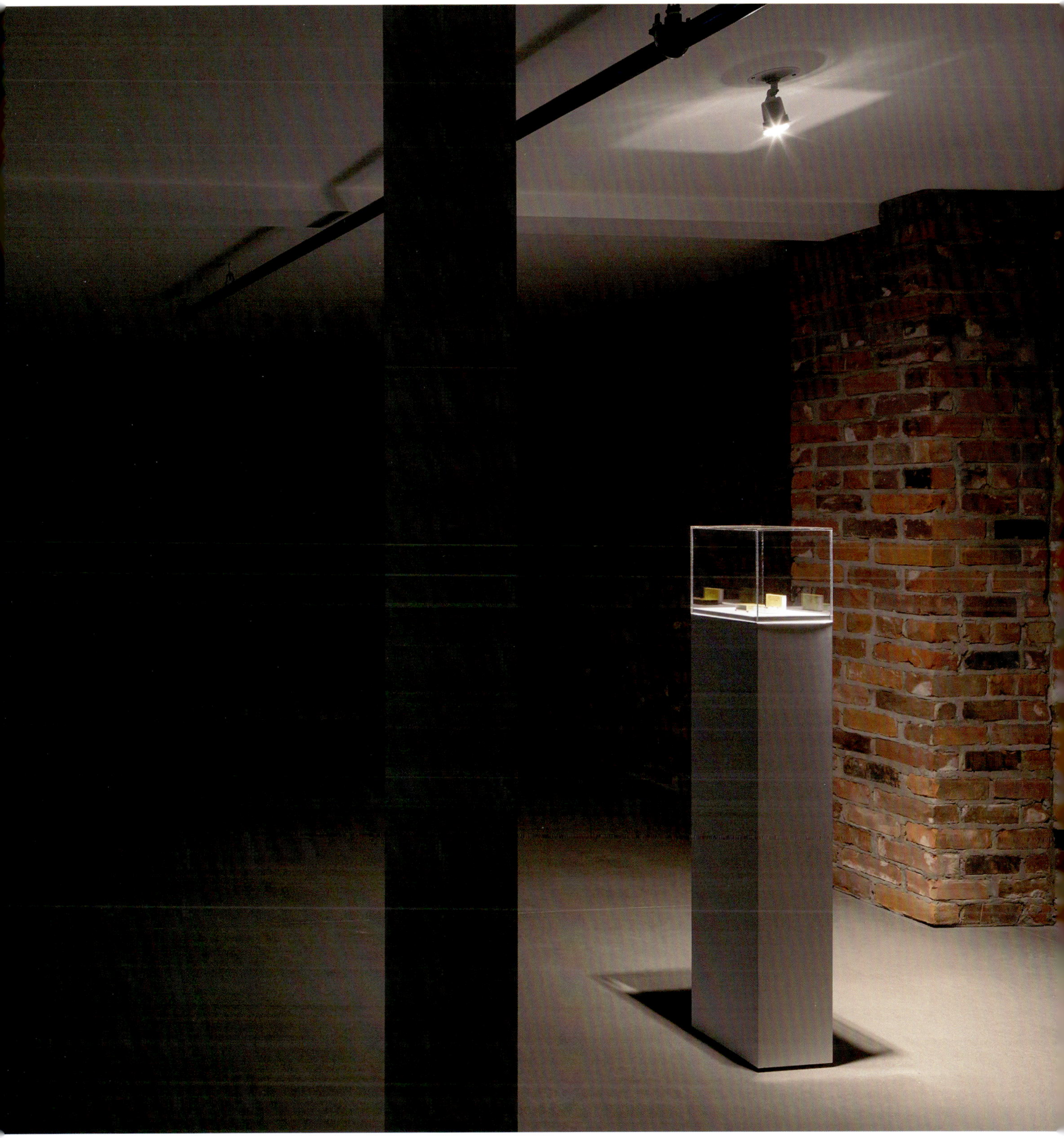

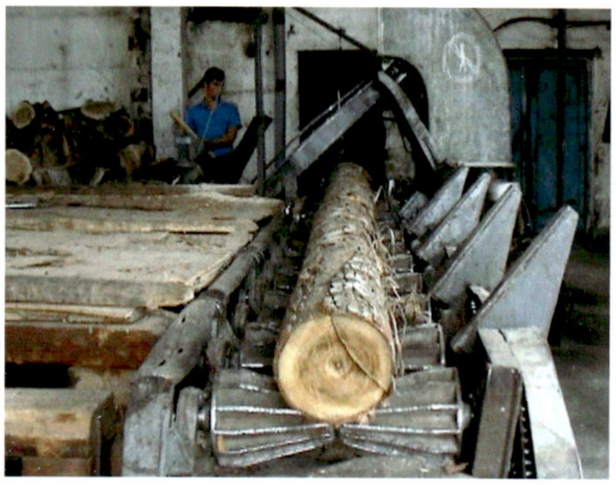

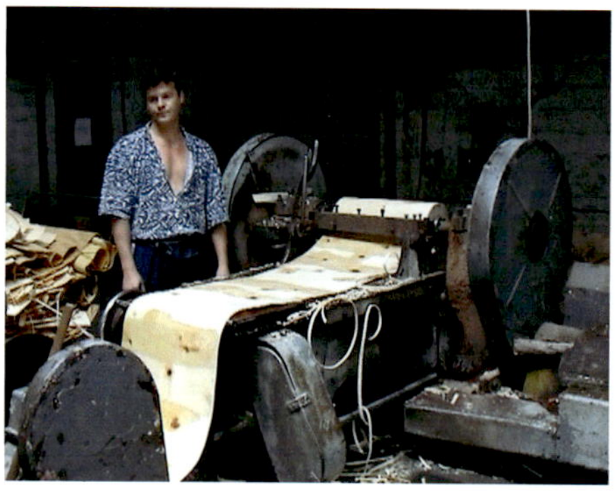

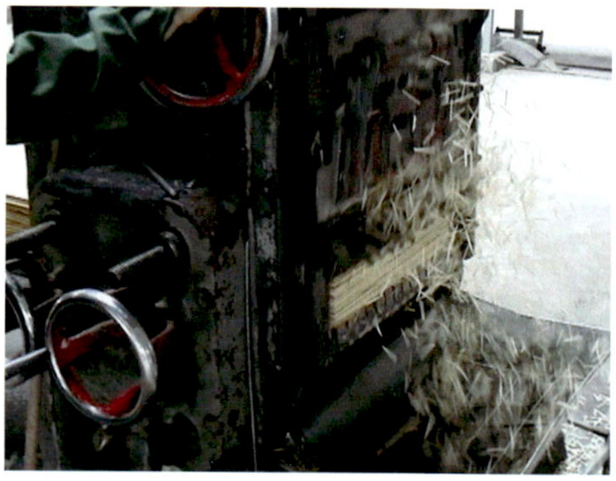

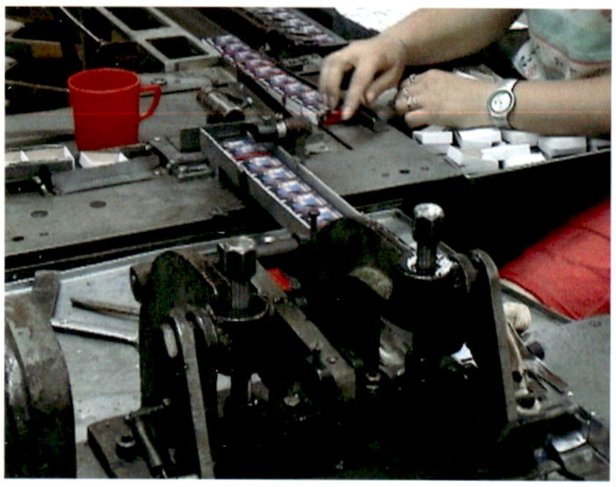

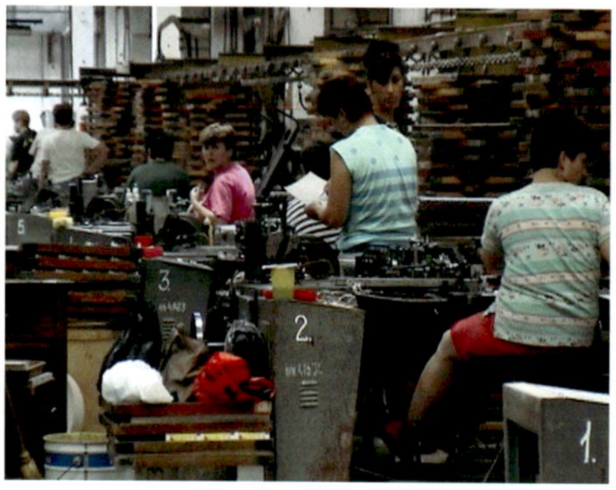
5
3
2.
1.

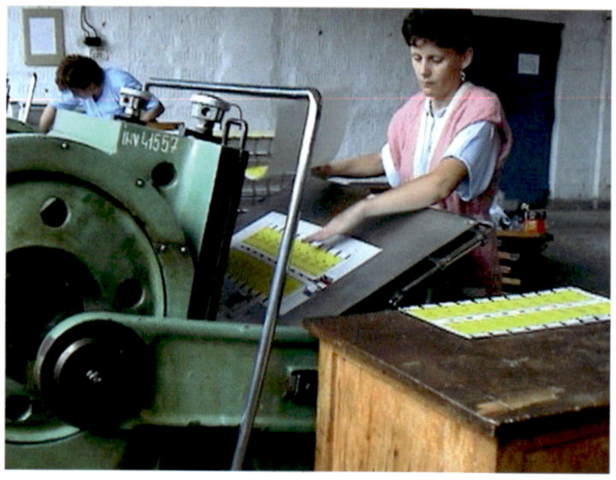

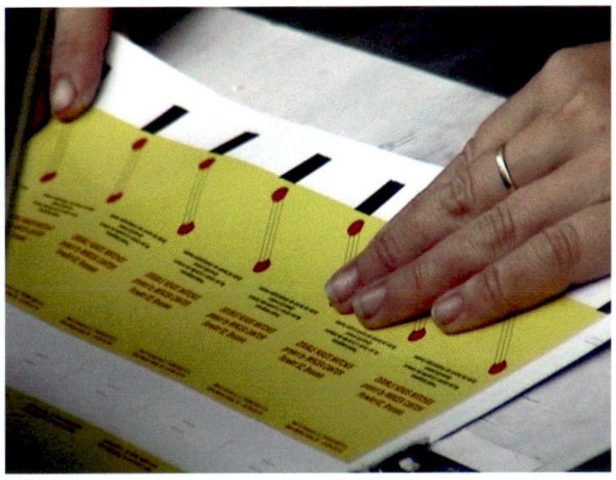
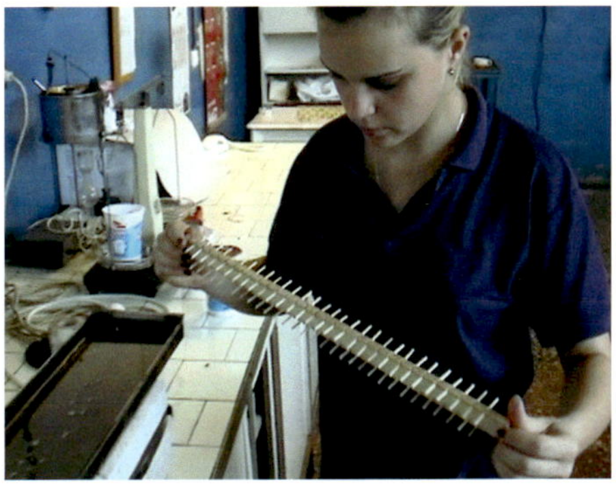
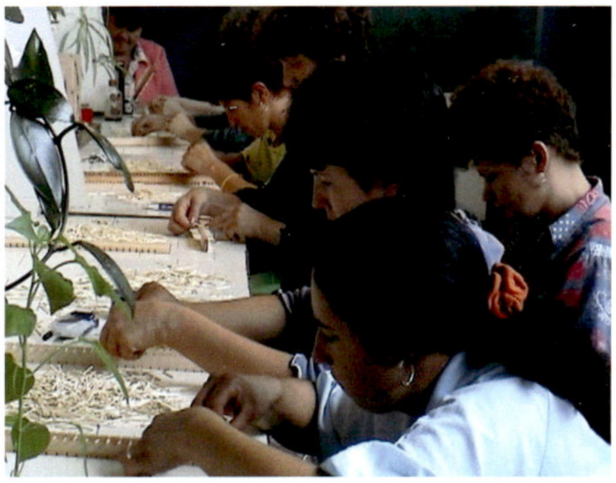
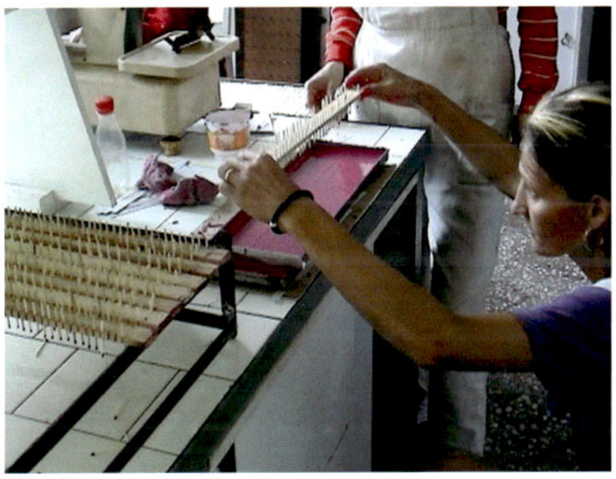
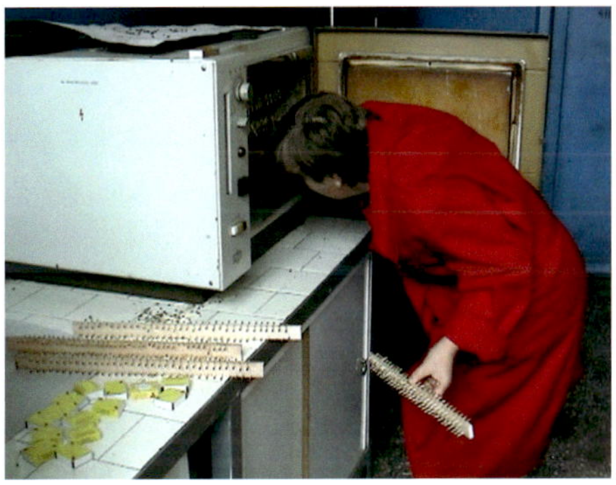
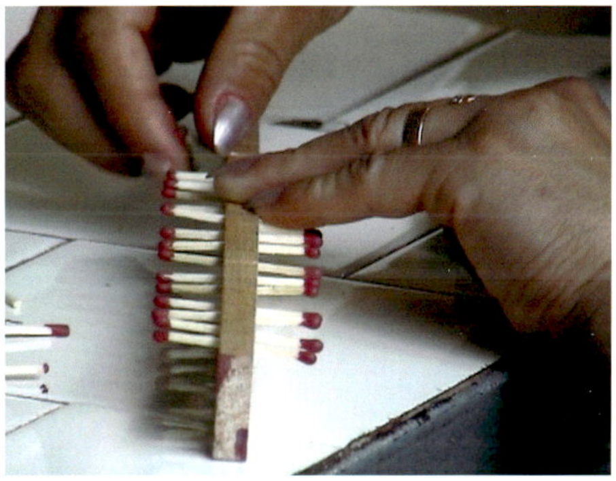

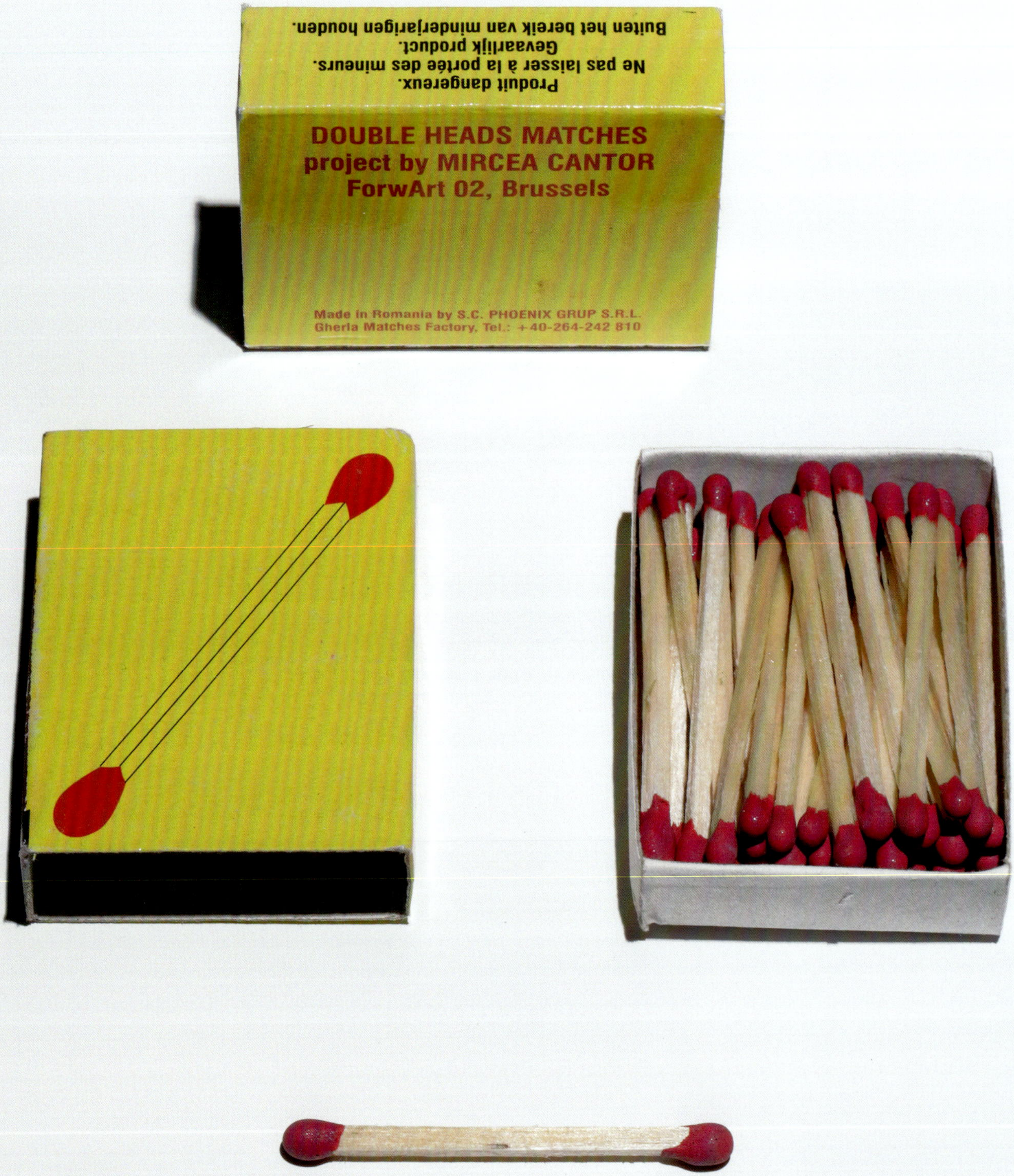
Produit dangereux.
Ne pas laisser à la portée des mineurs.
Gevaarlijk product.
Buiten het bereik van minderjarigen houden.
DOUBLE HEADS MATCHES
project by MIRCEA CANTOR
ForwArt 02, Brussels
Made in Romania by S.C. PHOENIX GRUP S.R.L.
Gherla Matches Factory, Tel.: +40-264-242 810

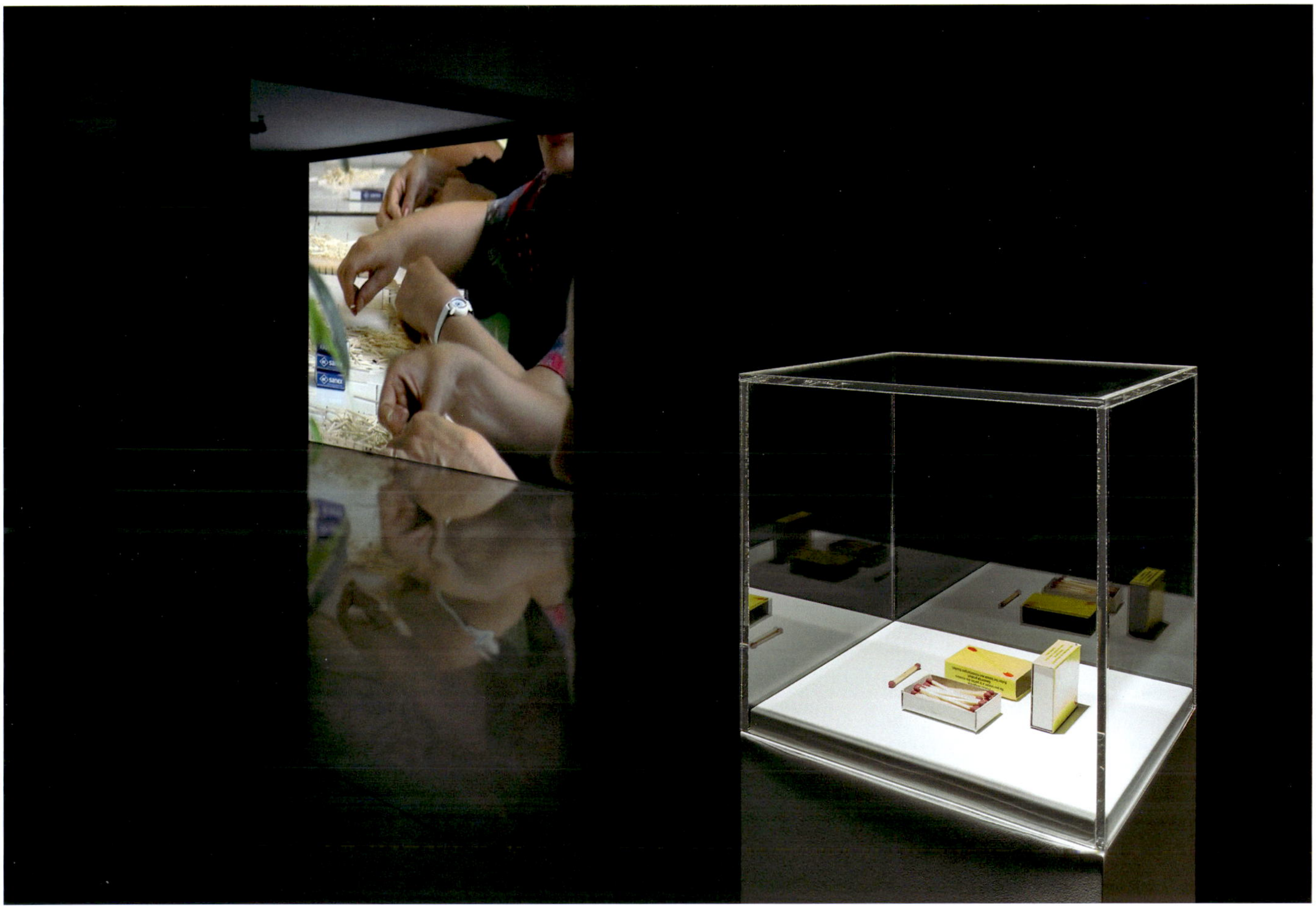

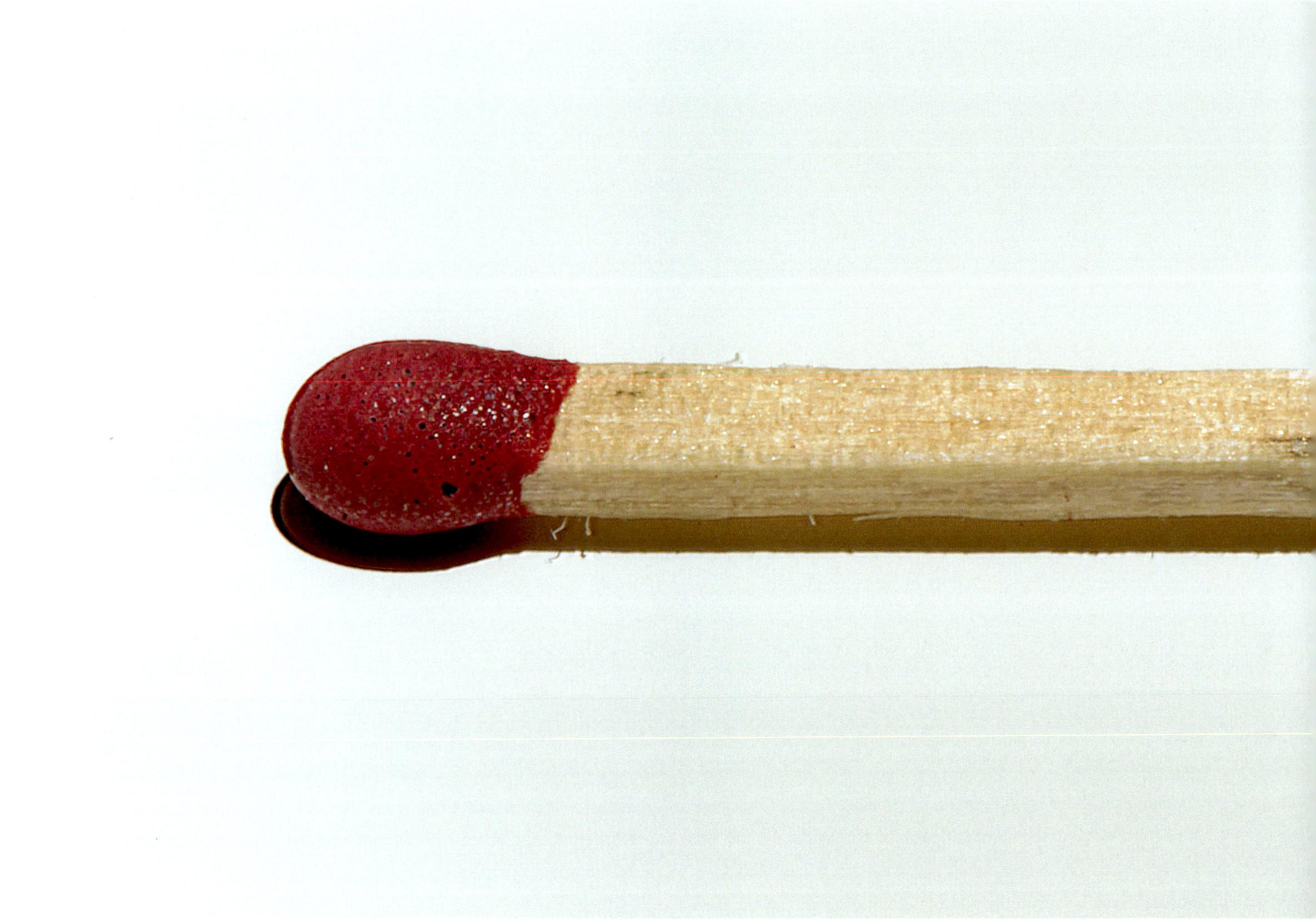

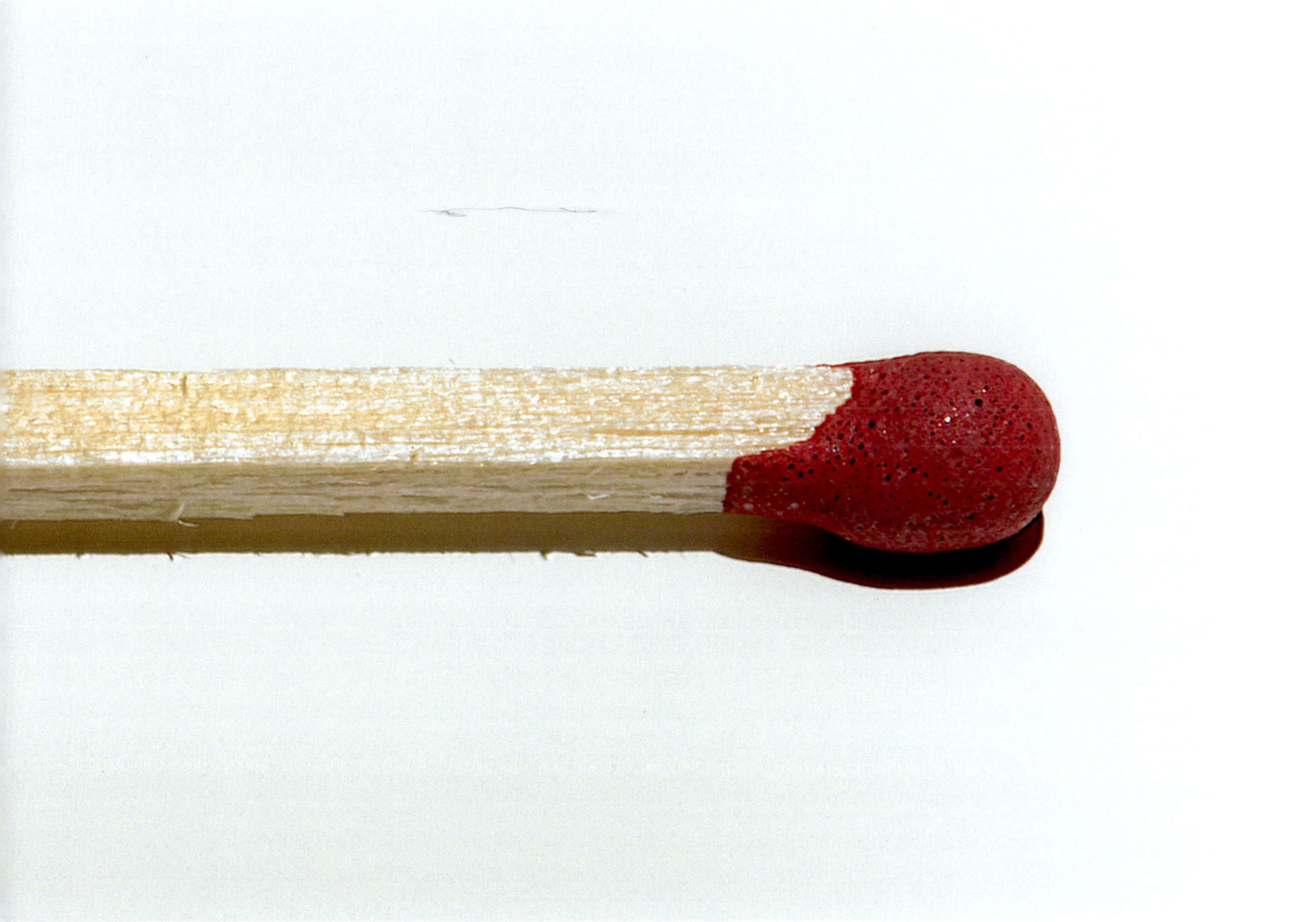

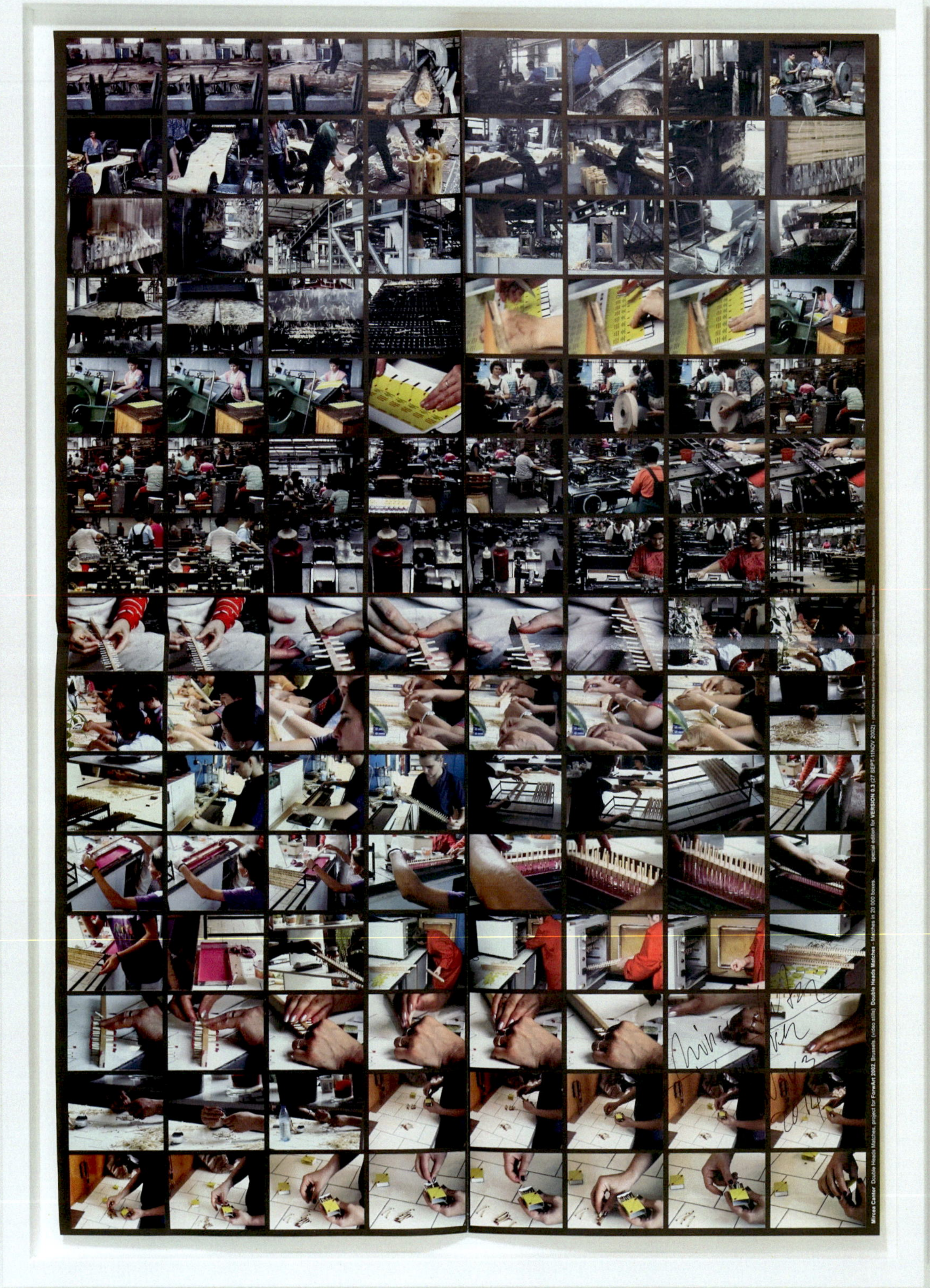
Mircea Cantor Double Heads Matches, project for ForwArt 2002, Brussels. (video stills) Double Heads Matches - Matches in 20 000 boxes. special edition for VERSION 0.3 (27 SEPT-11NOV 2002)

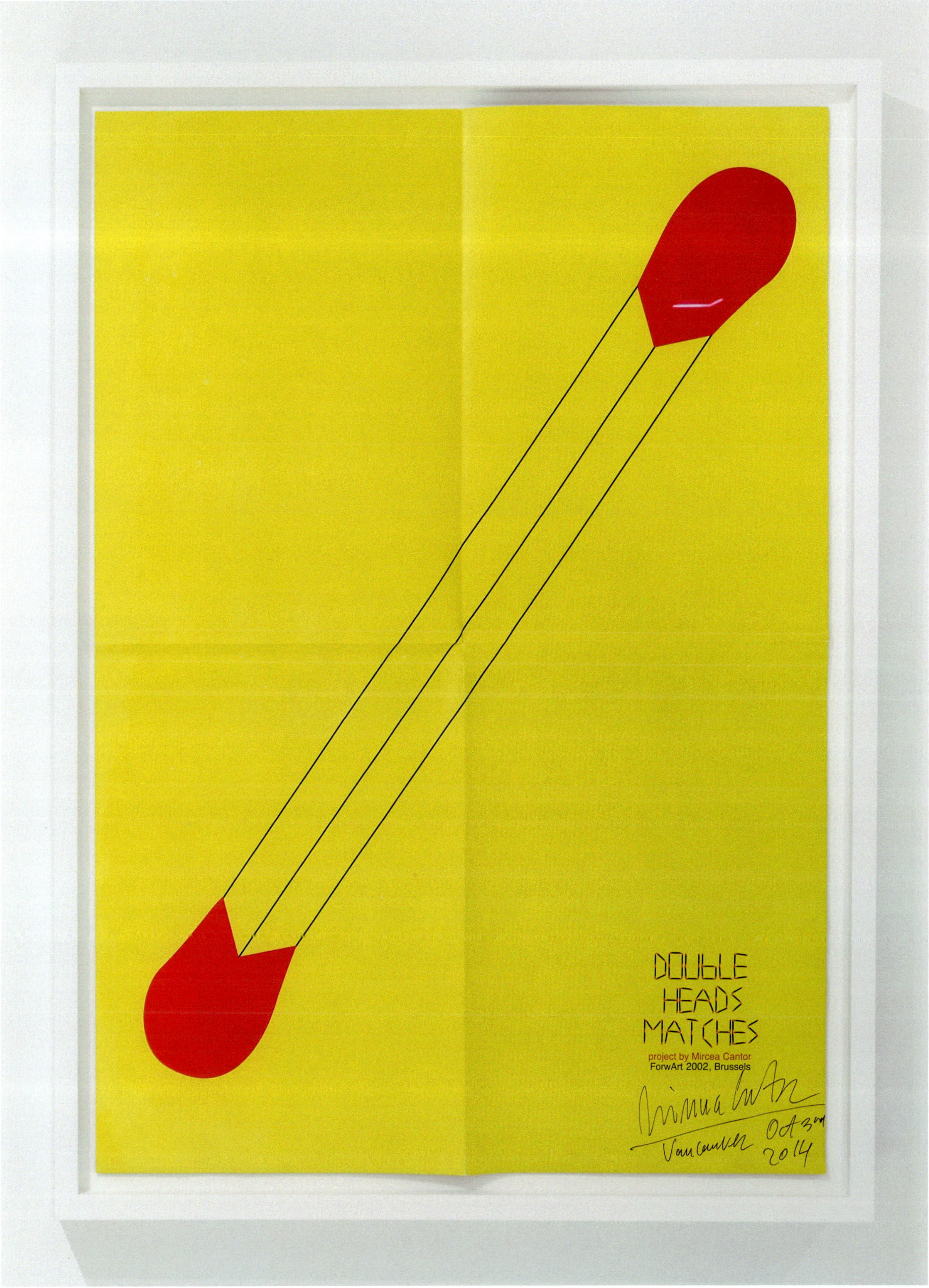
DOUBLE
HEADS
MATCHES
project by Mircea Cantor
ForwArt 2002, Brussels
Vancouver Oct 3rd
2014

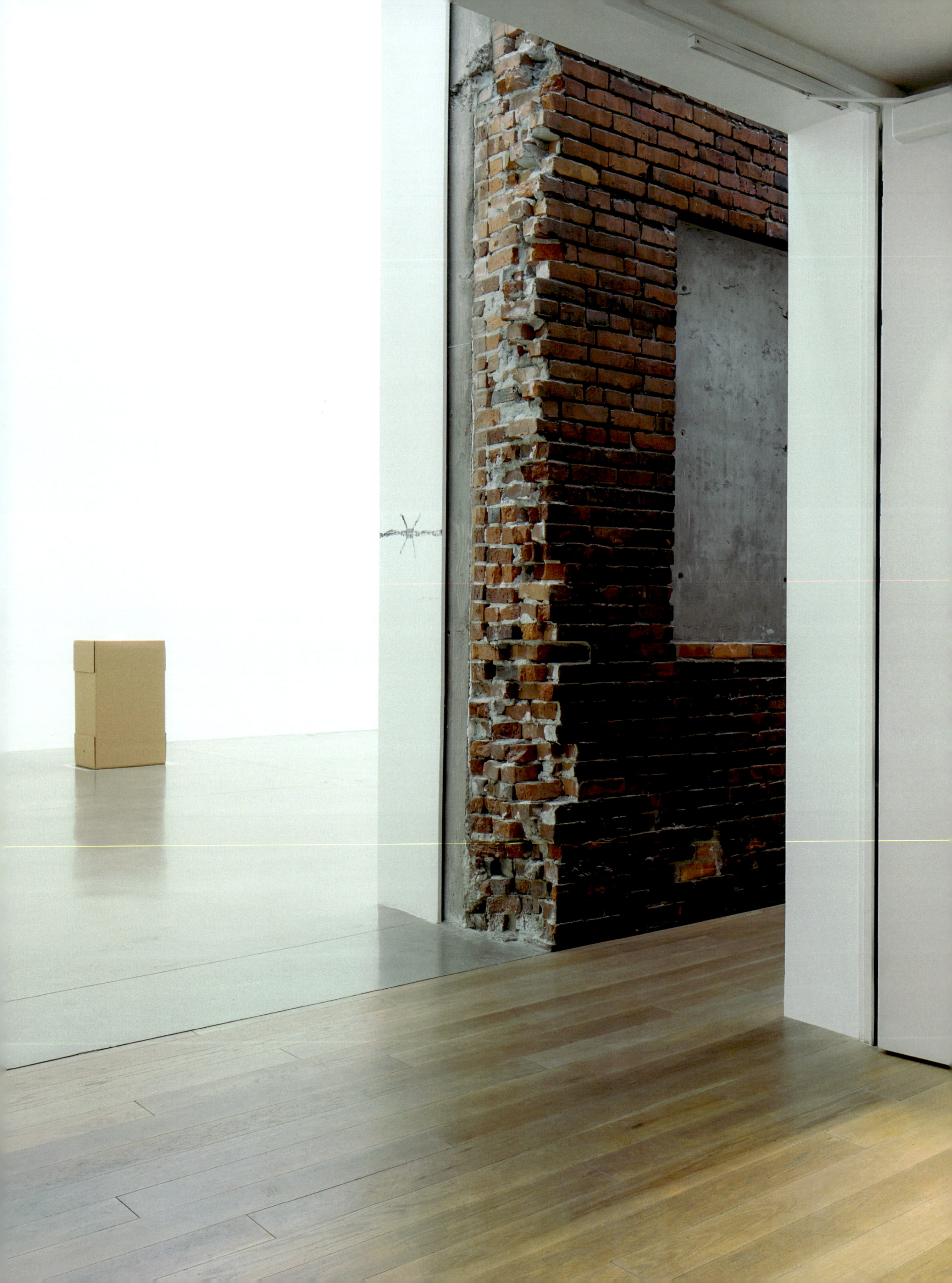

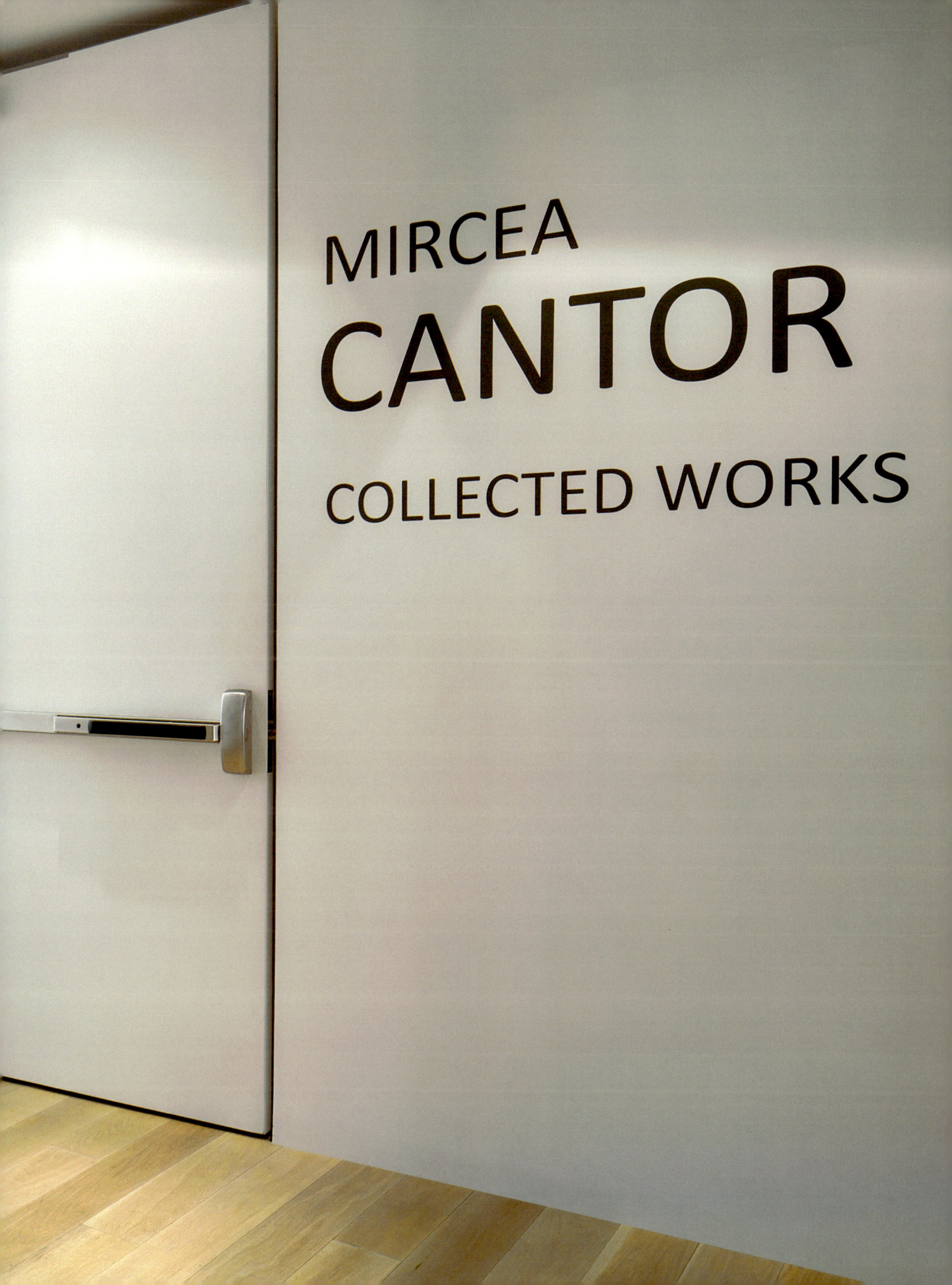
MIRCEA
CANTOR
COLLECTED WORKS

e masses on his ego. By

e preceding comments al

idual he knows himself

important for him to ma

in MIRCEA's personali

[redacted]. He may be [redacted]

with a penchant for [redacted]

[redacted], he is c[redacted] and [redacted]

es makes at others. How

nation, his capacity for s

ially attached to the one

full of st[redacted] and u[redacted]

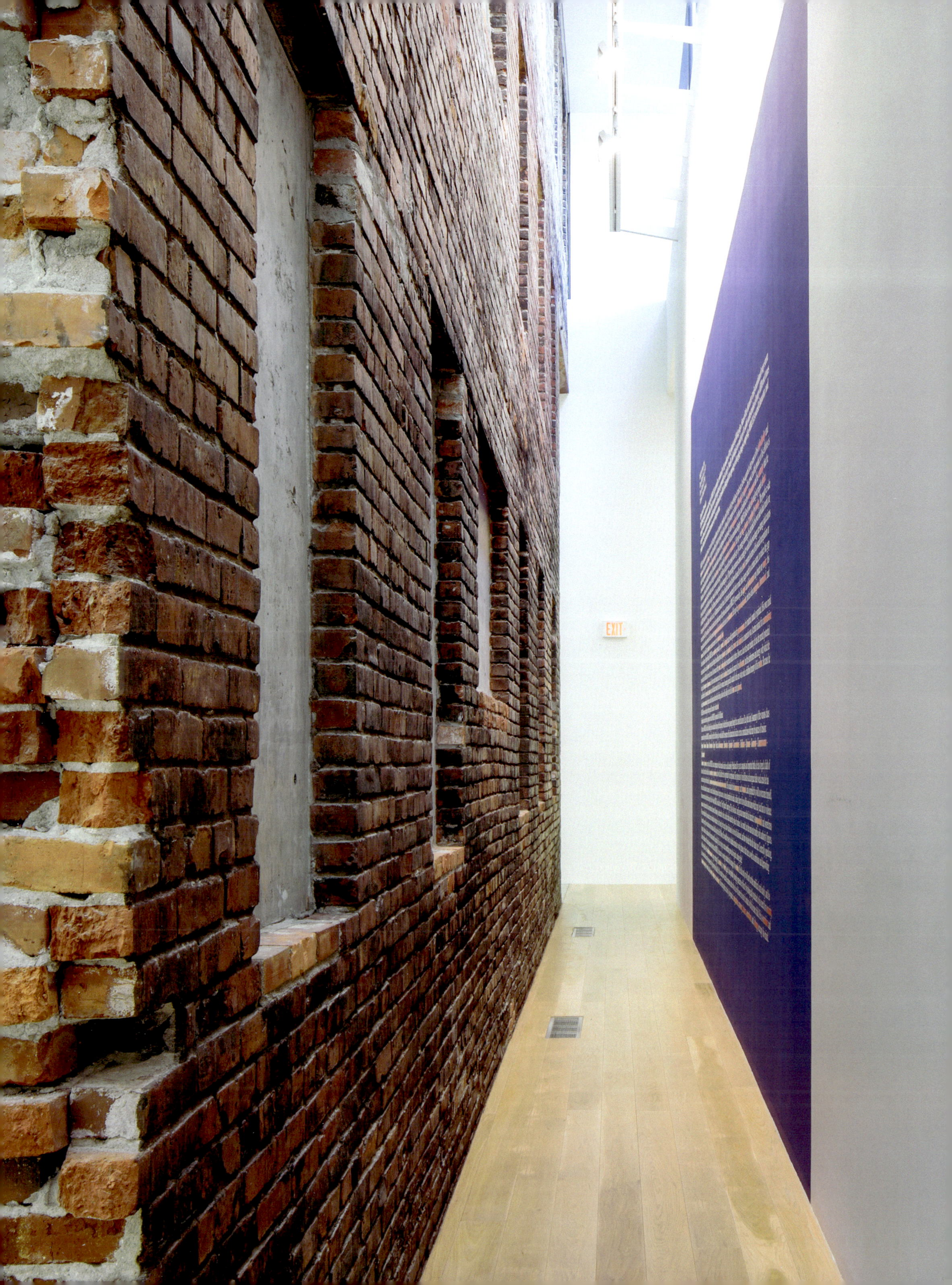
EXIT

ychological dynamic described earlier
combined with his somewhat [redacted]
of an [redacted] or an a[redacted]; moreover h
rpio Rising, MIRCEA has a [redacted]
ly s[redacted] viewpoint, and though he c
t to live with, at times. It is the source
nd d[redacted]. His other natural reso
[redacted] and se[redacted] and will dedicate mu
experiences and his instincts often ru
to other people. He cannot live witho
in groups are vital to MIRCEA's pers
rth, his Rising Sign was located in Sco
IRCEA's personality profile; the follo
[redacted] - D[redacted] - D[redacted] P[redacted]

a royal scale, MIRCEA has a tempera
bilities for c[redacted], o[redacted]
n himself (a s[redacted]
encounters. As a result, he holds the pr
er the rising of the New Moon, MIRCE
buck convention and innovate. Mono

xplains many of the pluses and minuse
[redacted] incline him to be [redacted]
is [redacted] l[redacted].
ersonality, a p[redacted], f[redacted] natu
cillates between o[redacted] and [redacted]
f the c[redacted], m[redacted] [redacted] he someti
rces are his r[redacted] and u[redacted] determ
h of his life to women, becoming espe
his feelings, his love life is likely to b
l[redacted]!
al self-fulfillment.
pio (the Scorpion), while the Sun was
ing key words distill the essence of hi
[redacted] and se[redacted] S[redacted] - Su[redacted]

ent which demands initiative and lead
and work find their best opportunity f
[redacted]). He is i
mise of great success, as long as he pu
is said to be a ‘First Quarter’ lunar typ
ny is unbearable to him, and he chafe

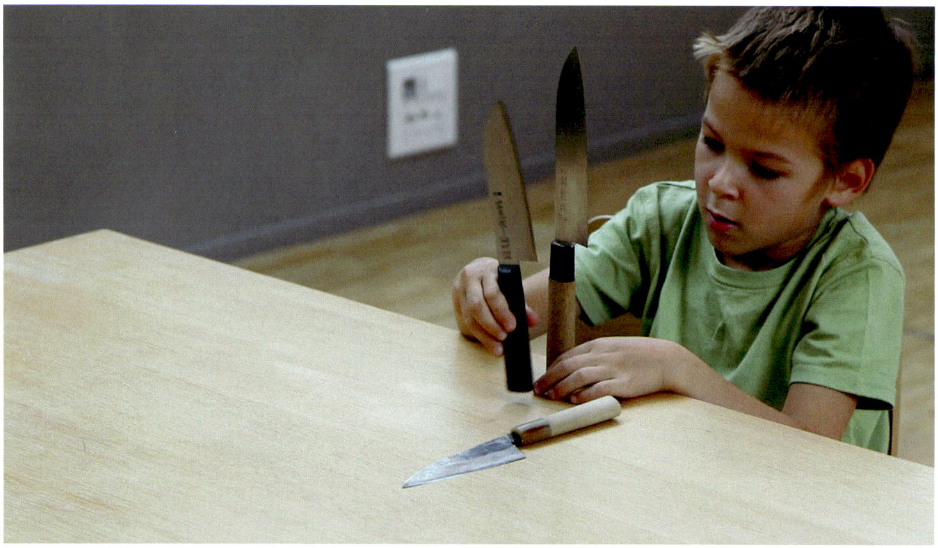

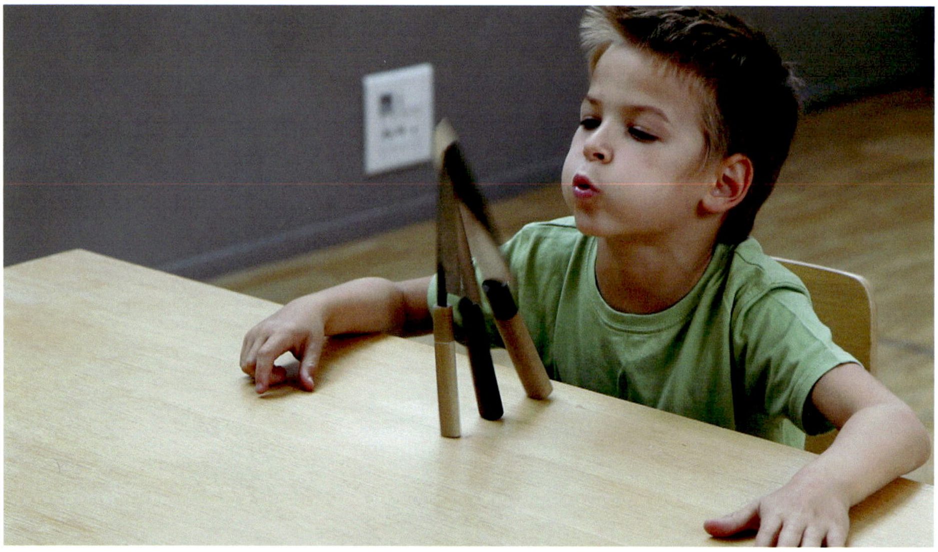

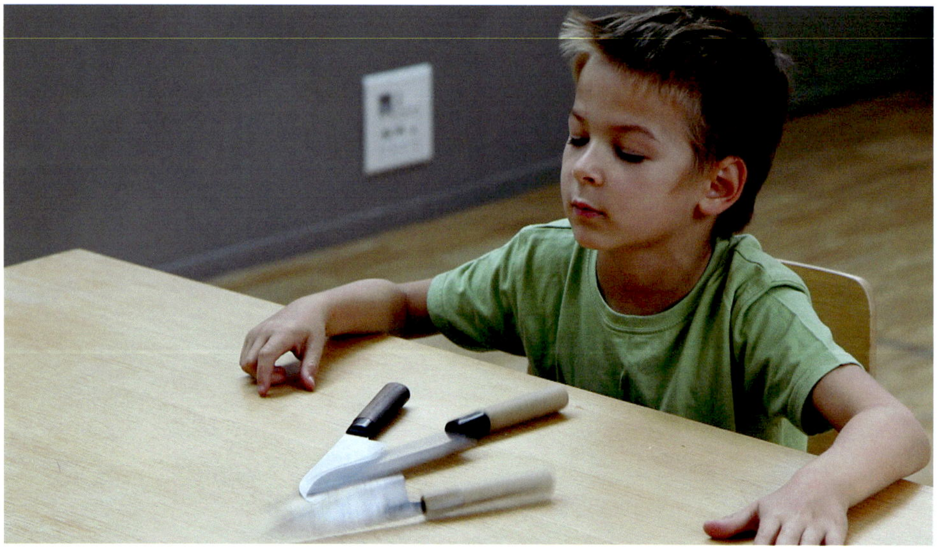

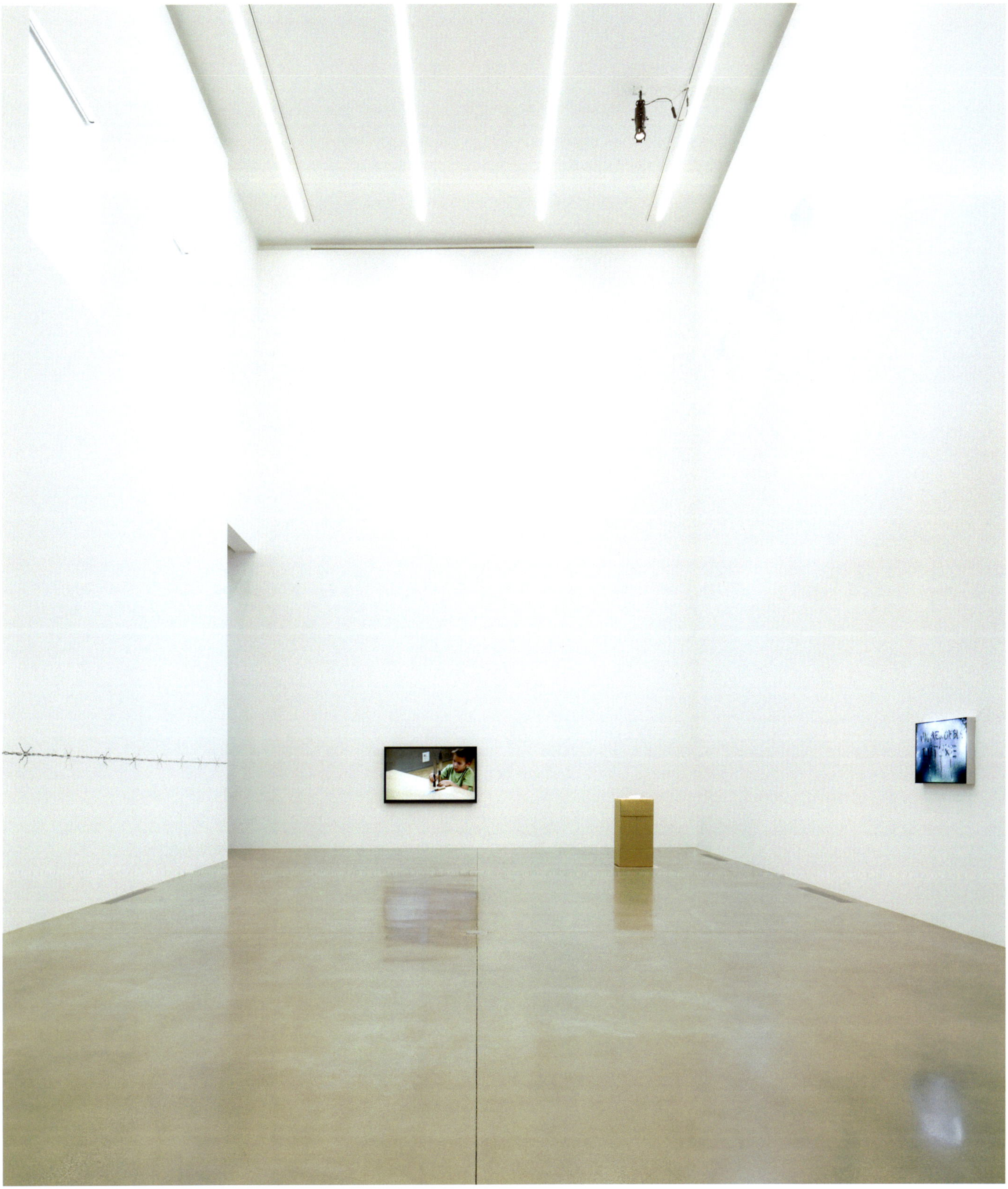

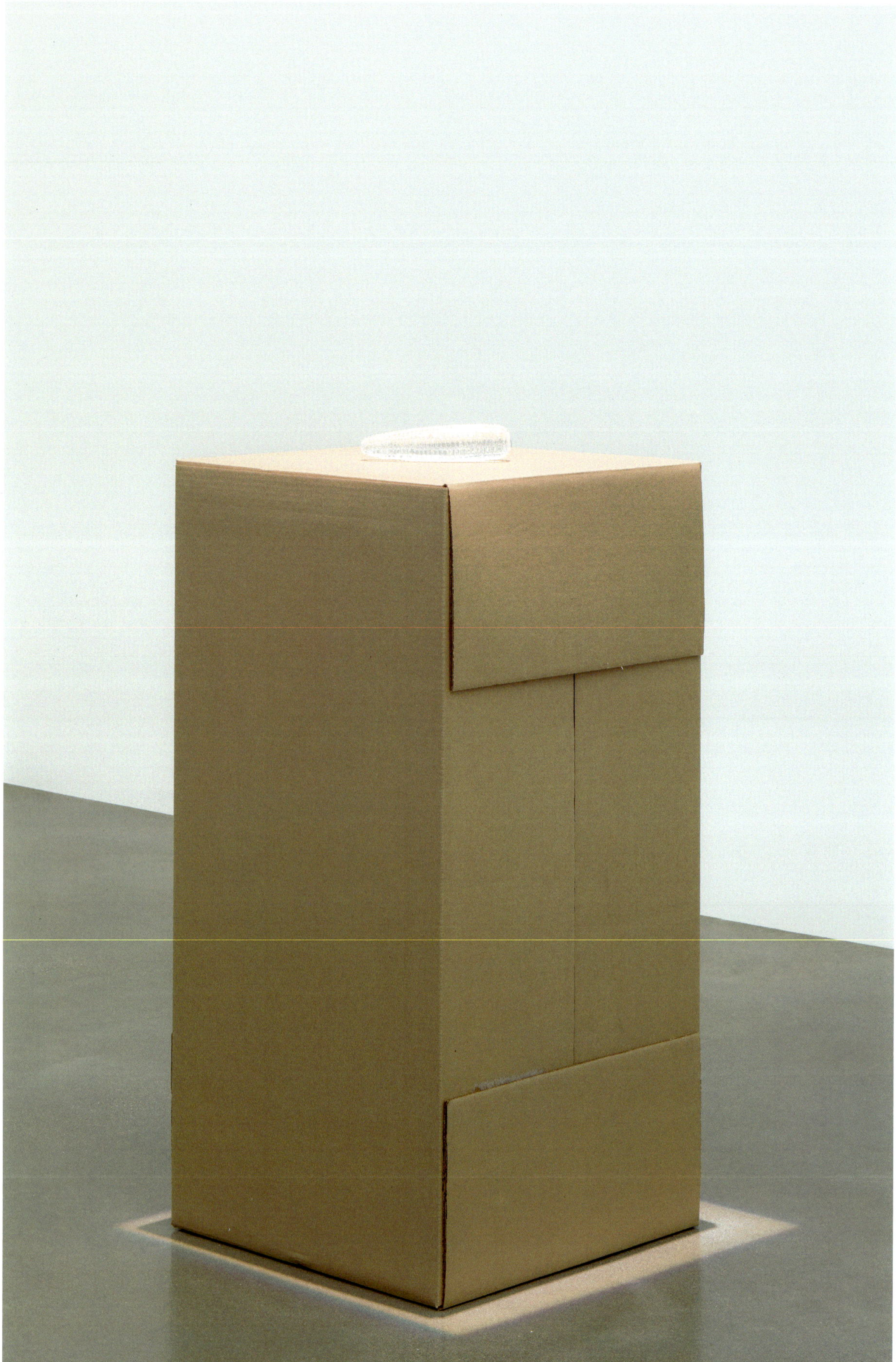

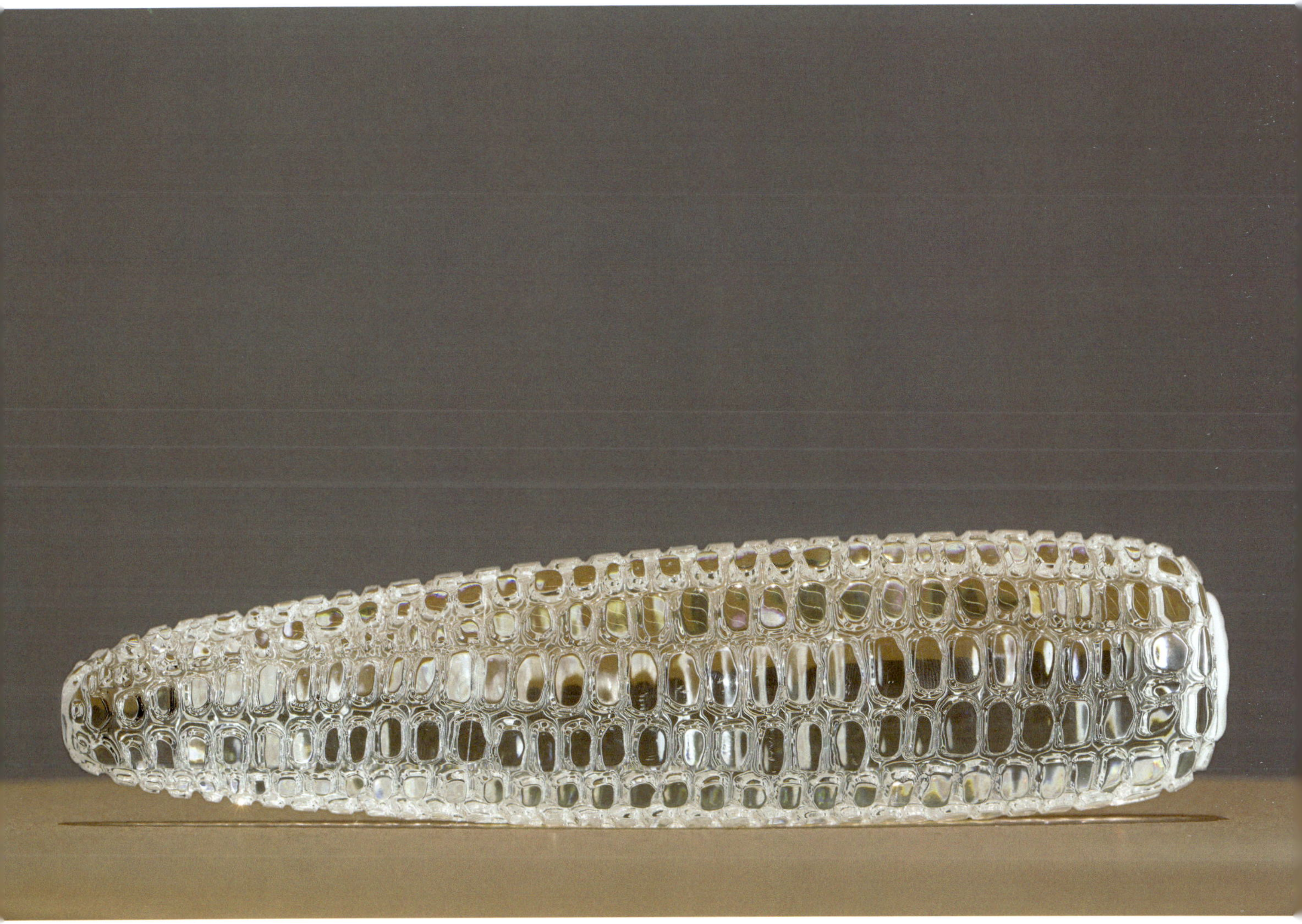

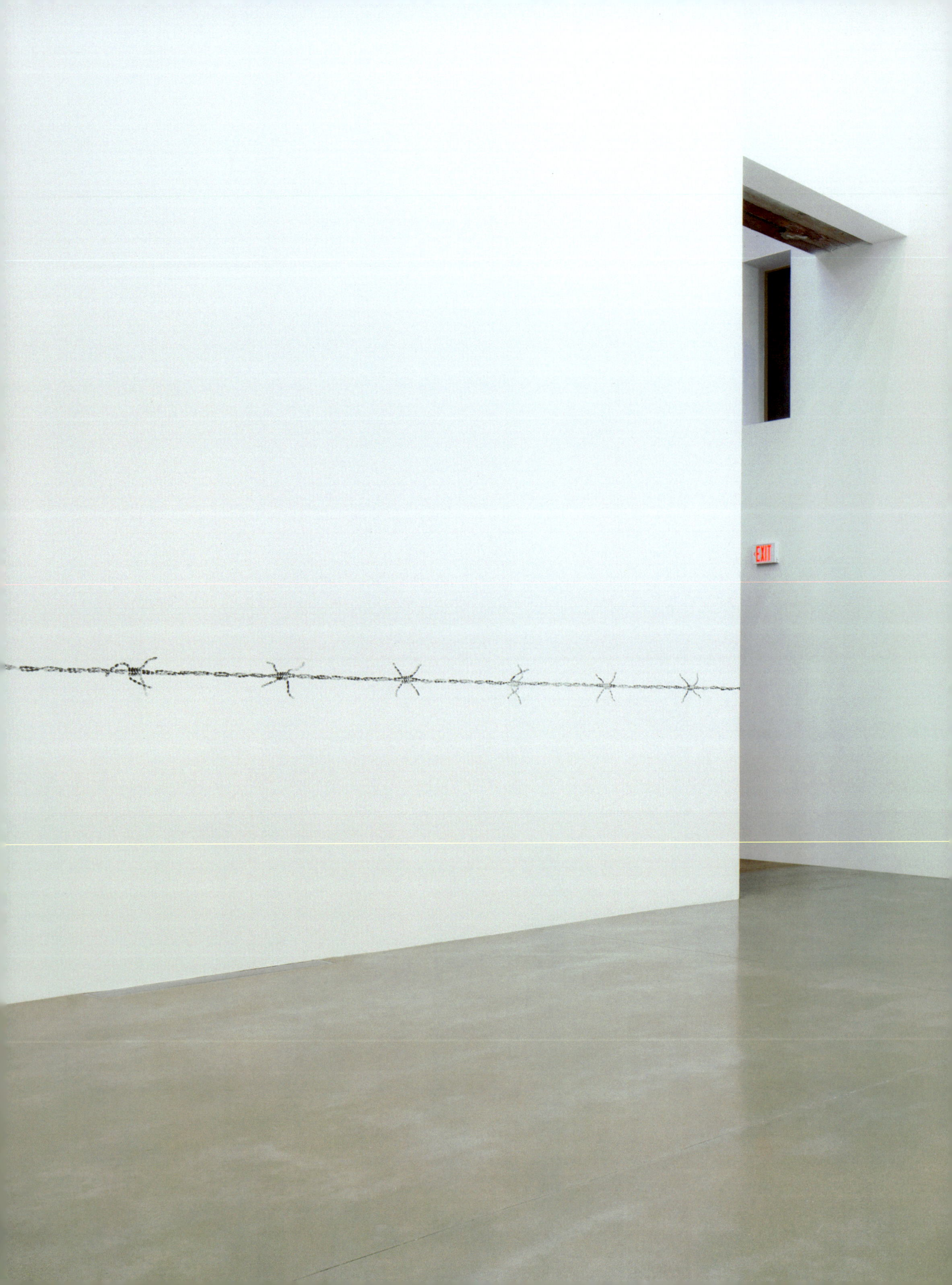
EXIT

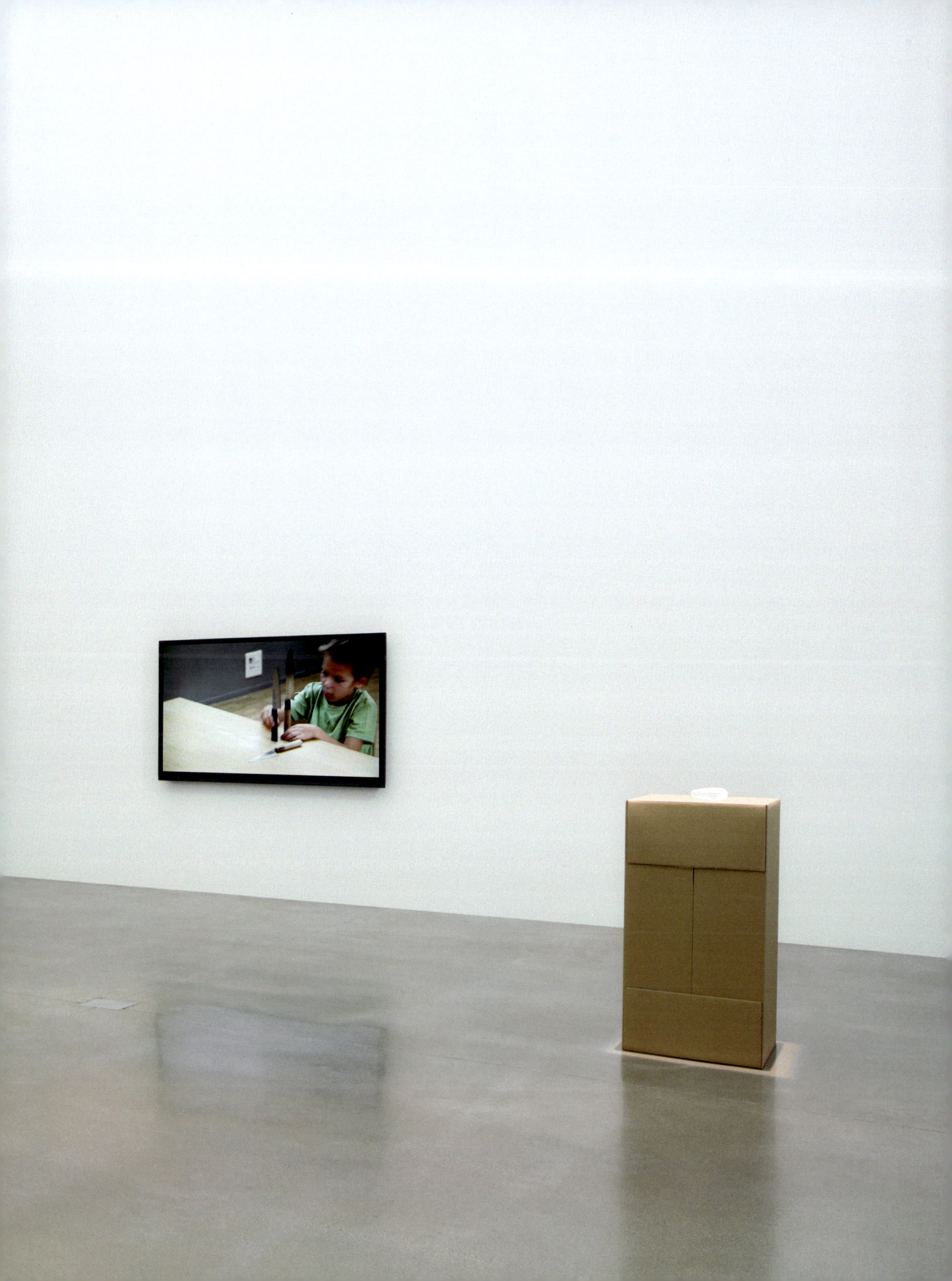

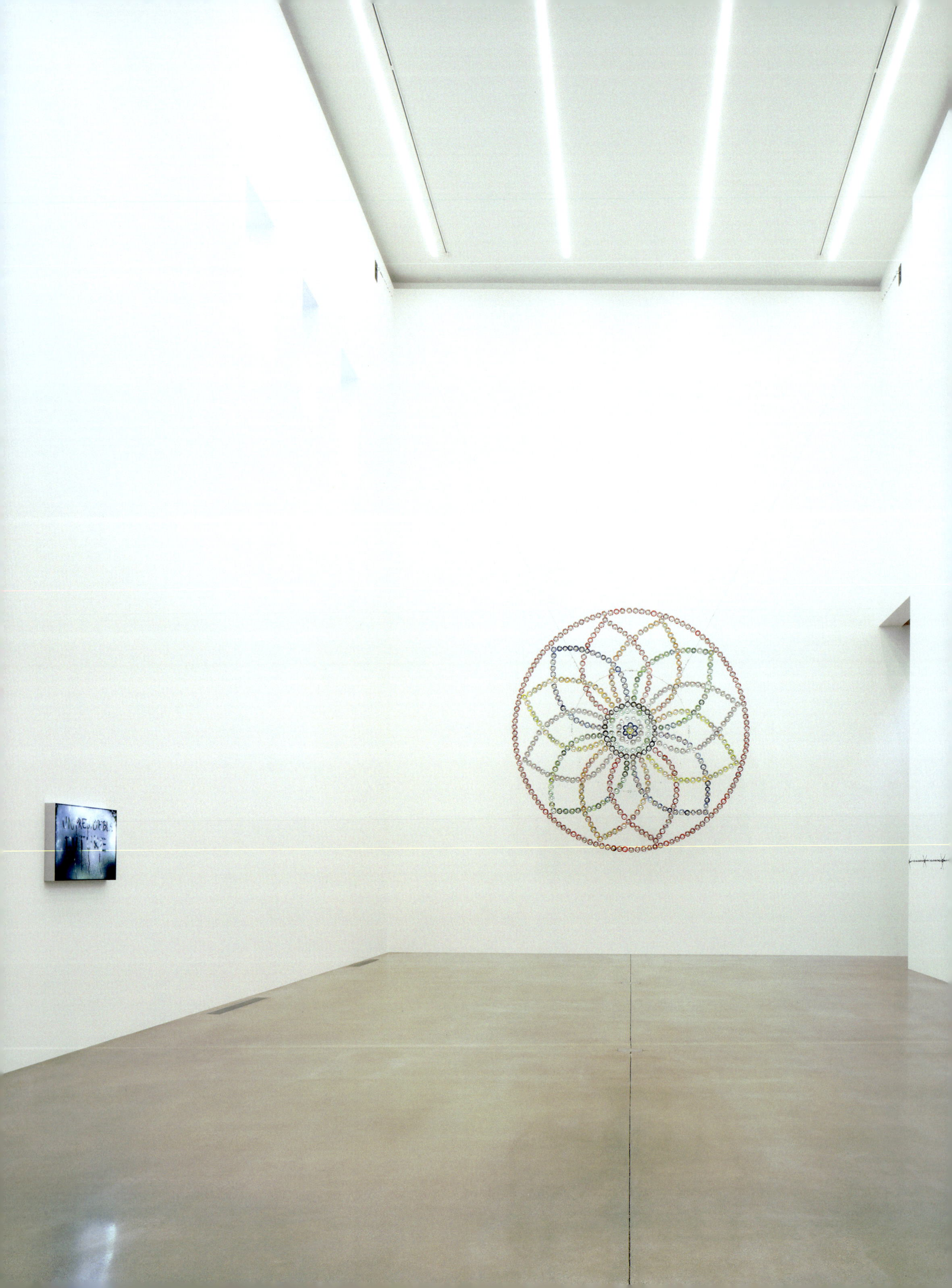

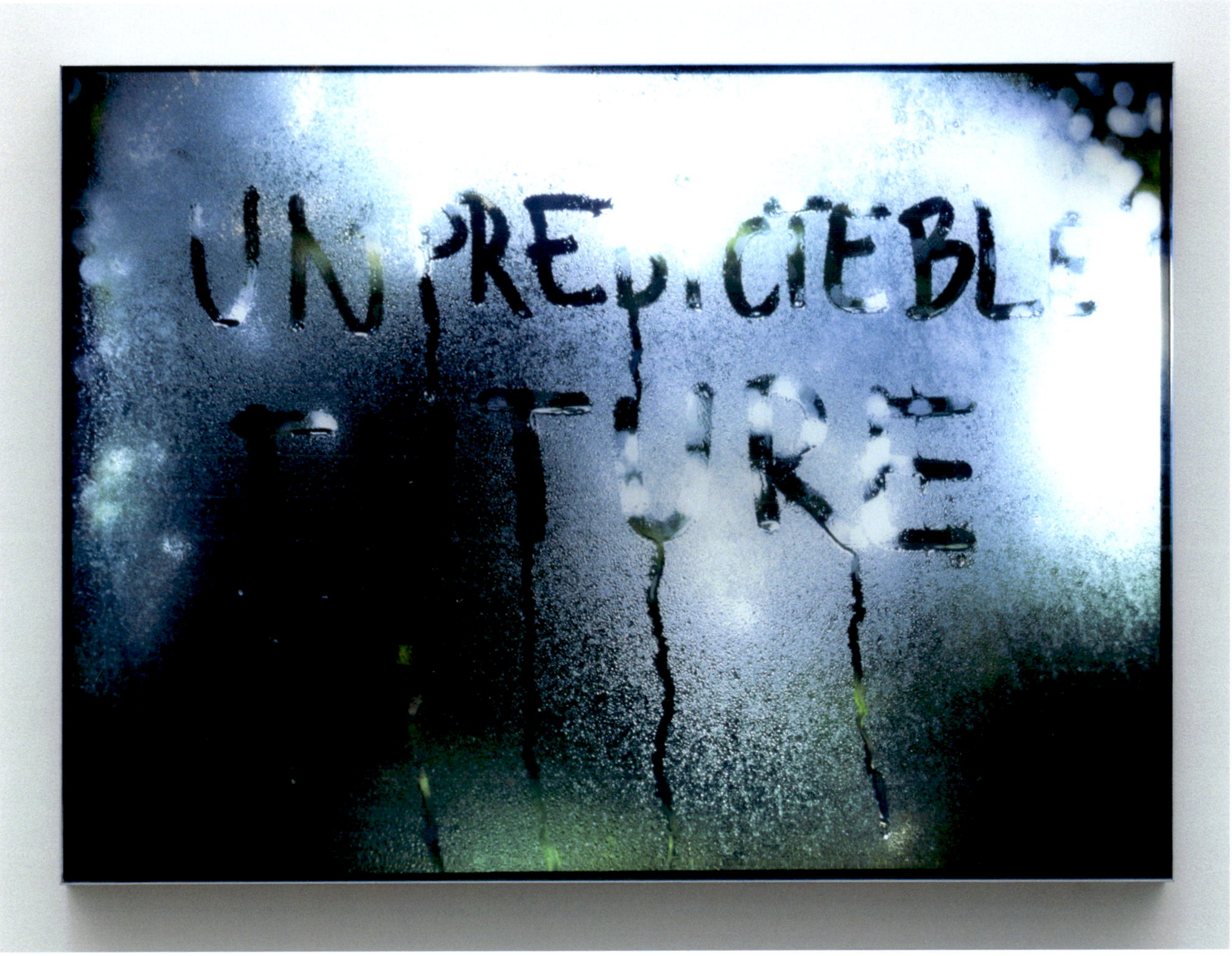
UNPREDICTEBLE
TURE

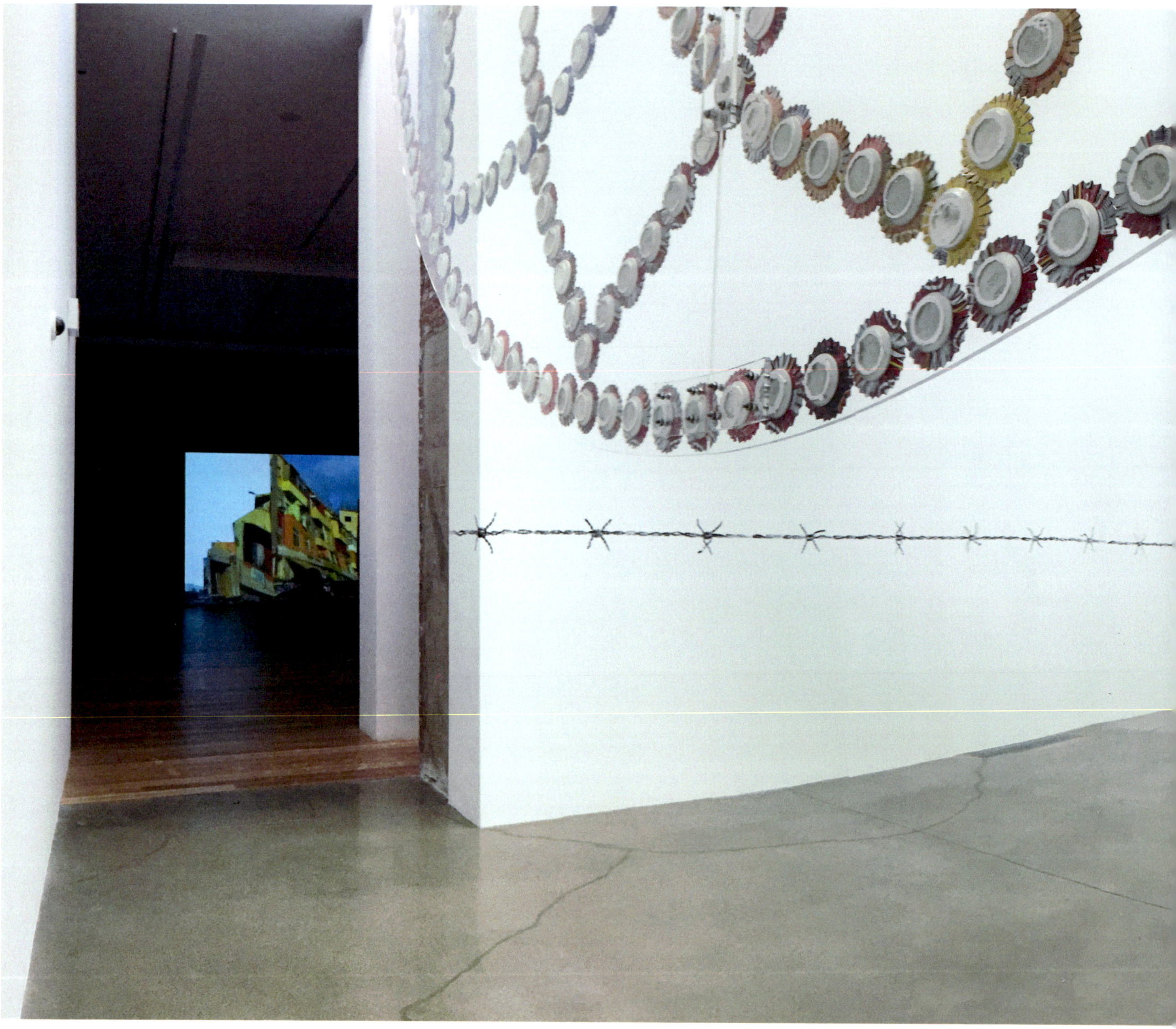

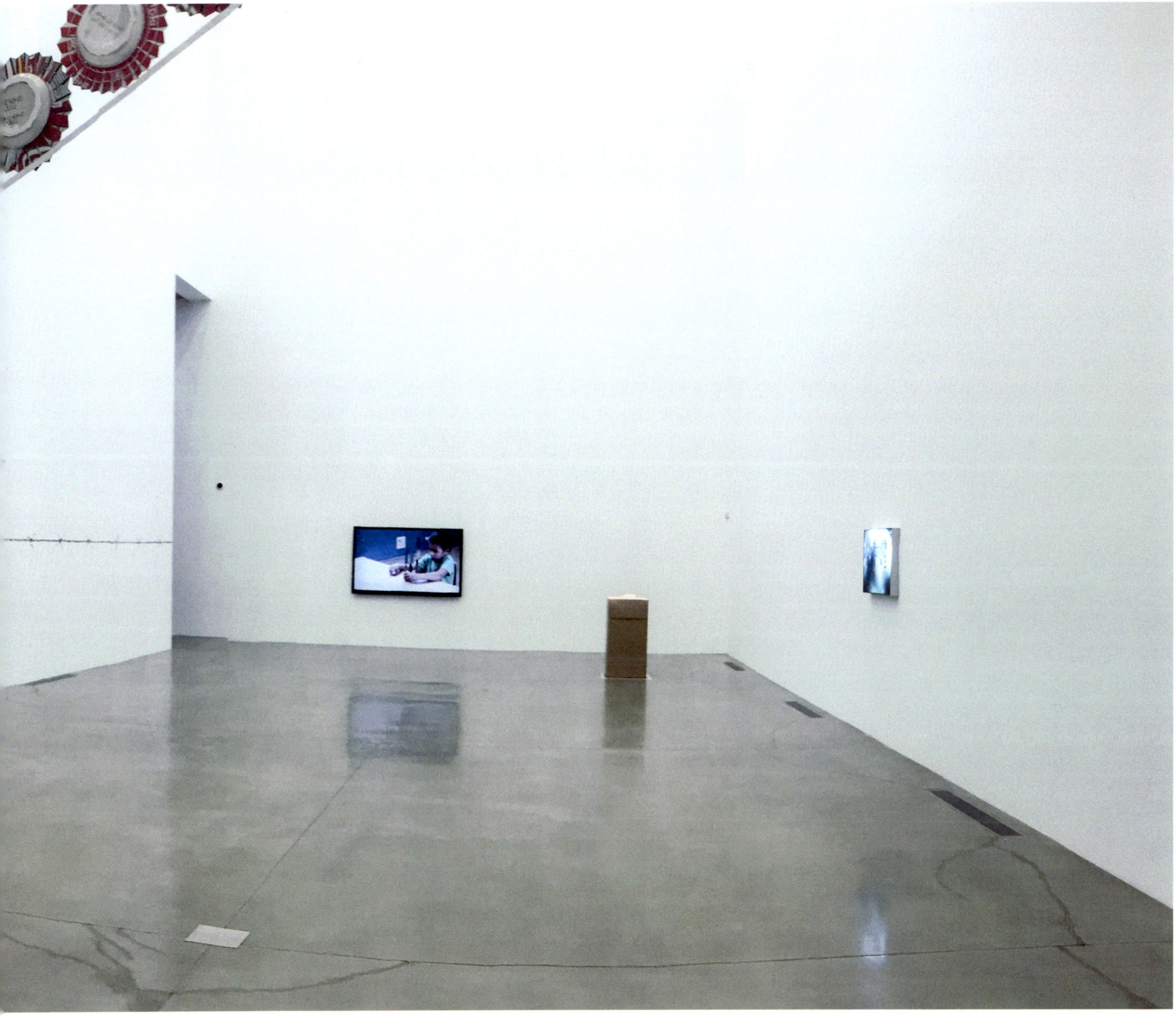

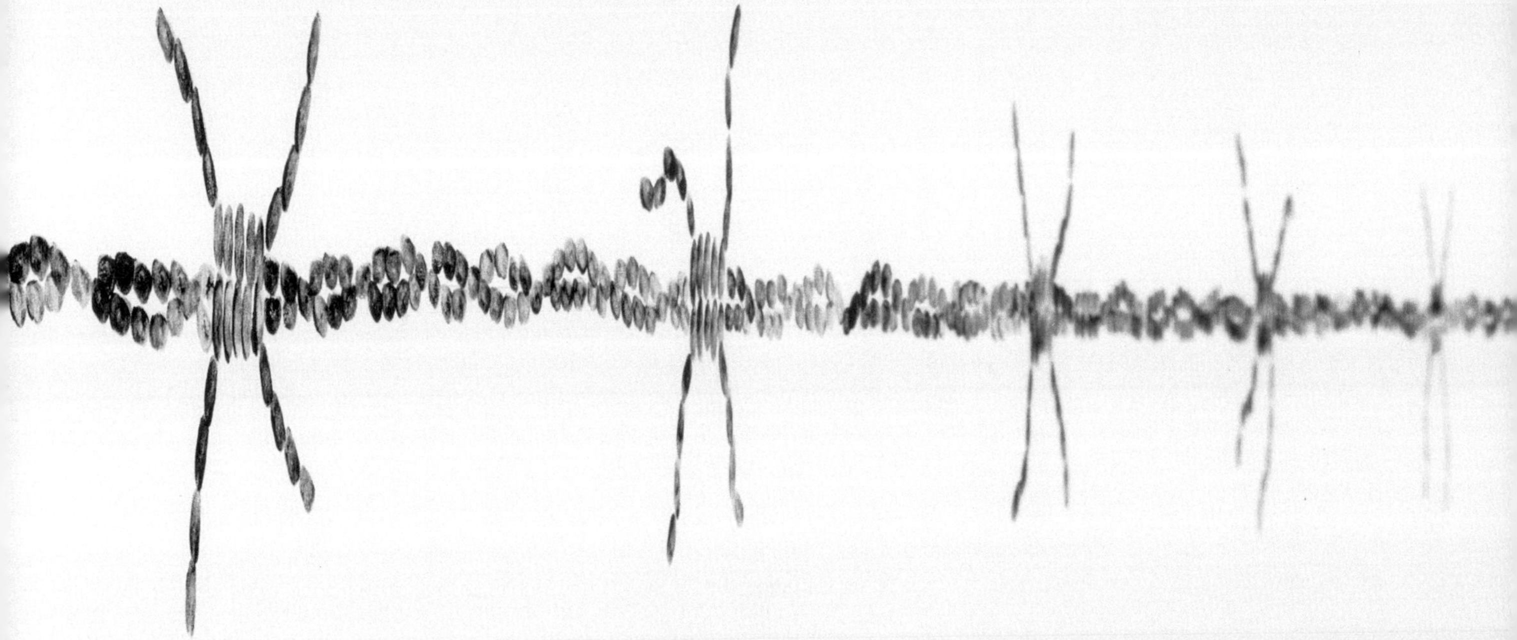

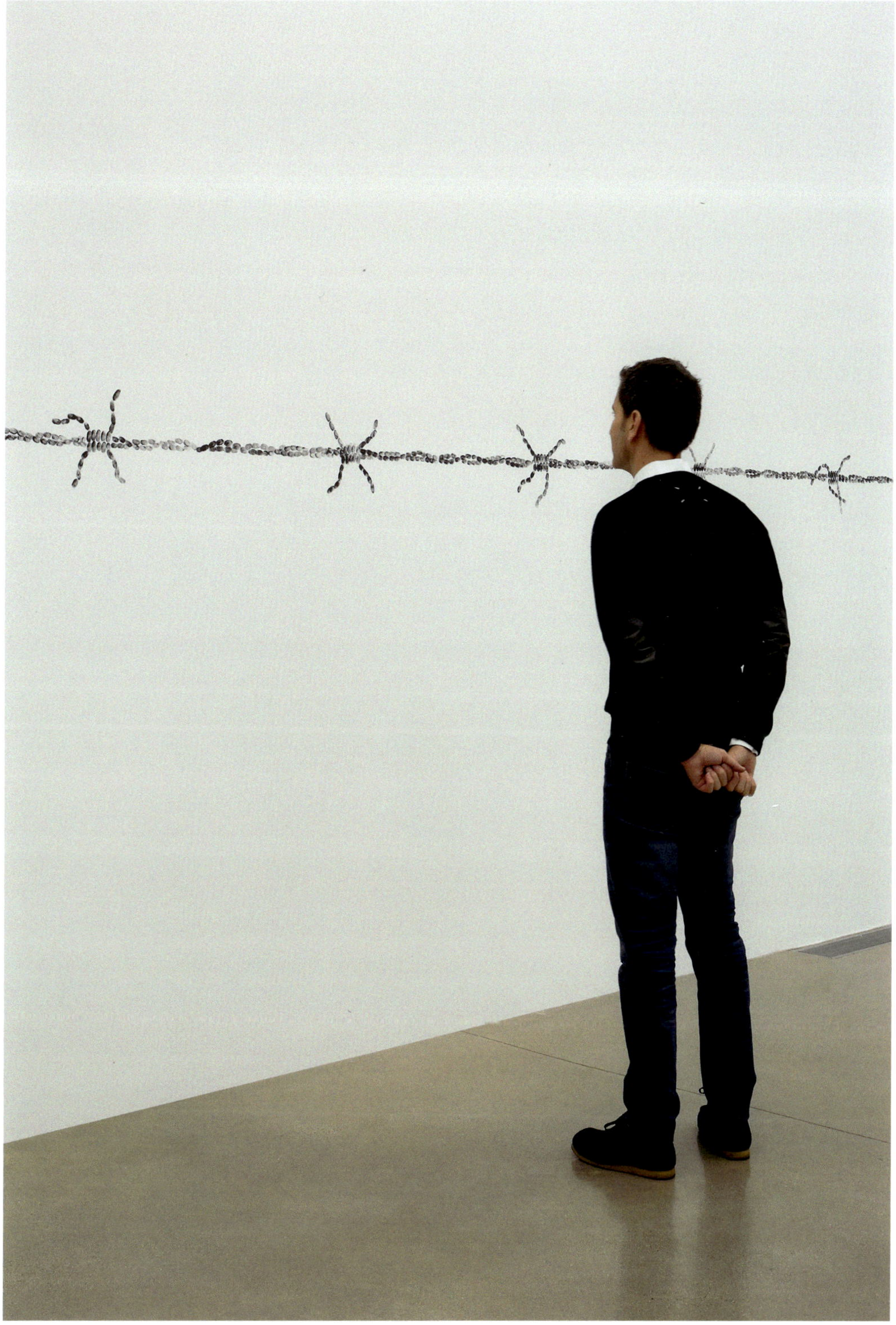

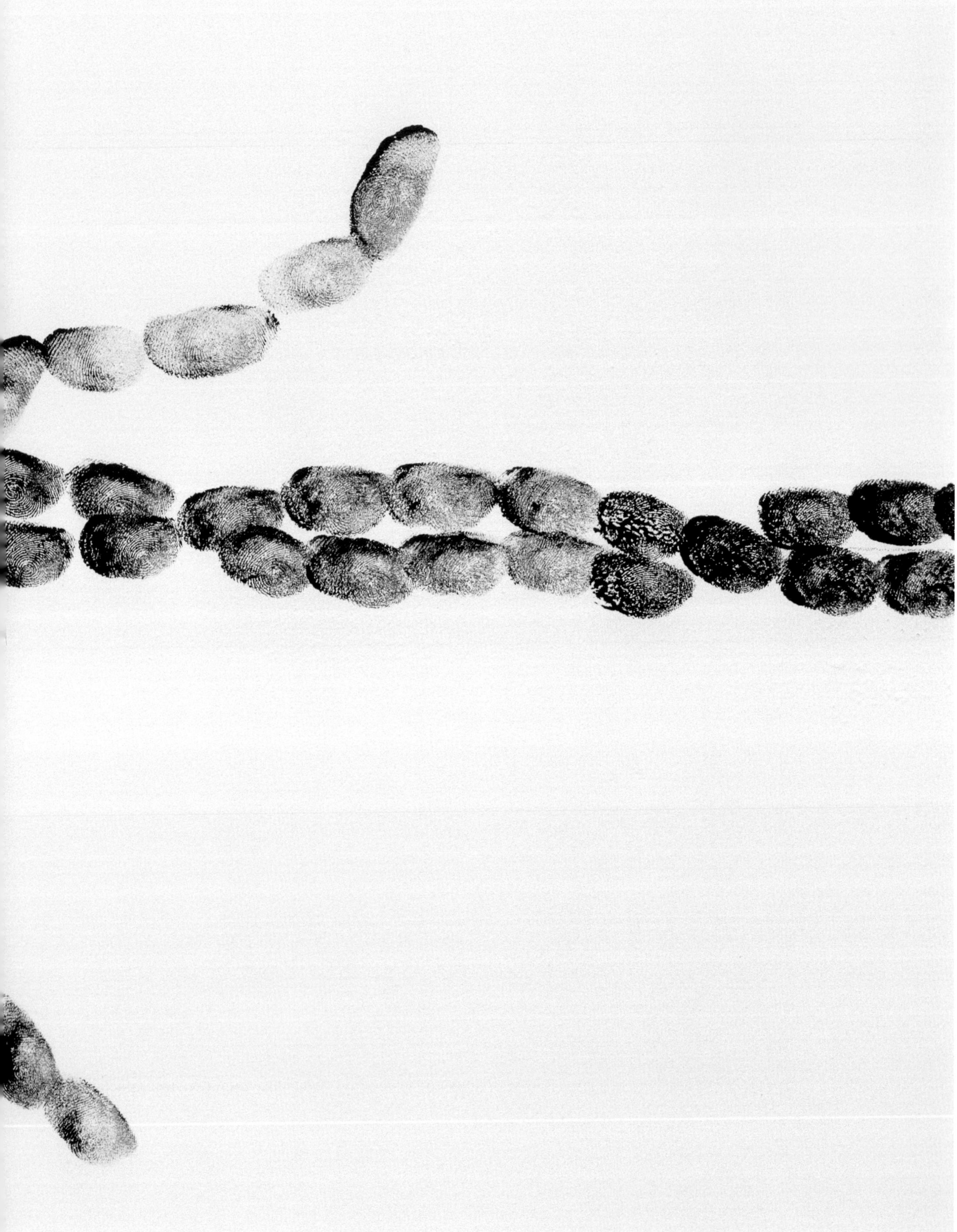

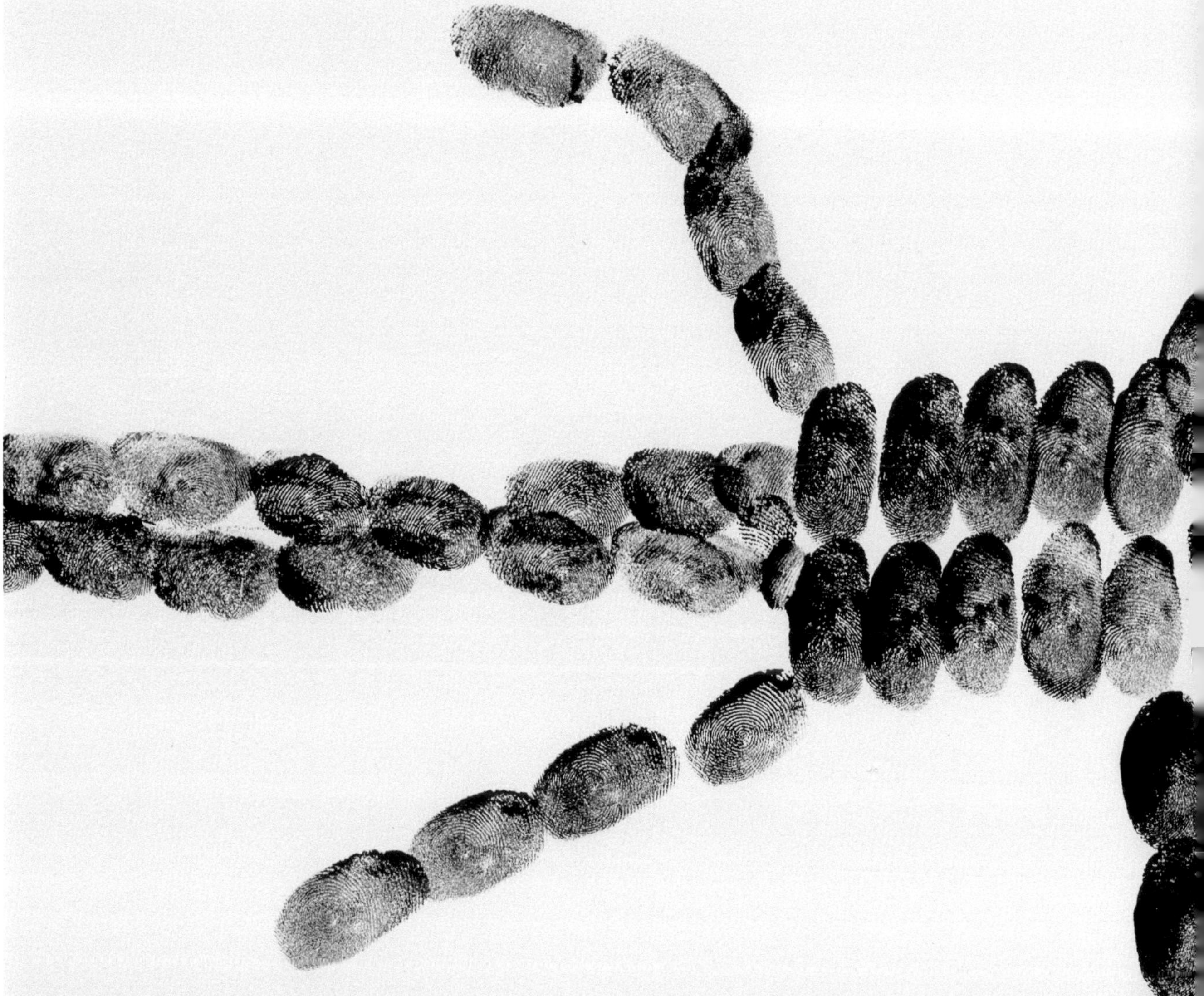

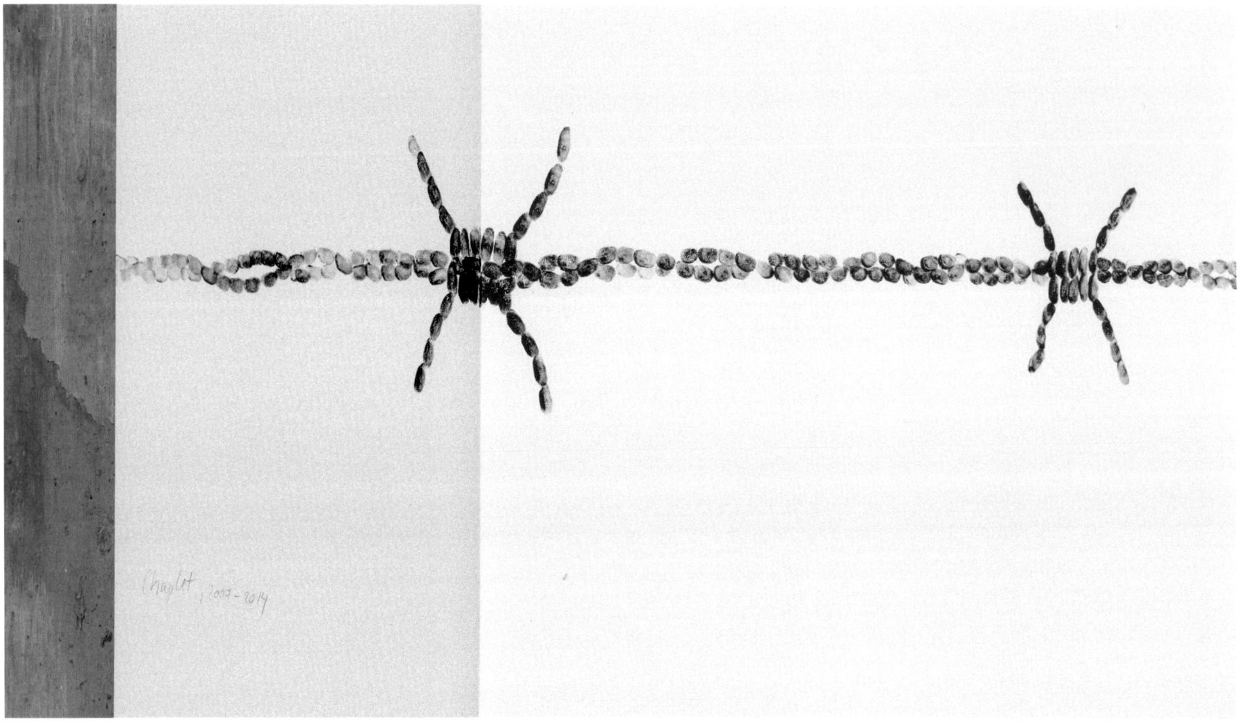
Chaplet, 2007–2014

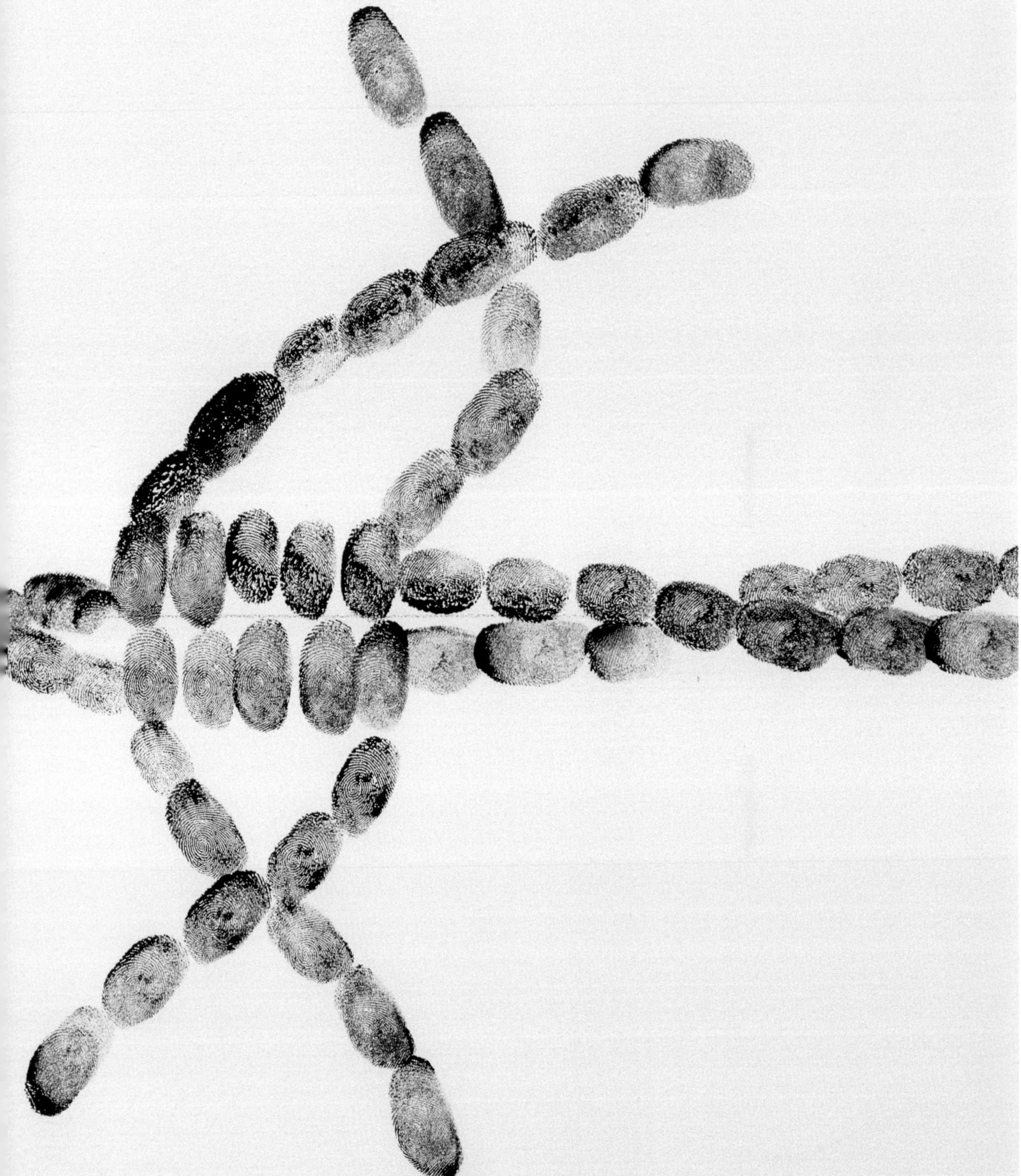

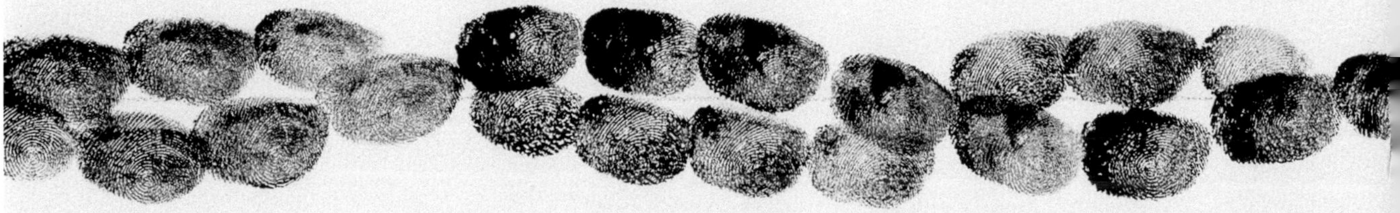

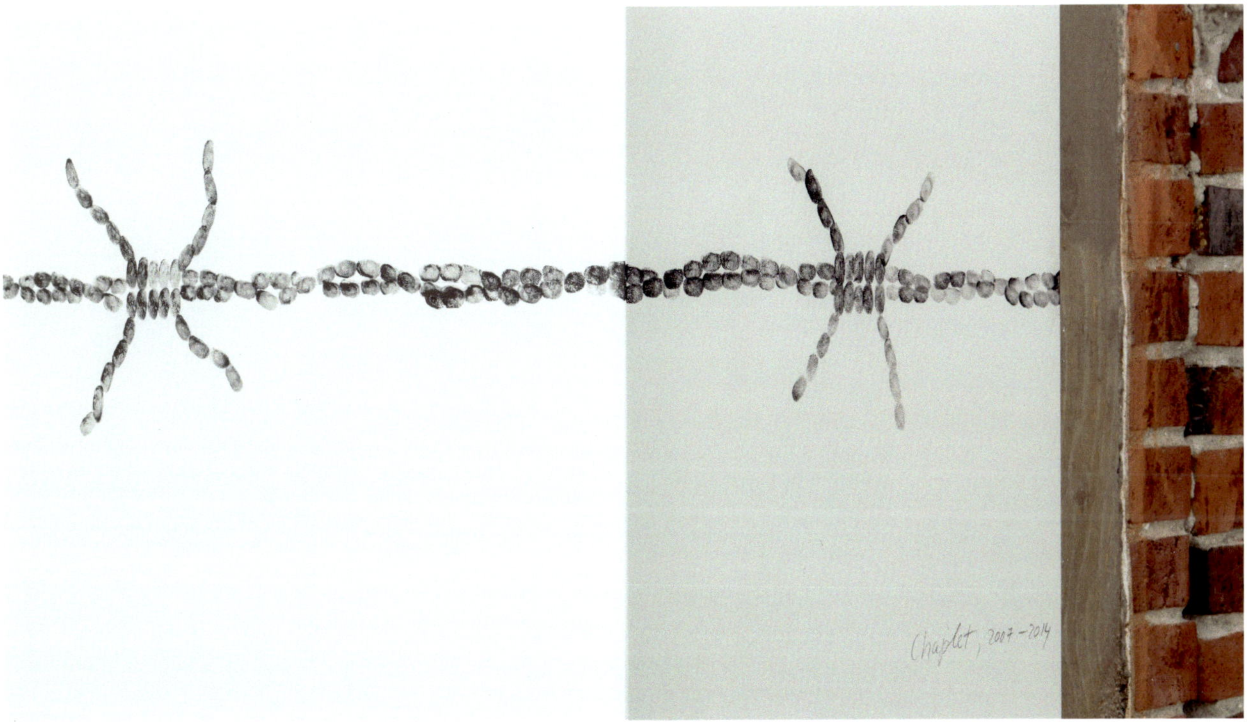
Chaplet, 2007–2014

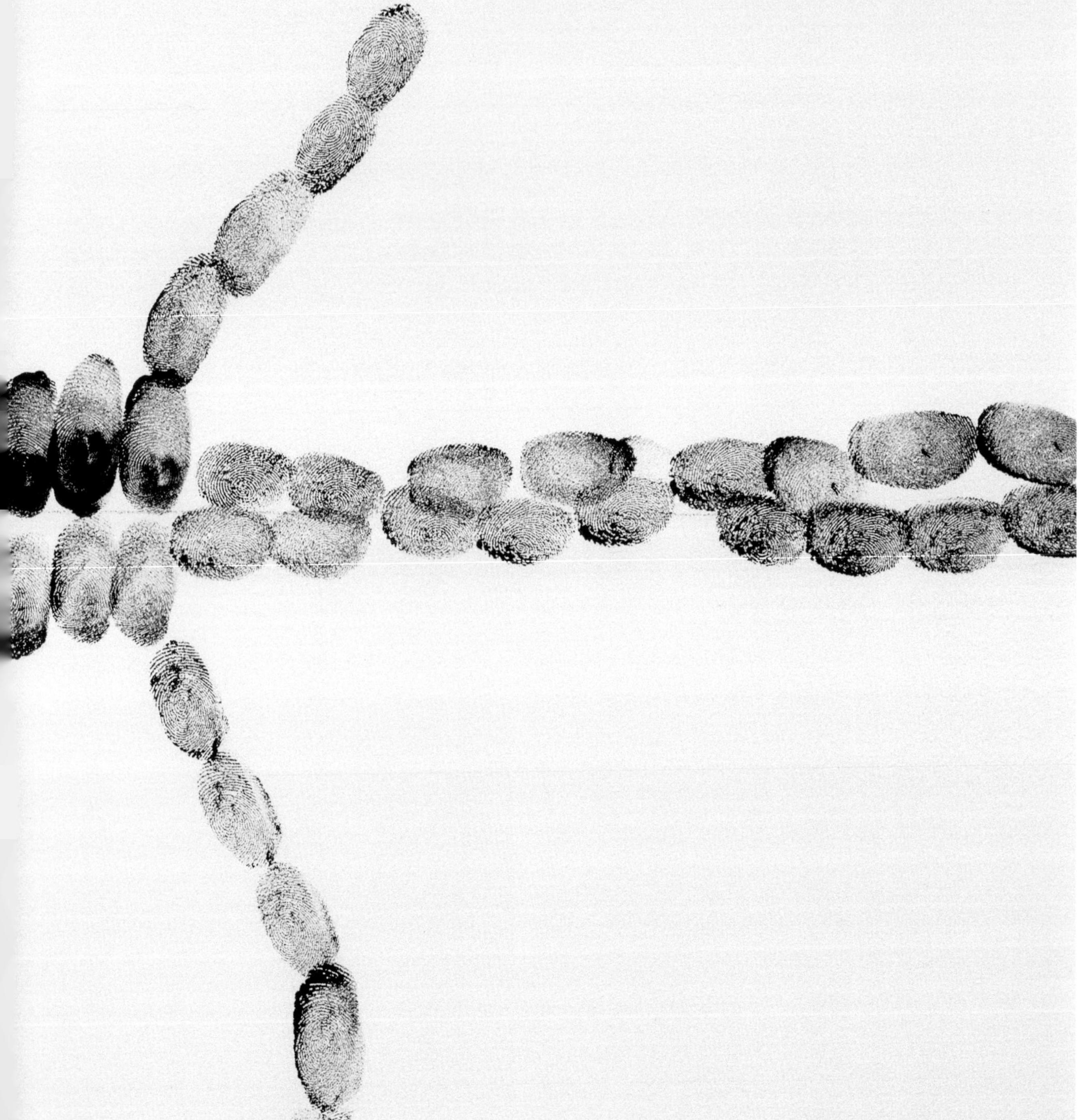

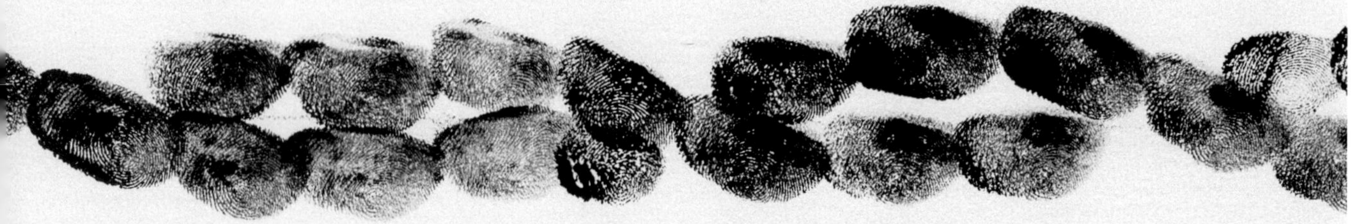

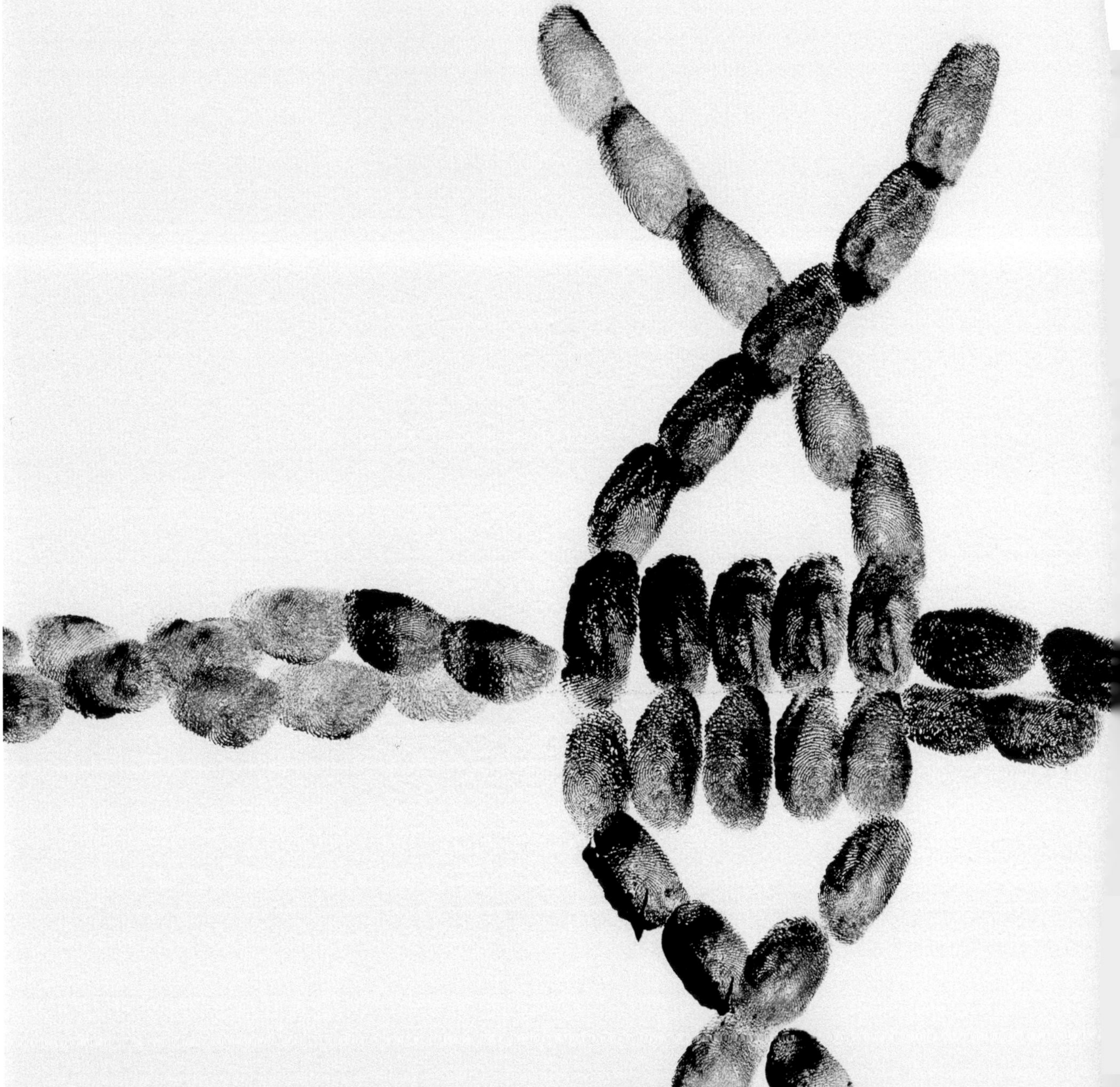

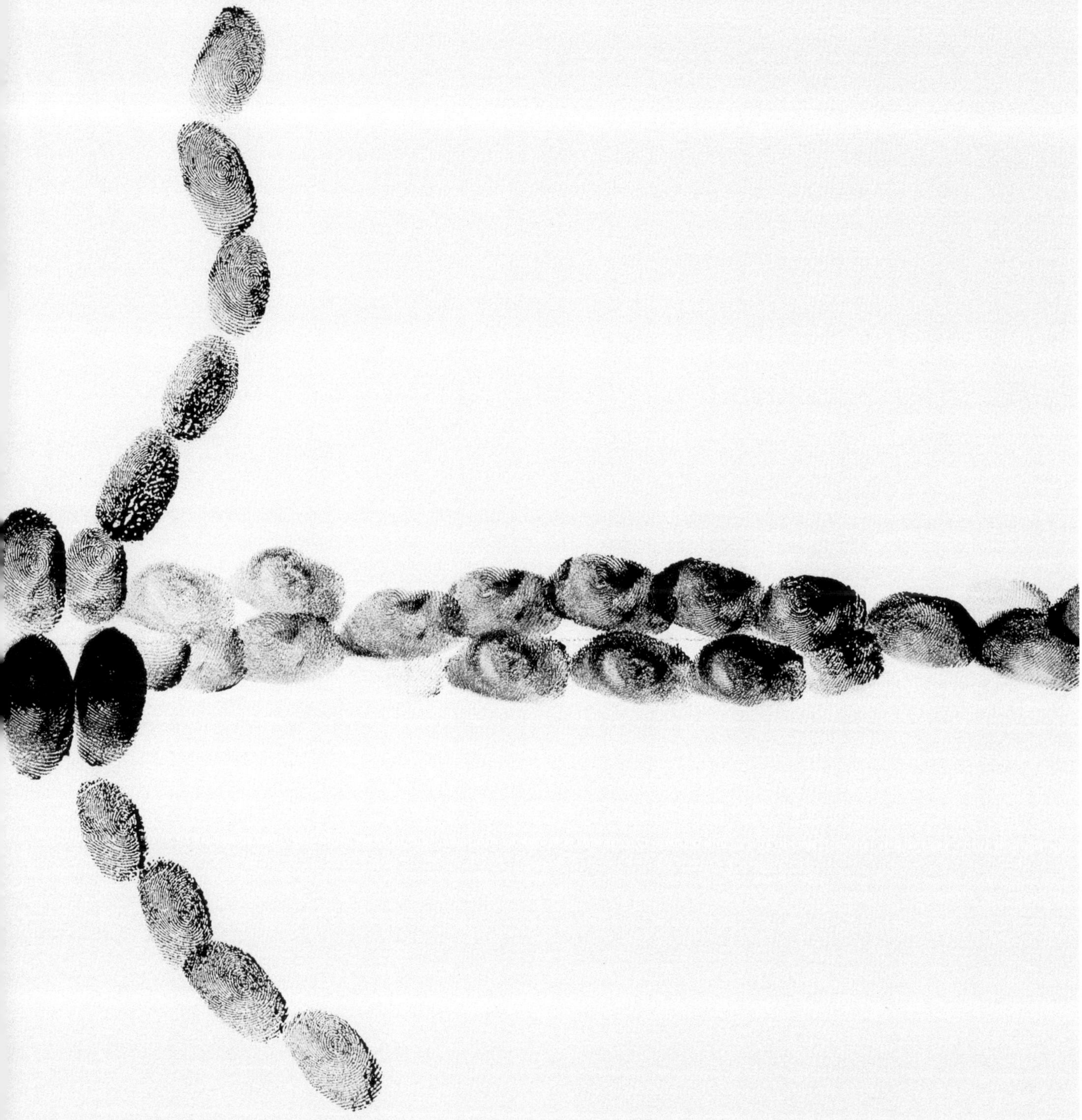

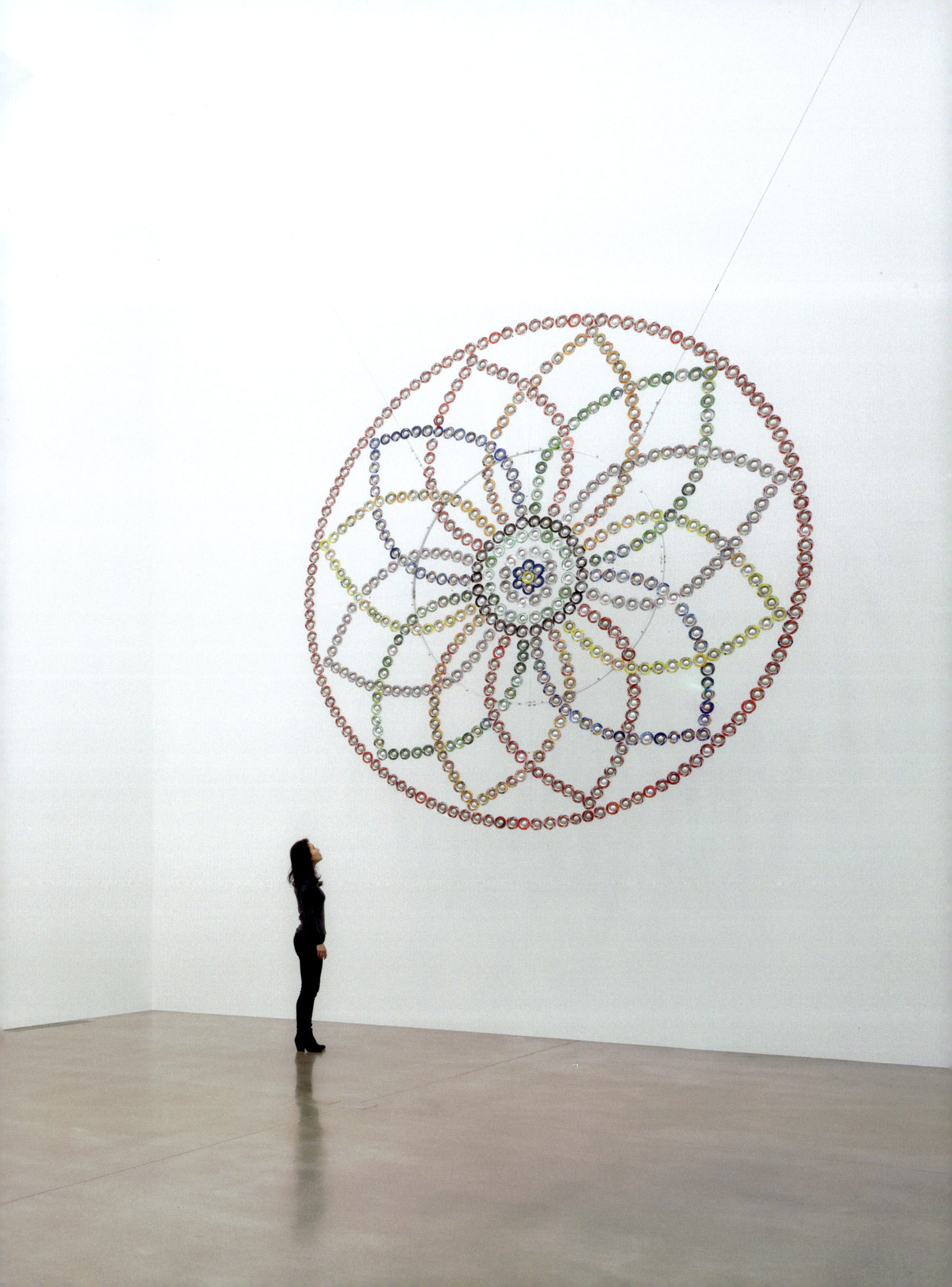

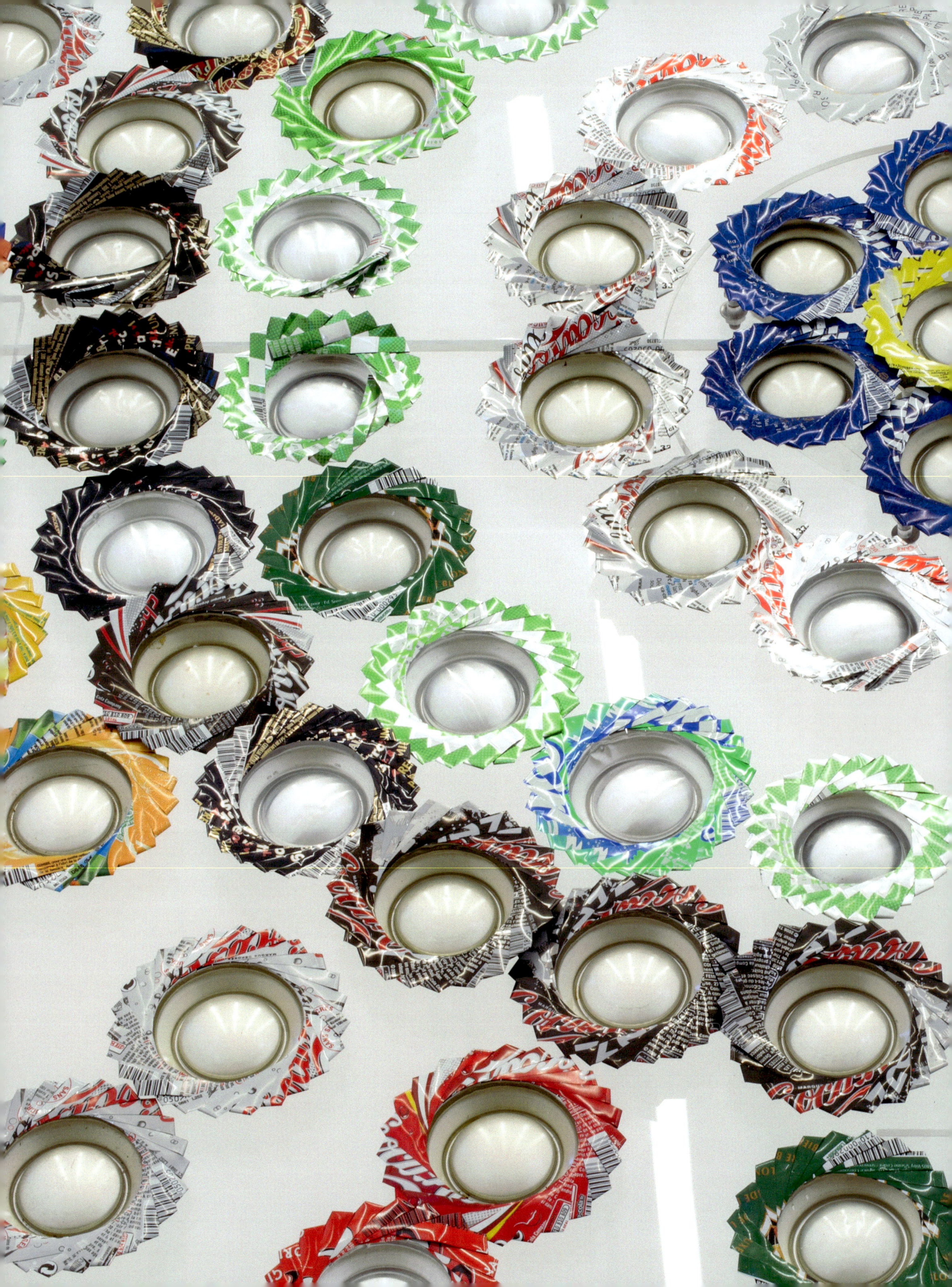

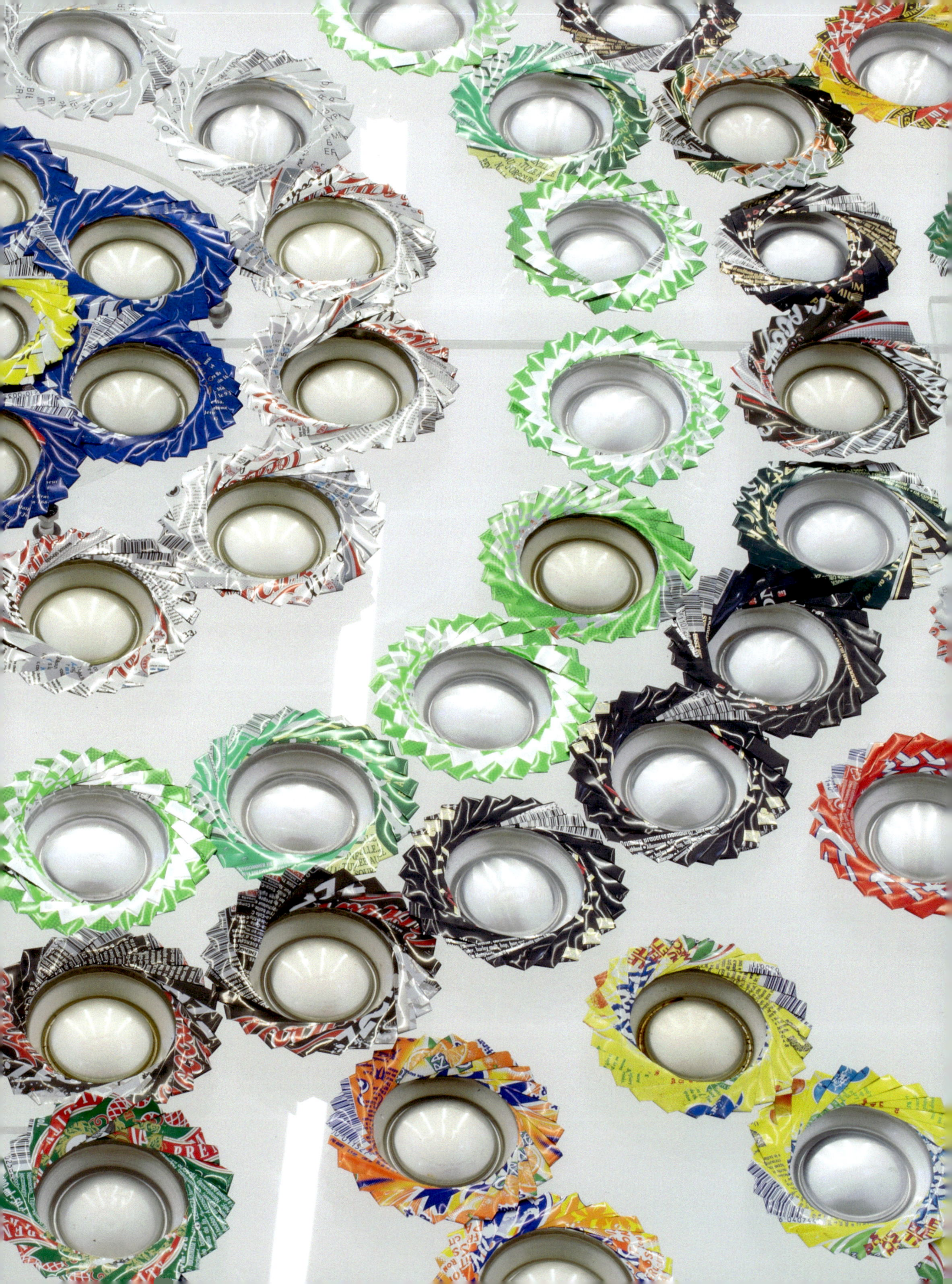

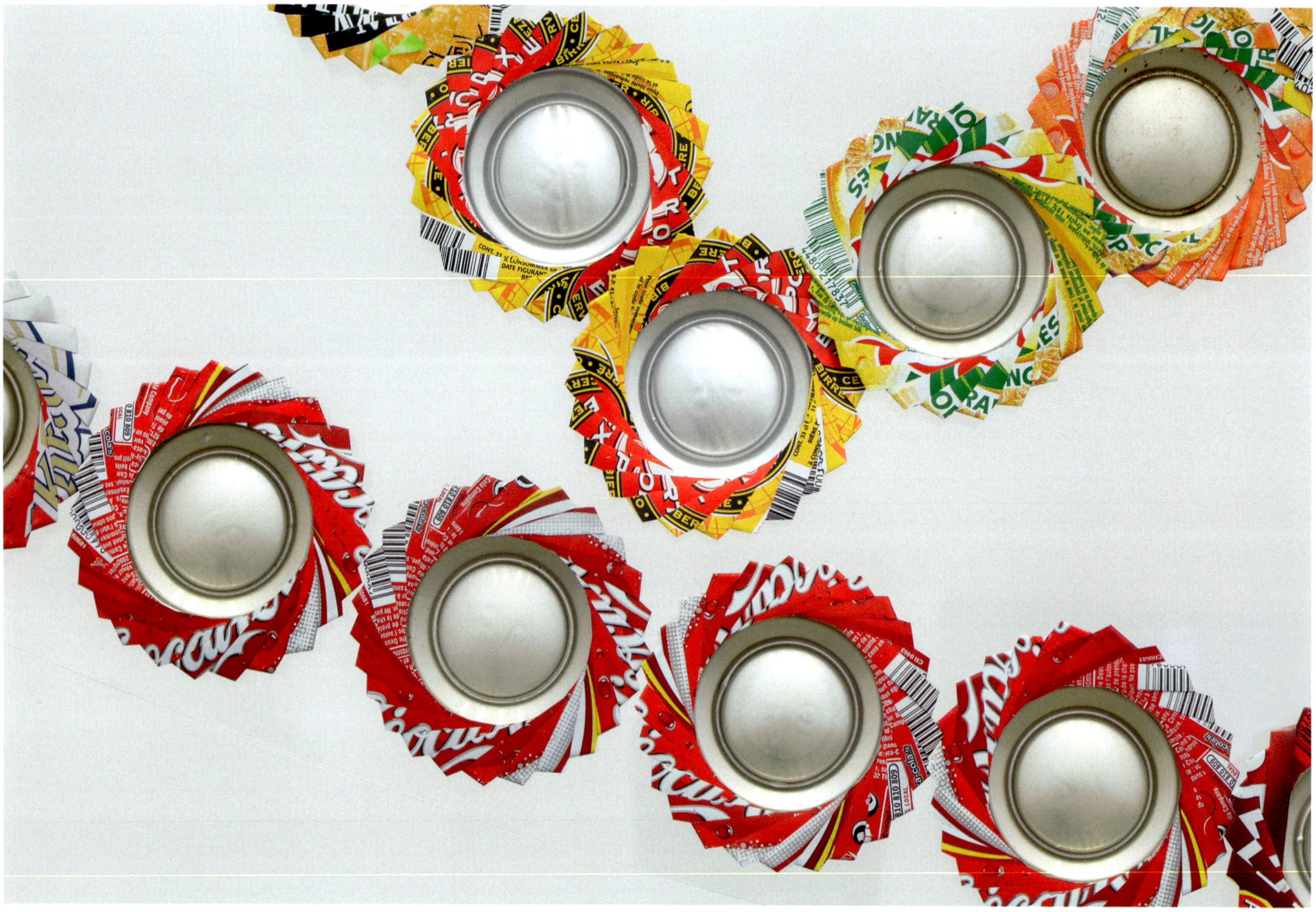

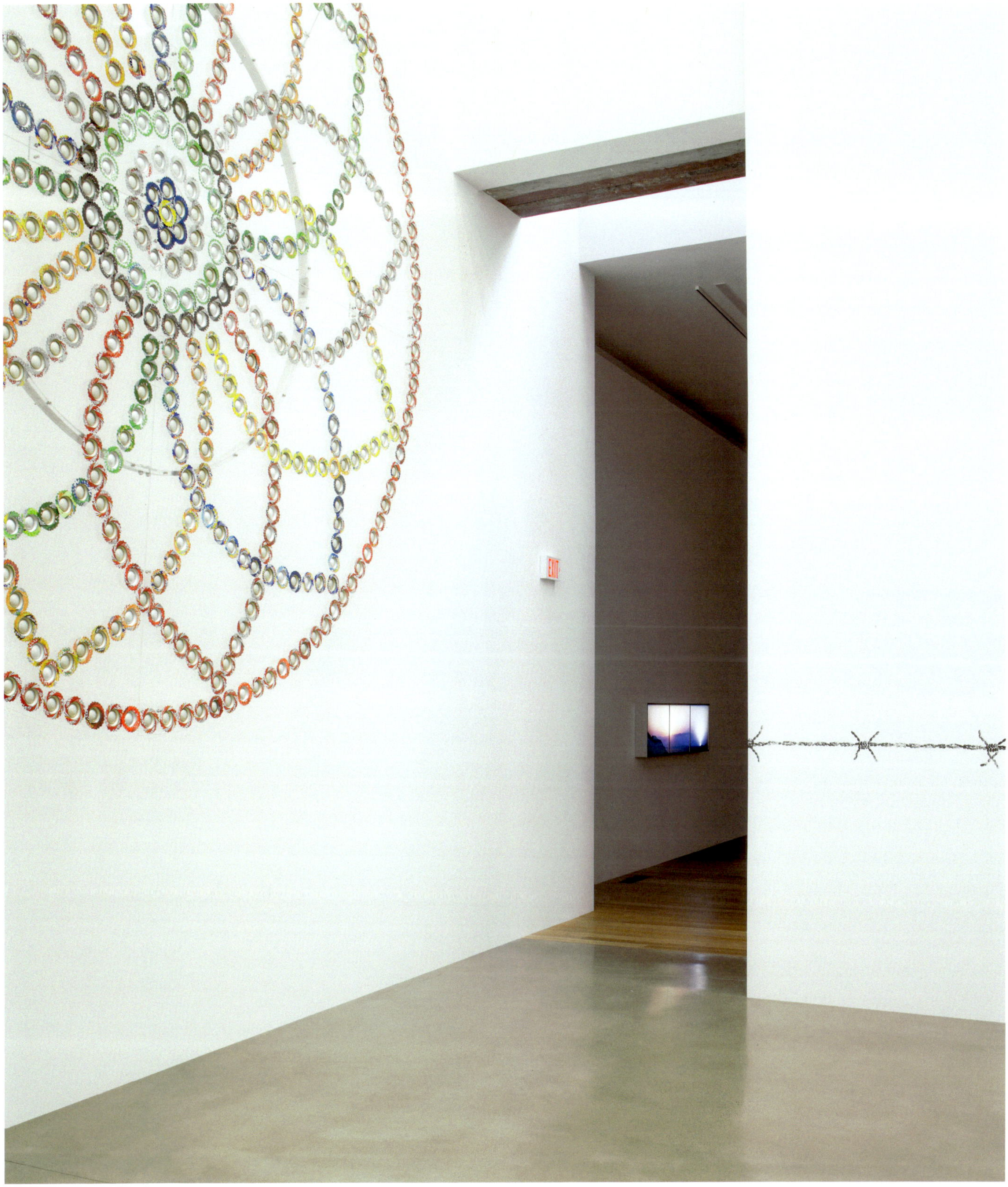
EXIT

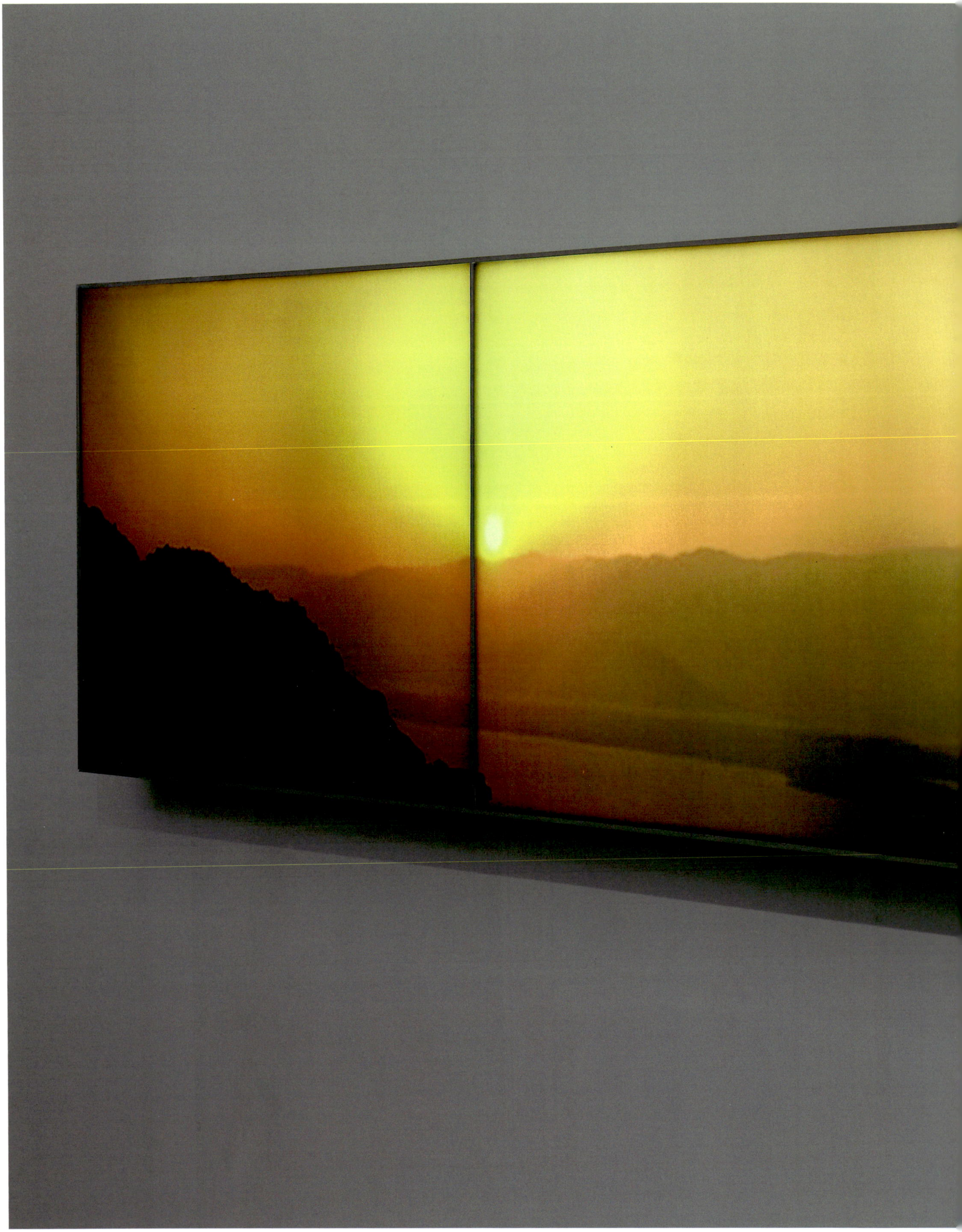

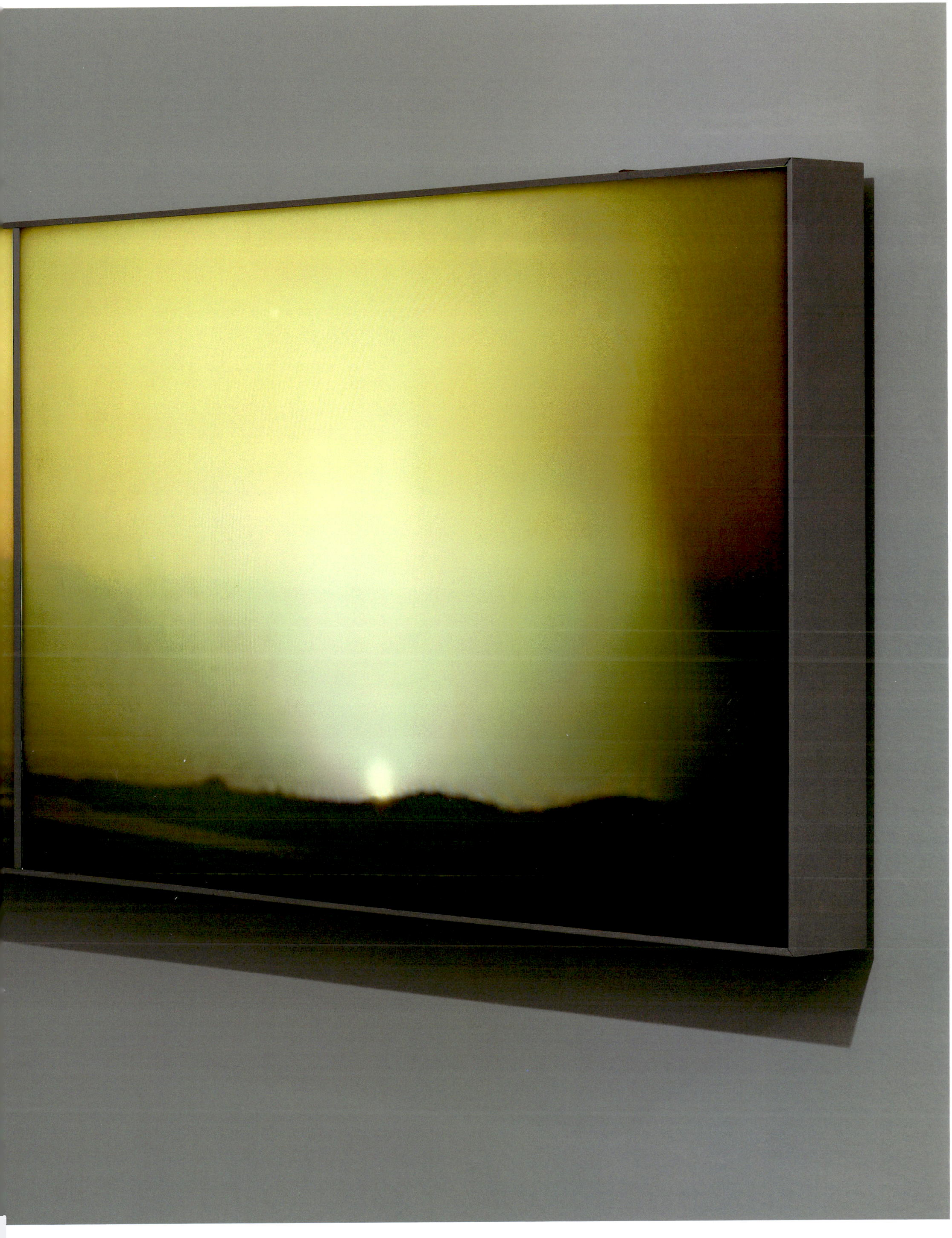

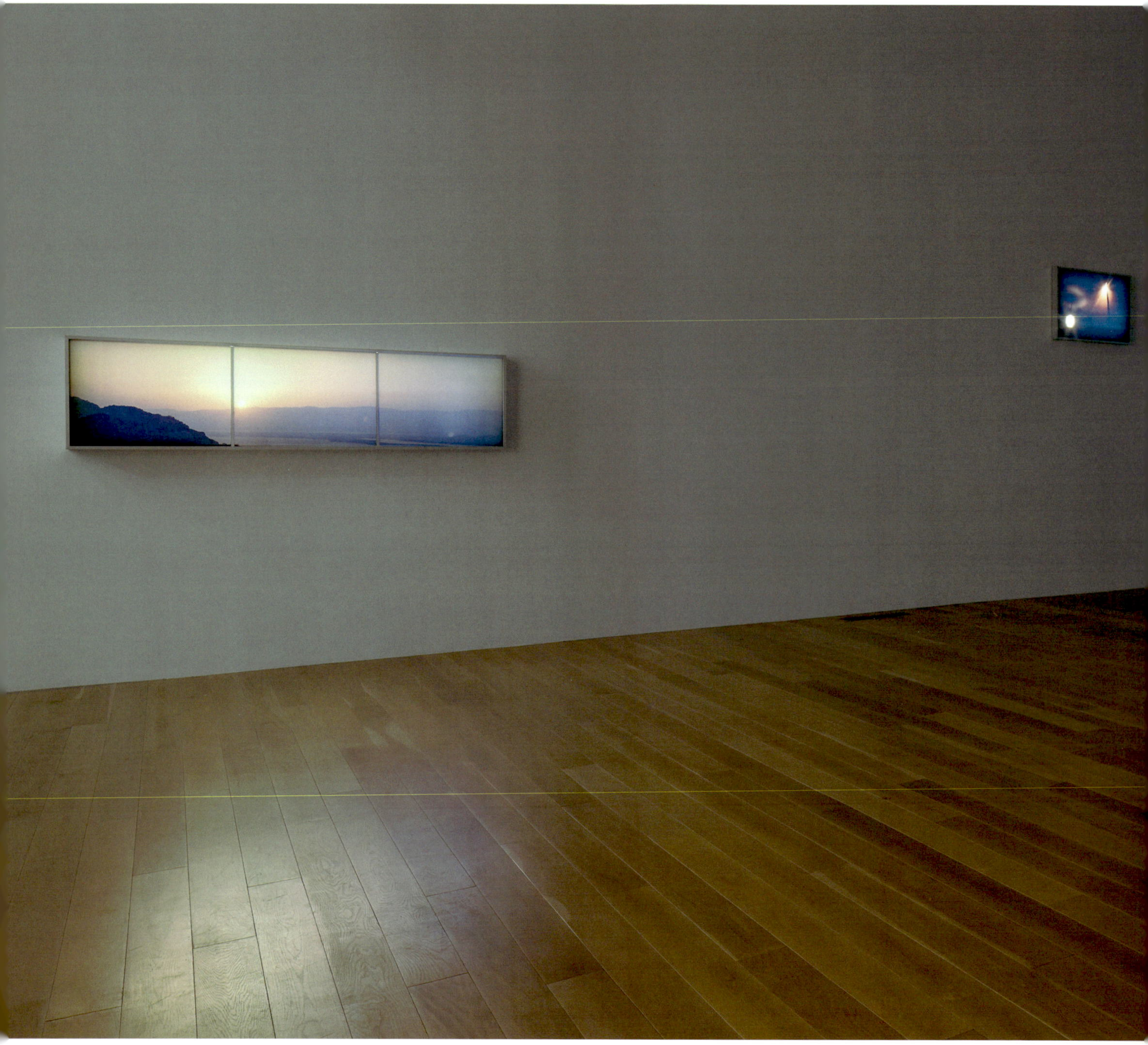

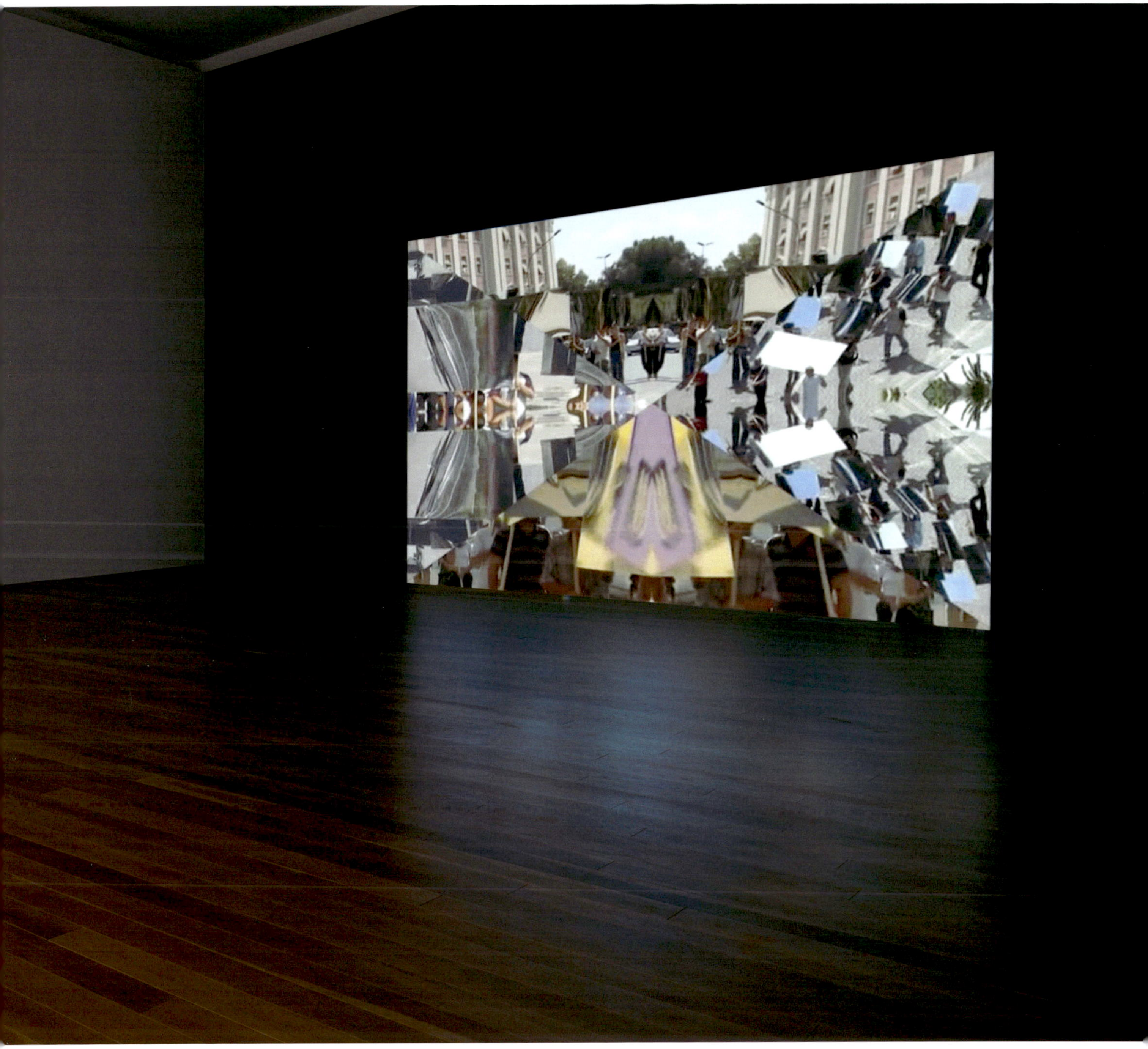

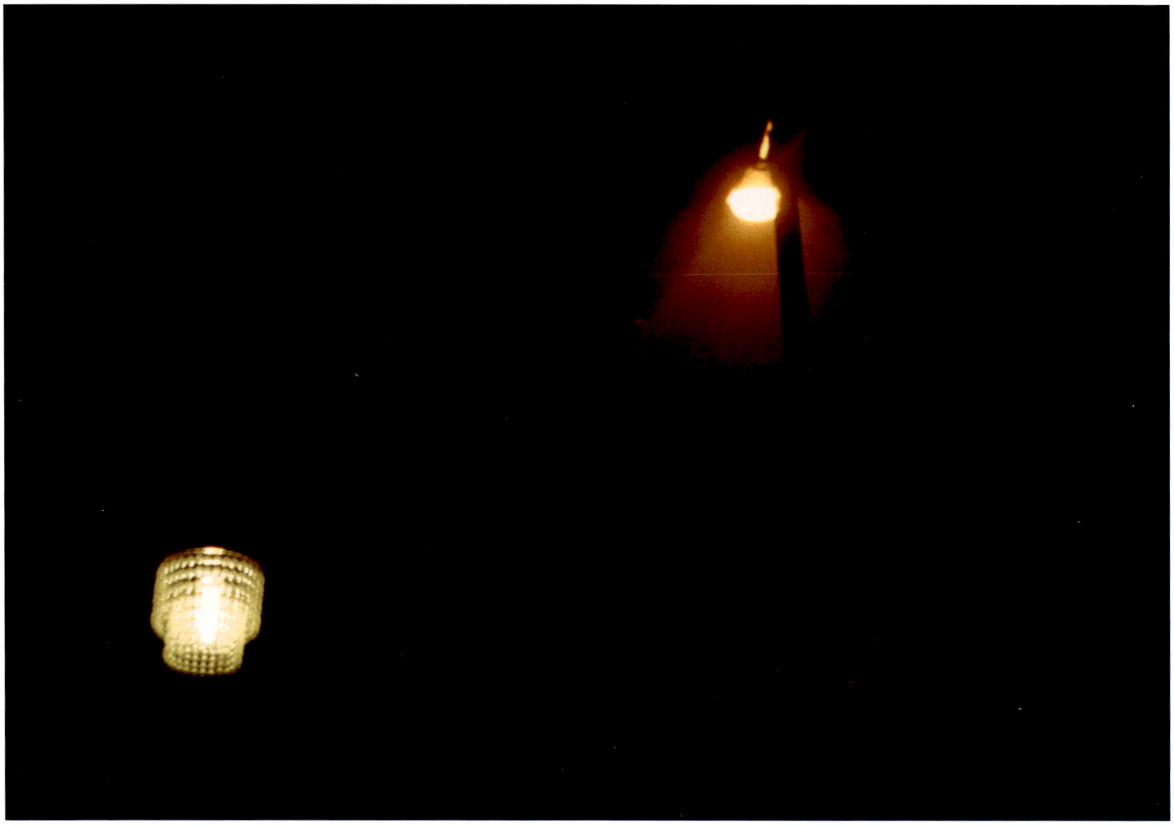

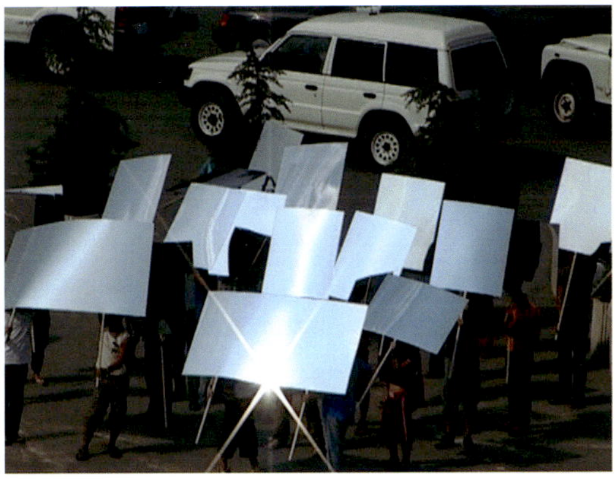
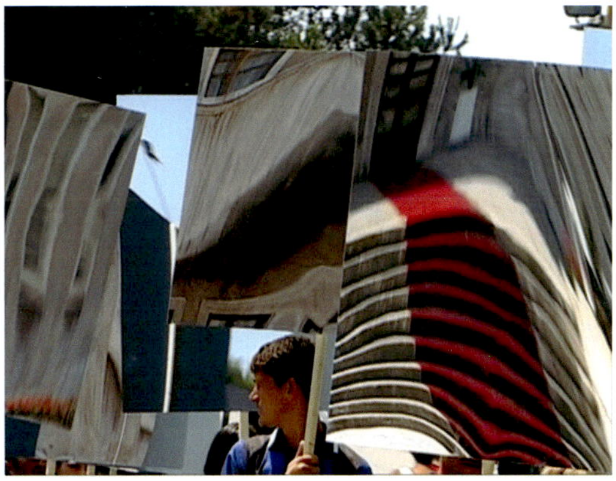
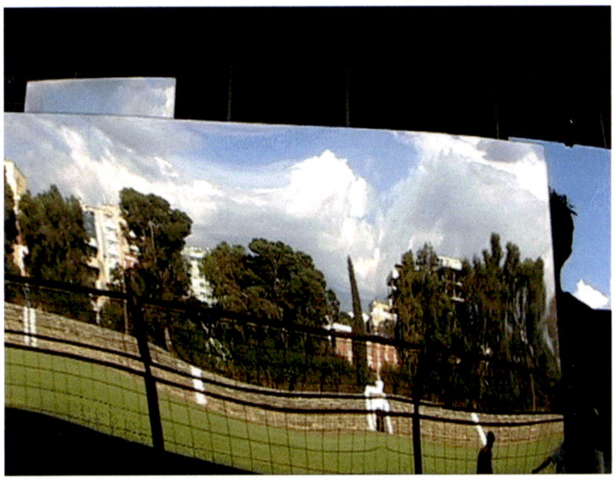
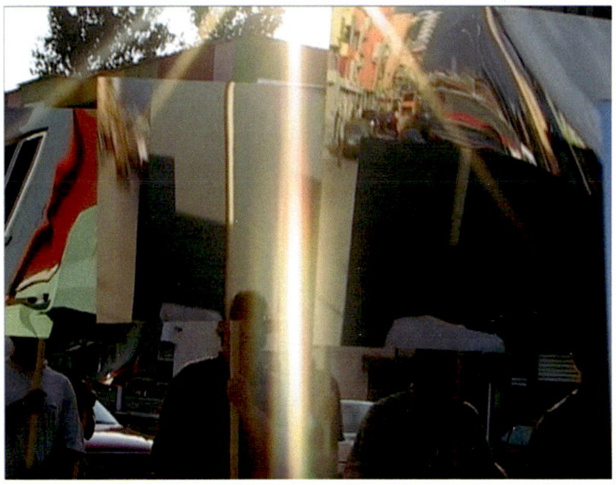
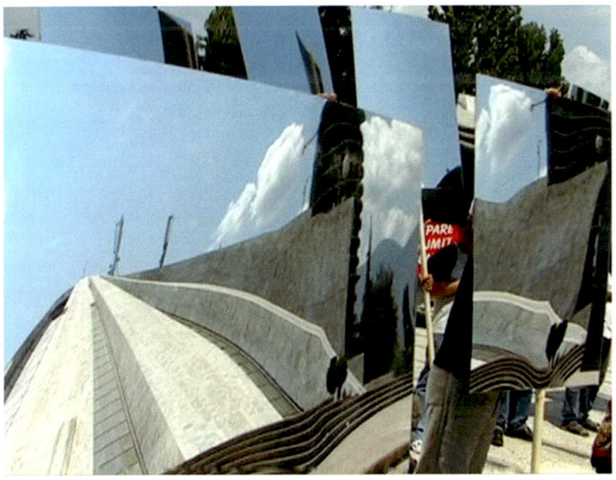
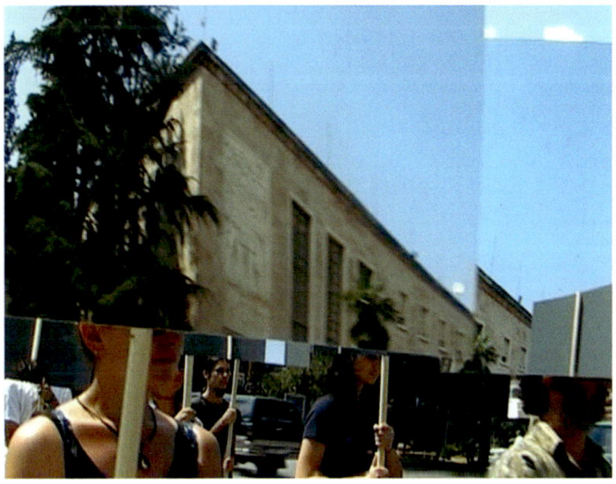
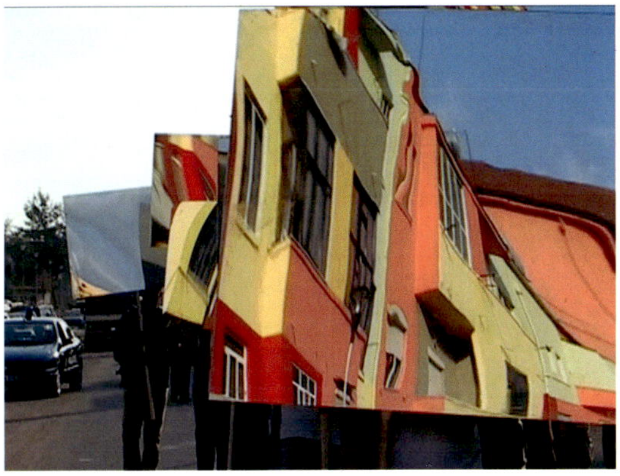
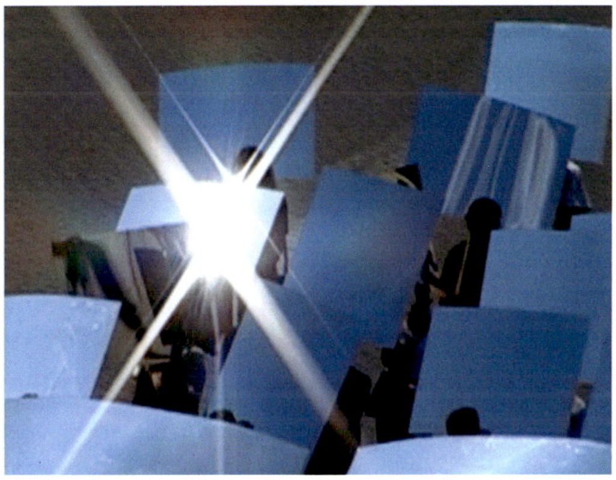

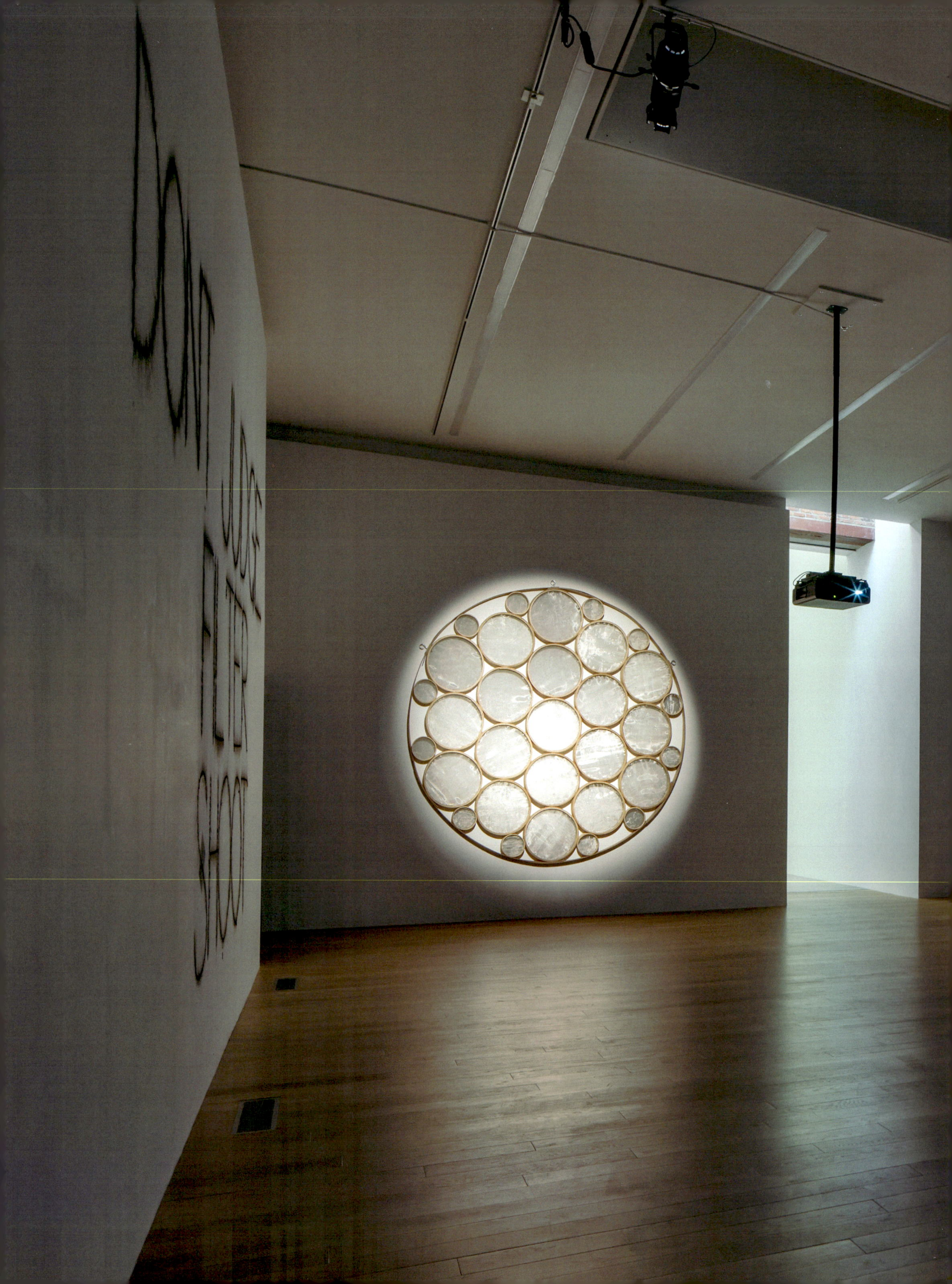
JUDGE
FILTER
SHOOT

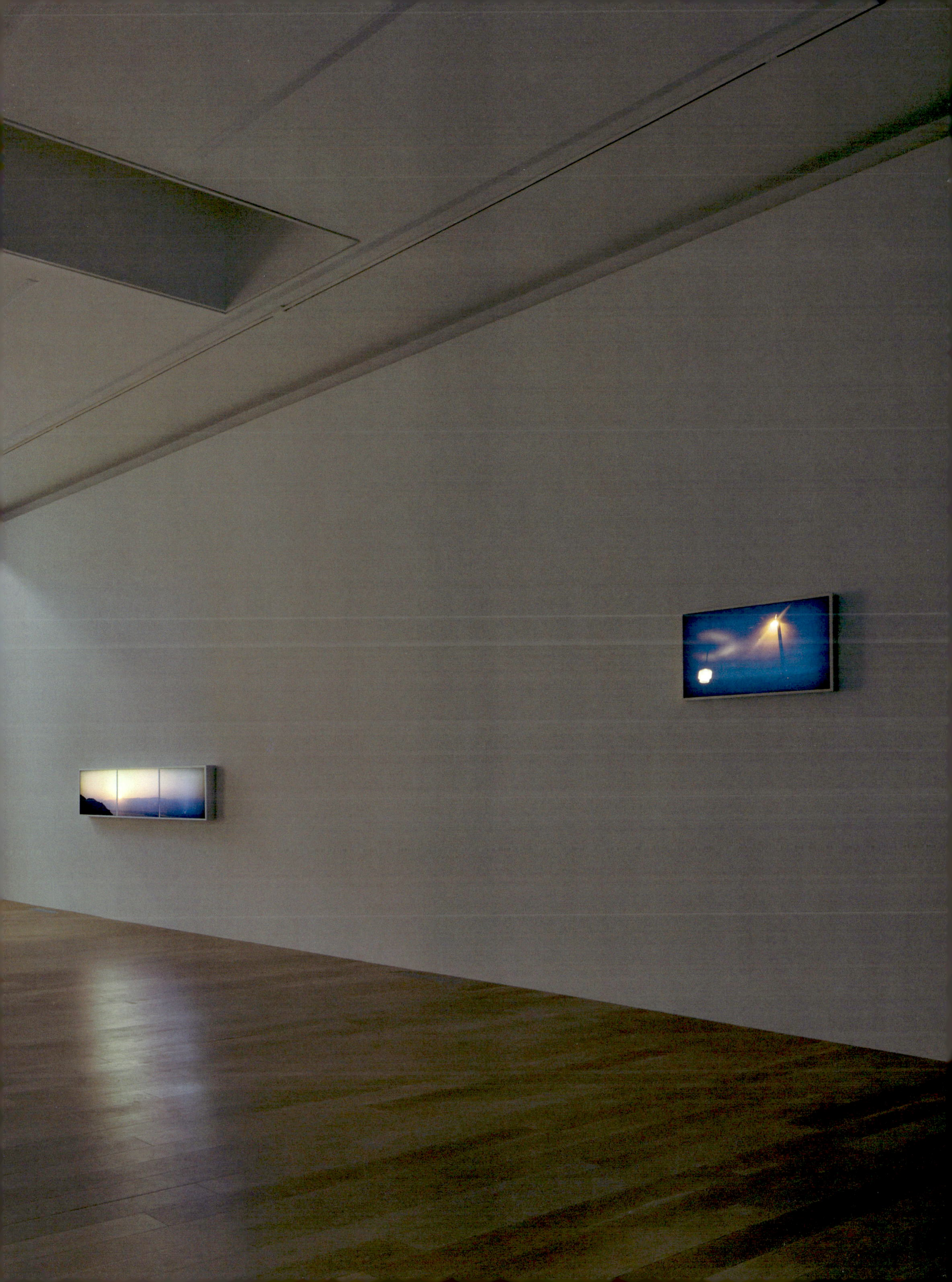

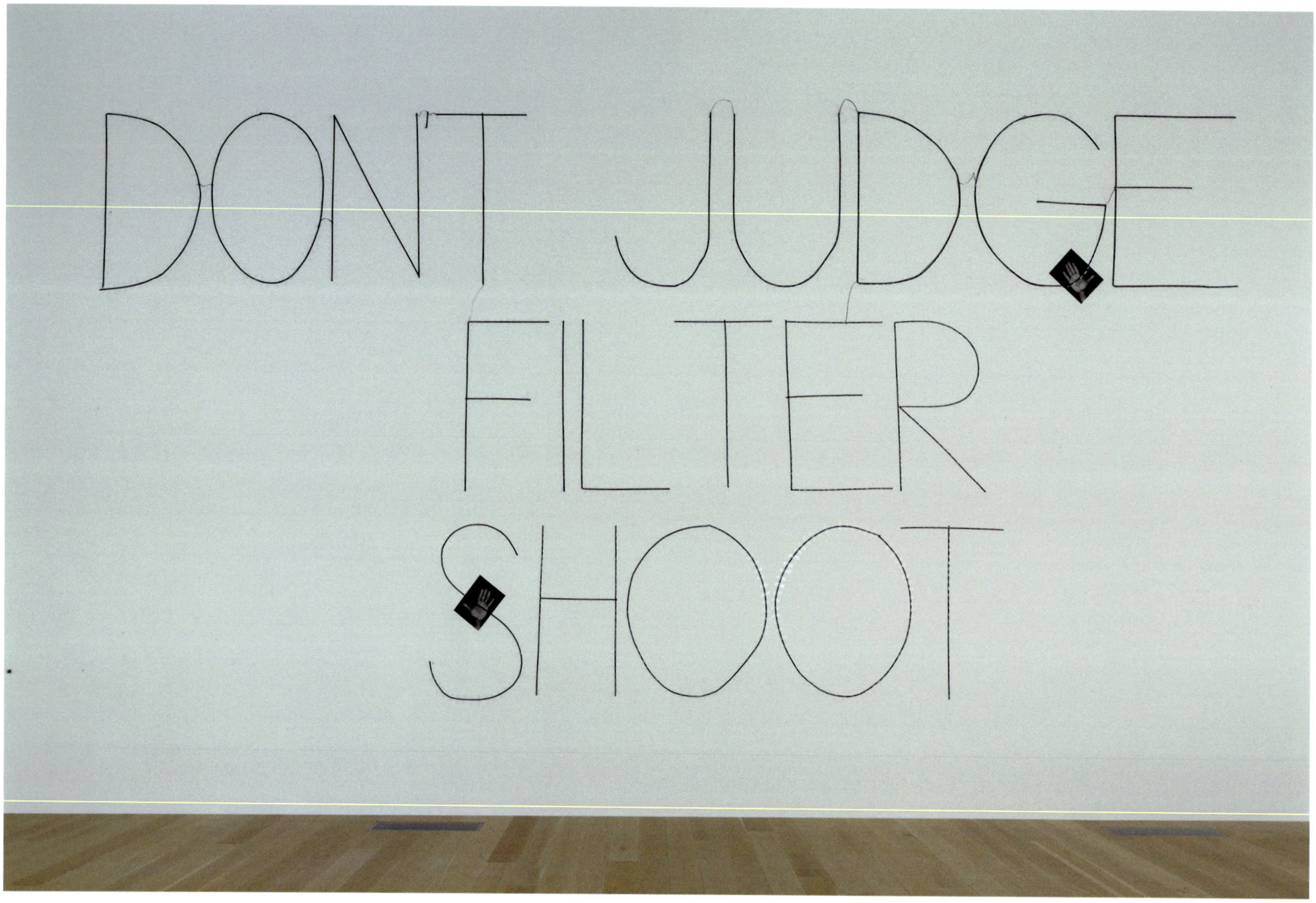
DON'T JUDGE
FILTER
SHOOT

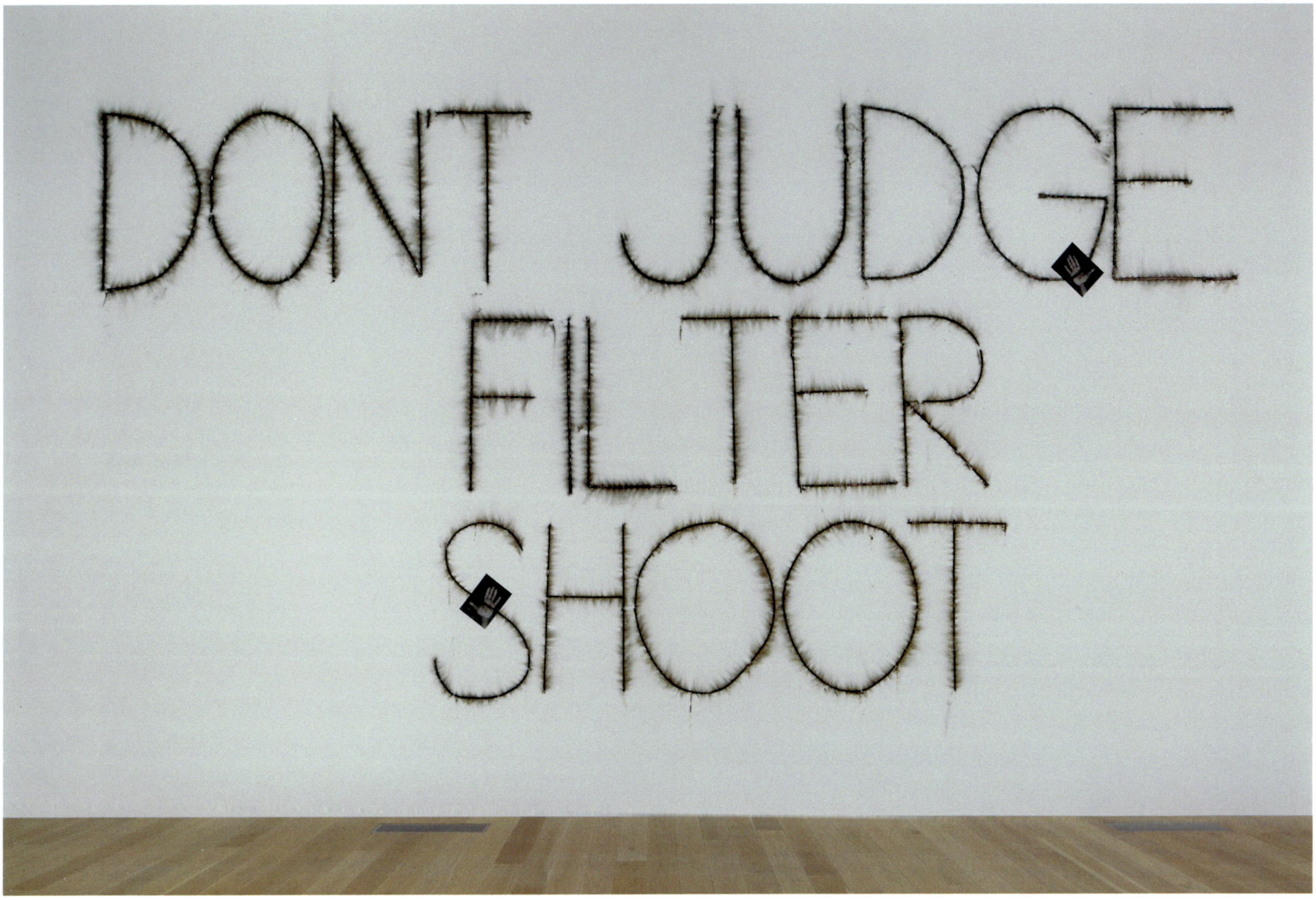
DON'T JUDGE
FILTER
SHOOT

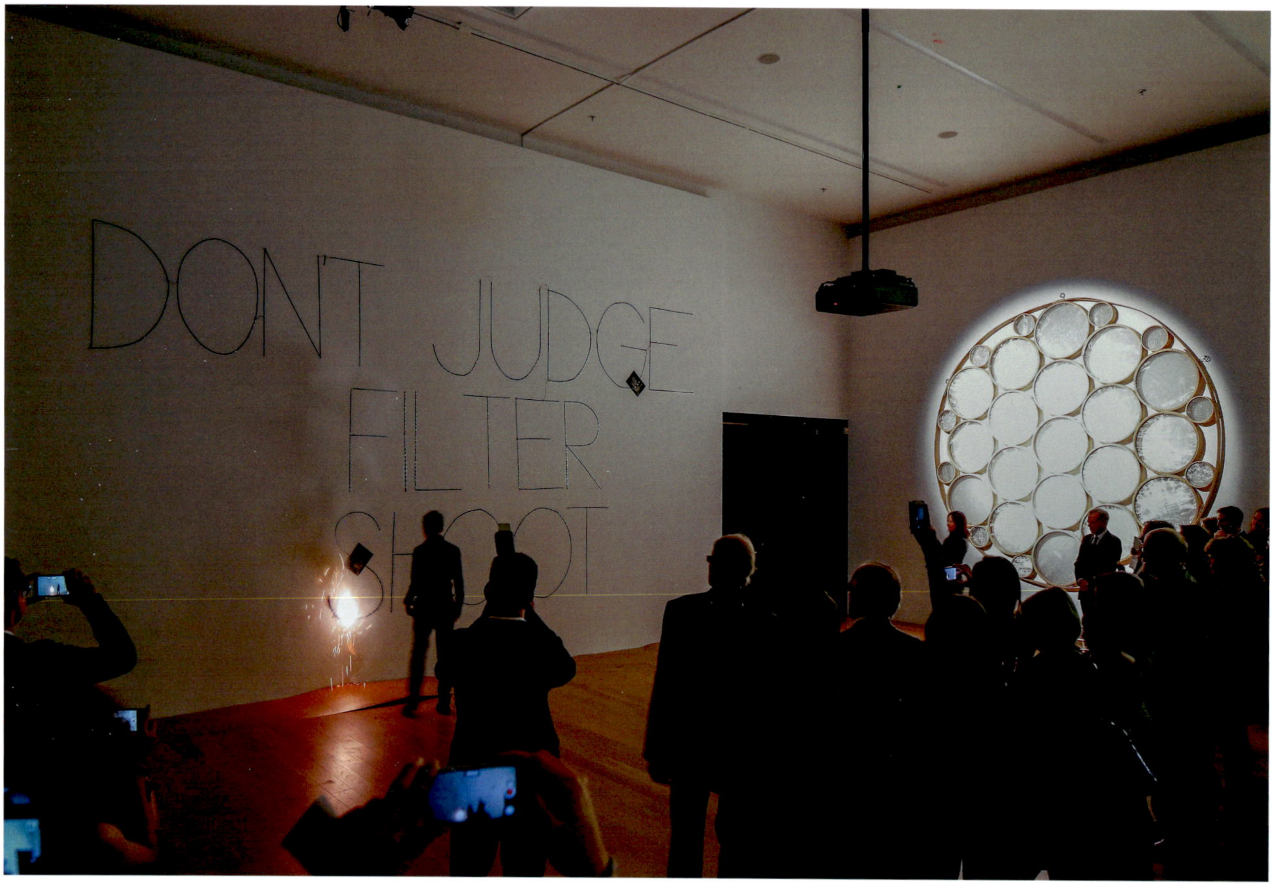
DON'T JUDGE
FILTER
SHOOT

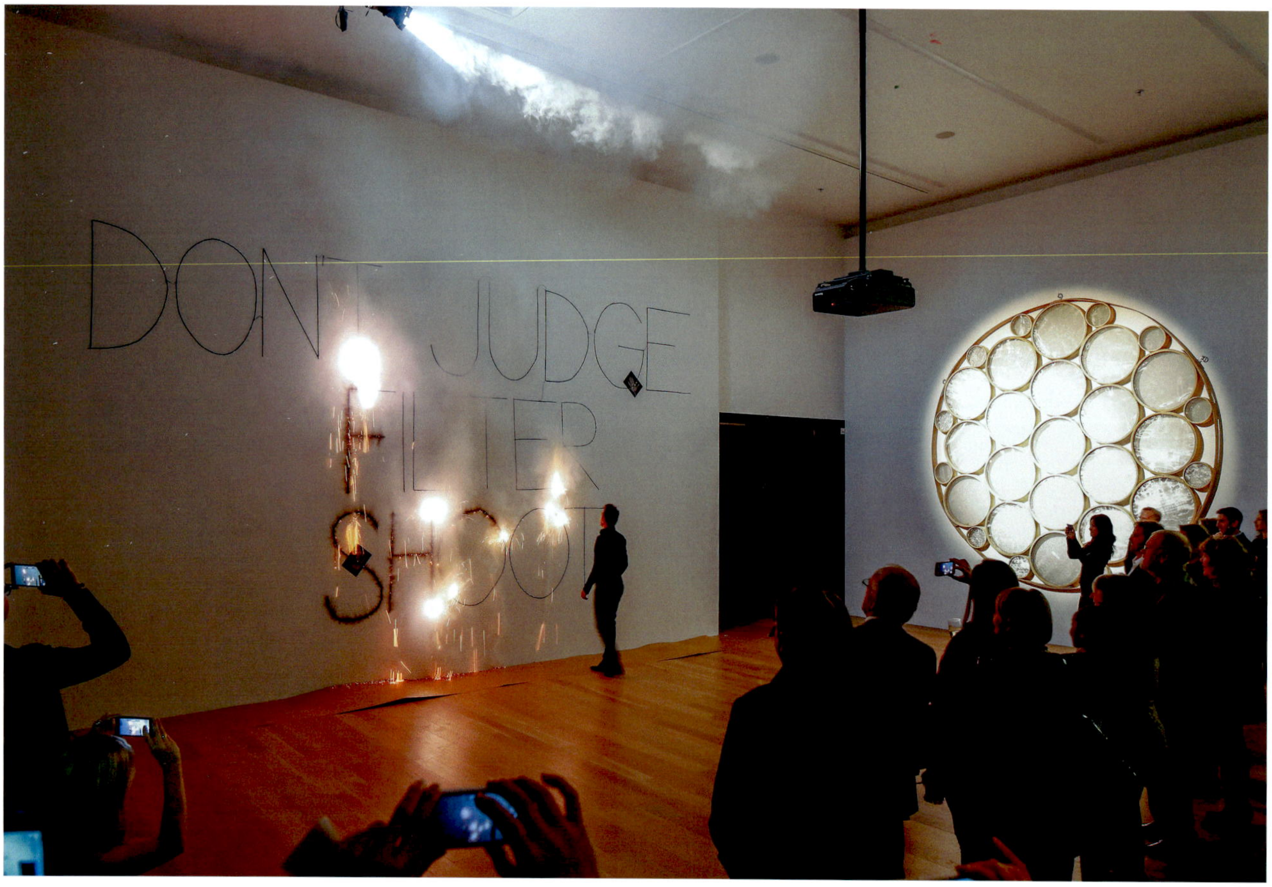
DON'T JUDGE
FILTER
SHOOT

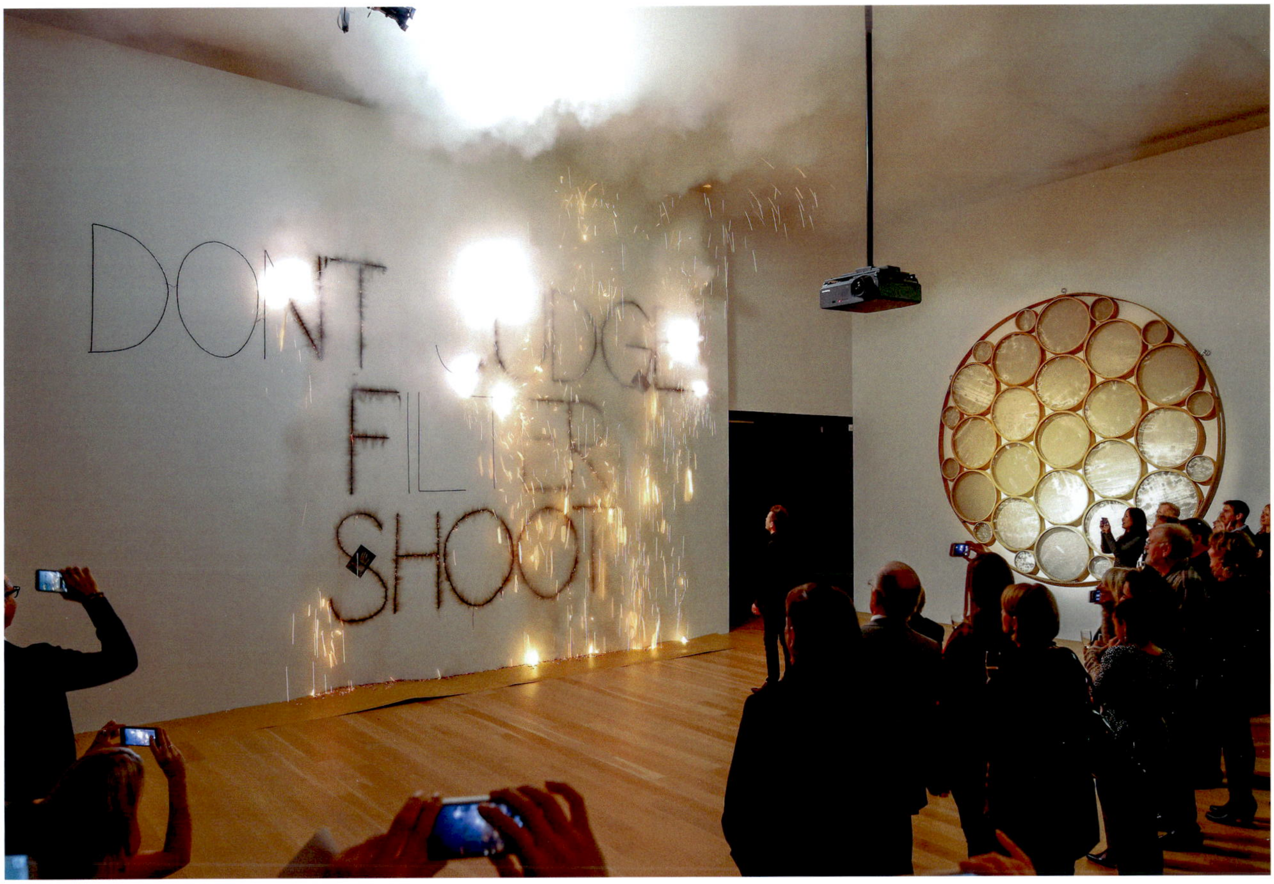
DON'T JUDGE
FILTER
SHOOT

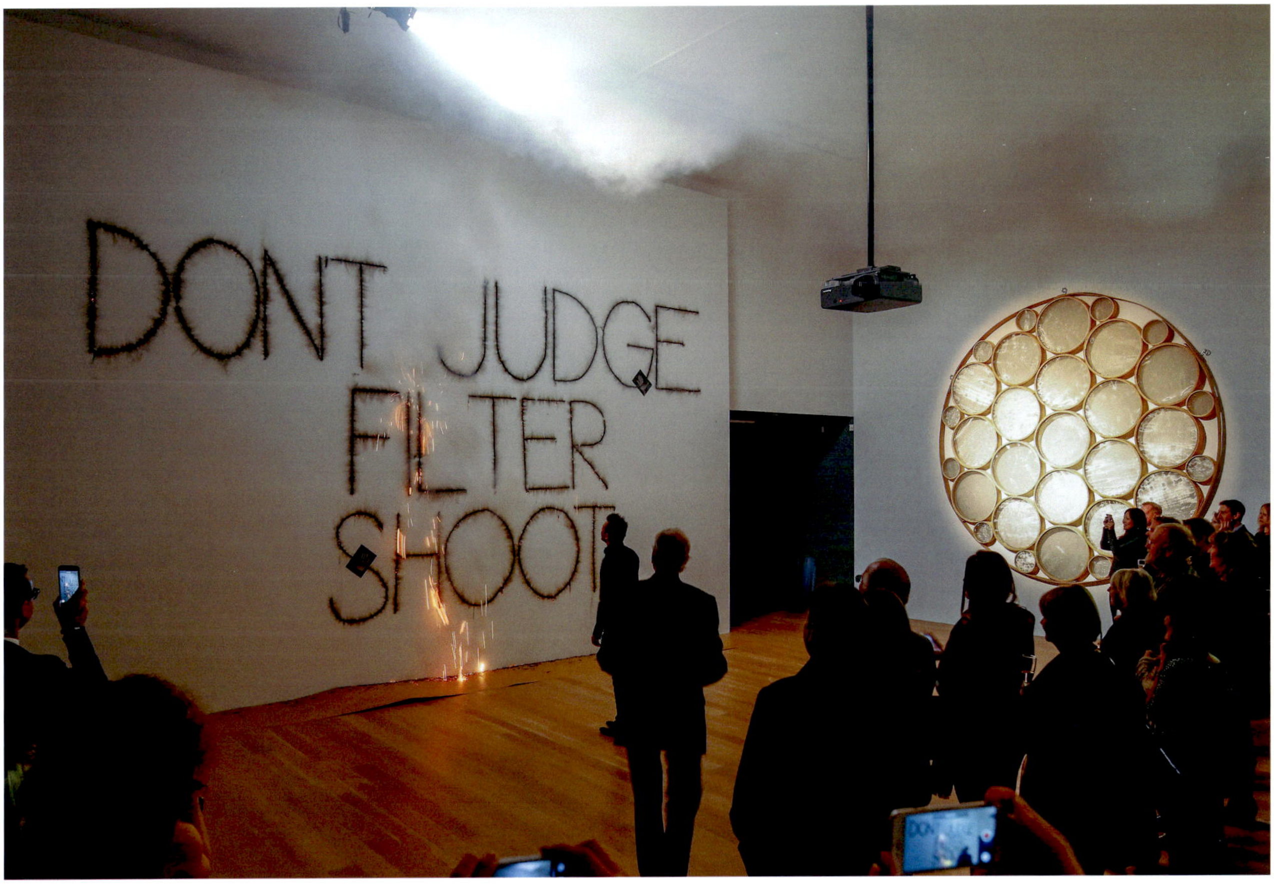
DON'T JUDGE
FILTER
SHOOT

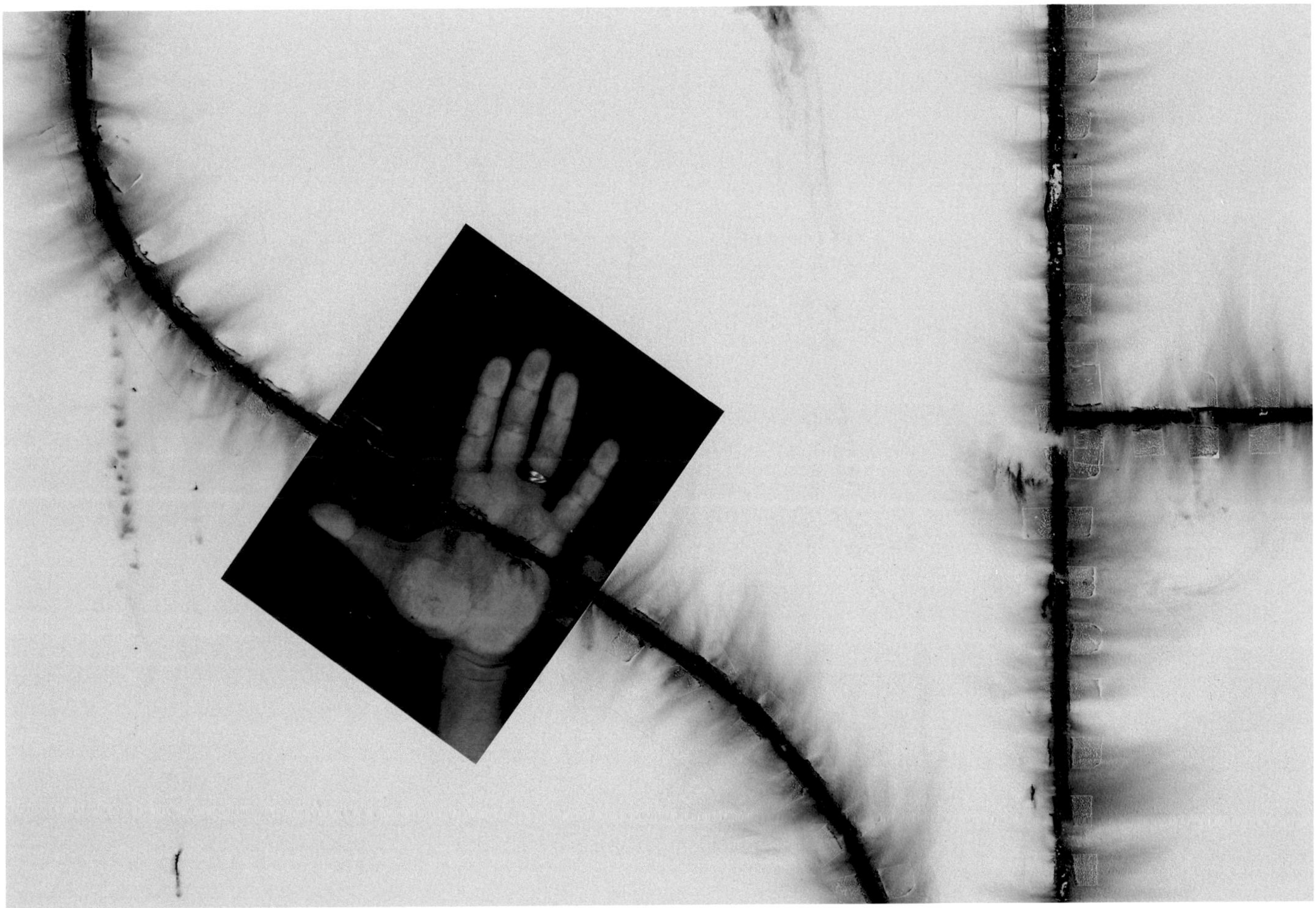

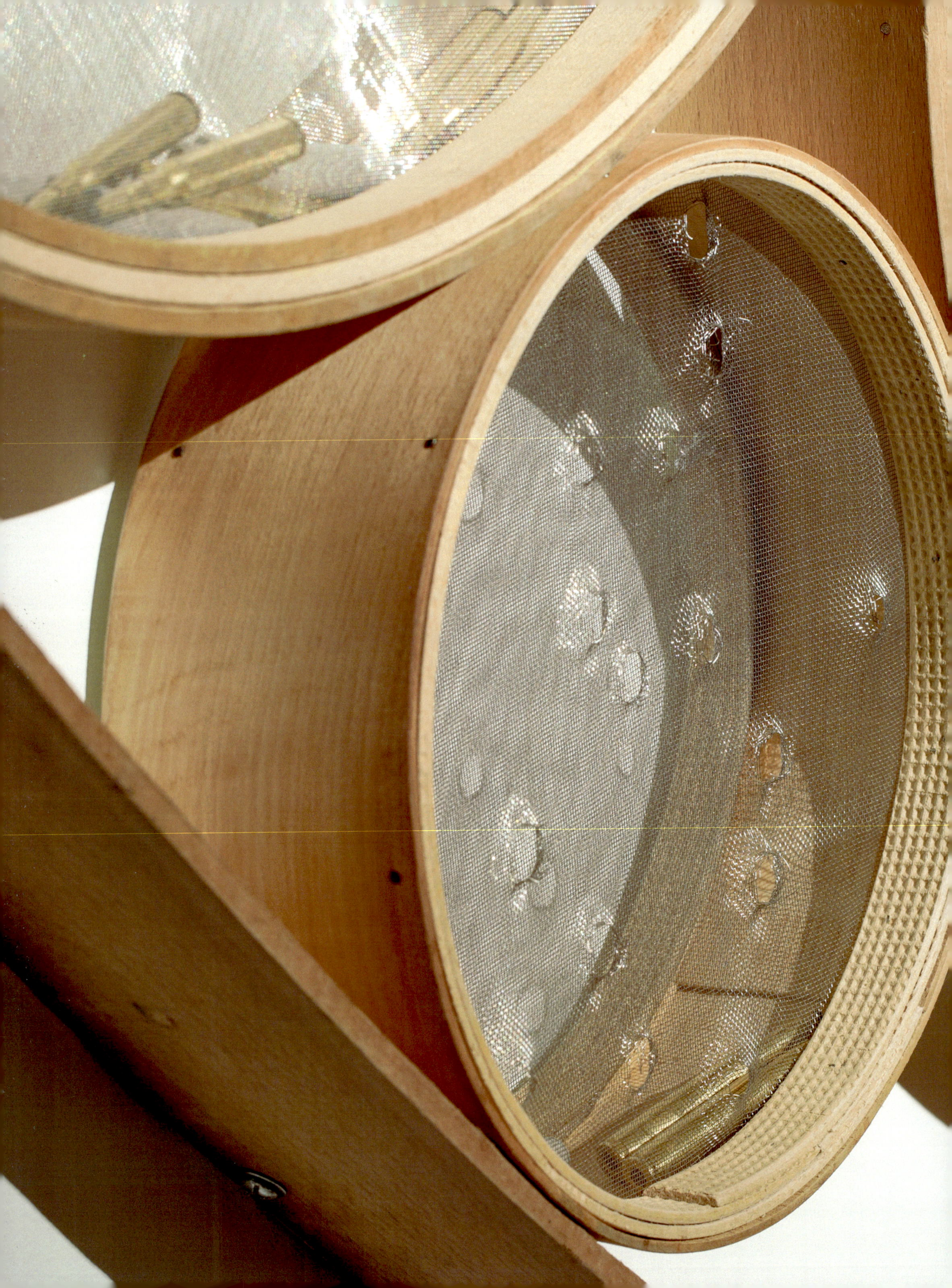

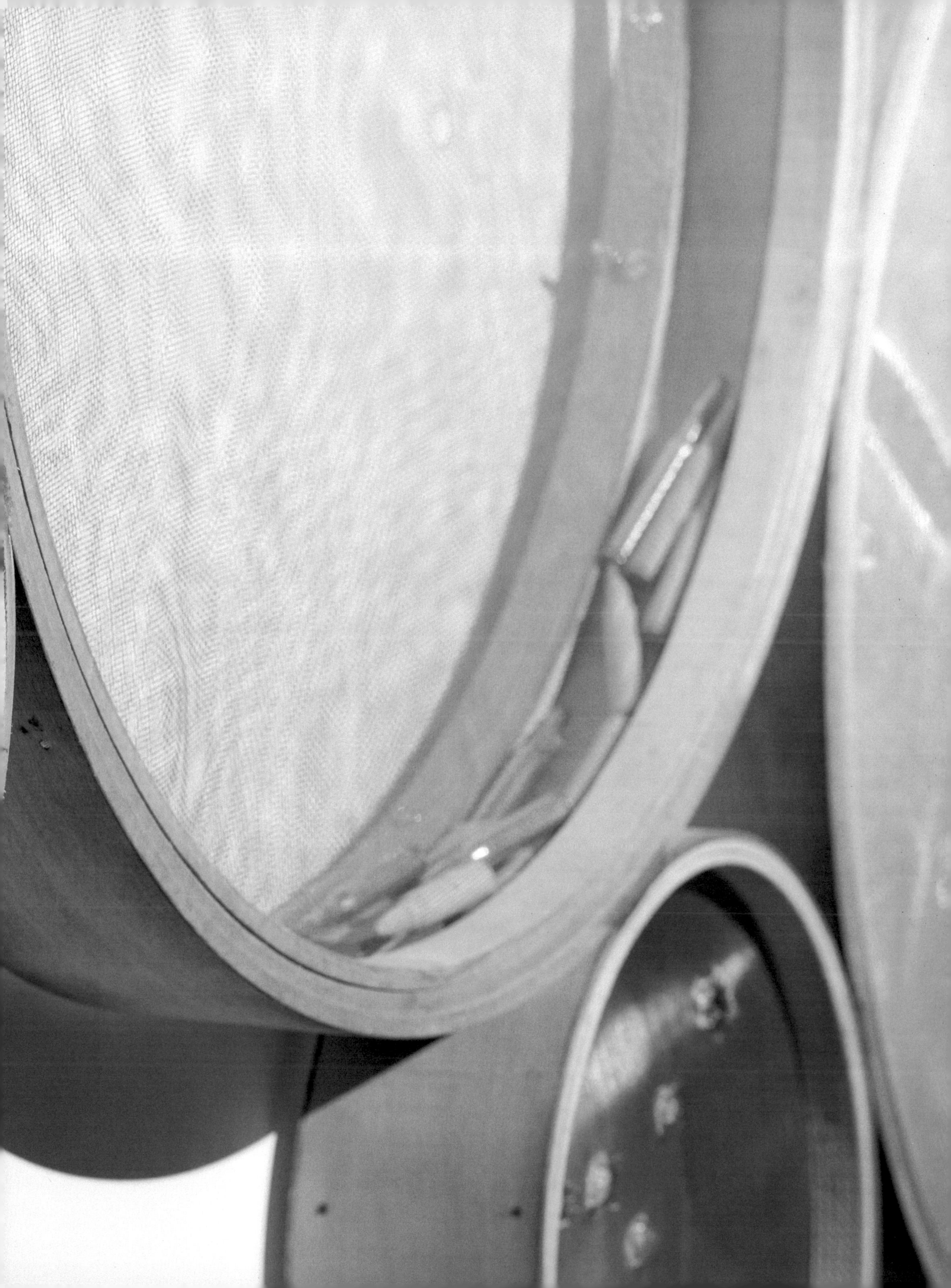

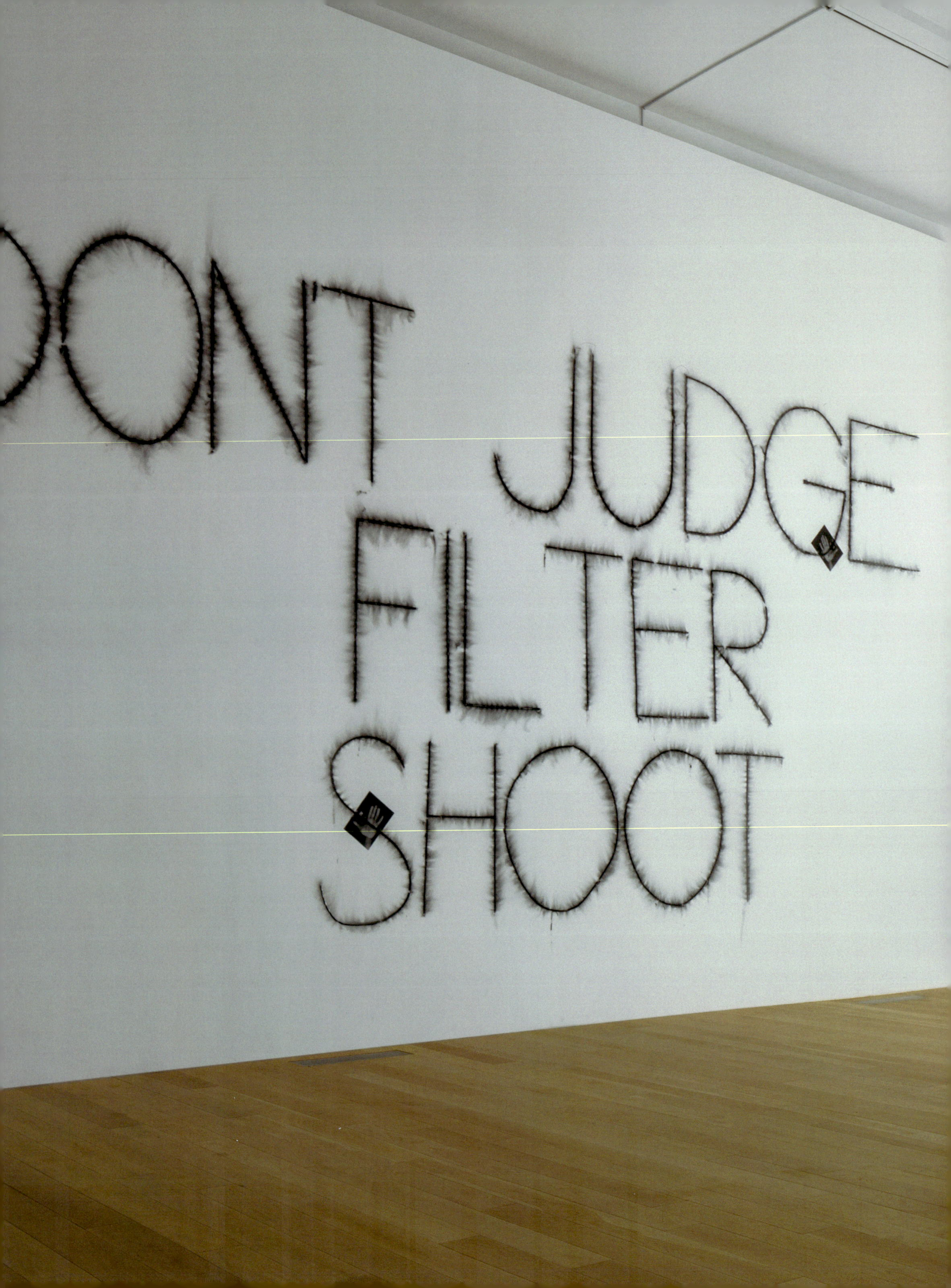
DON'T JUDGE
FILTER
SHOOT

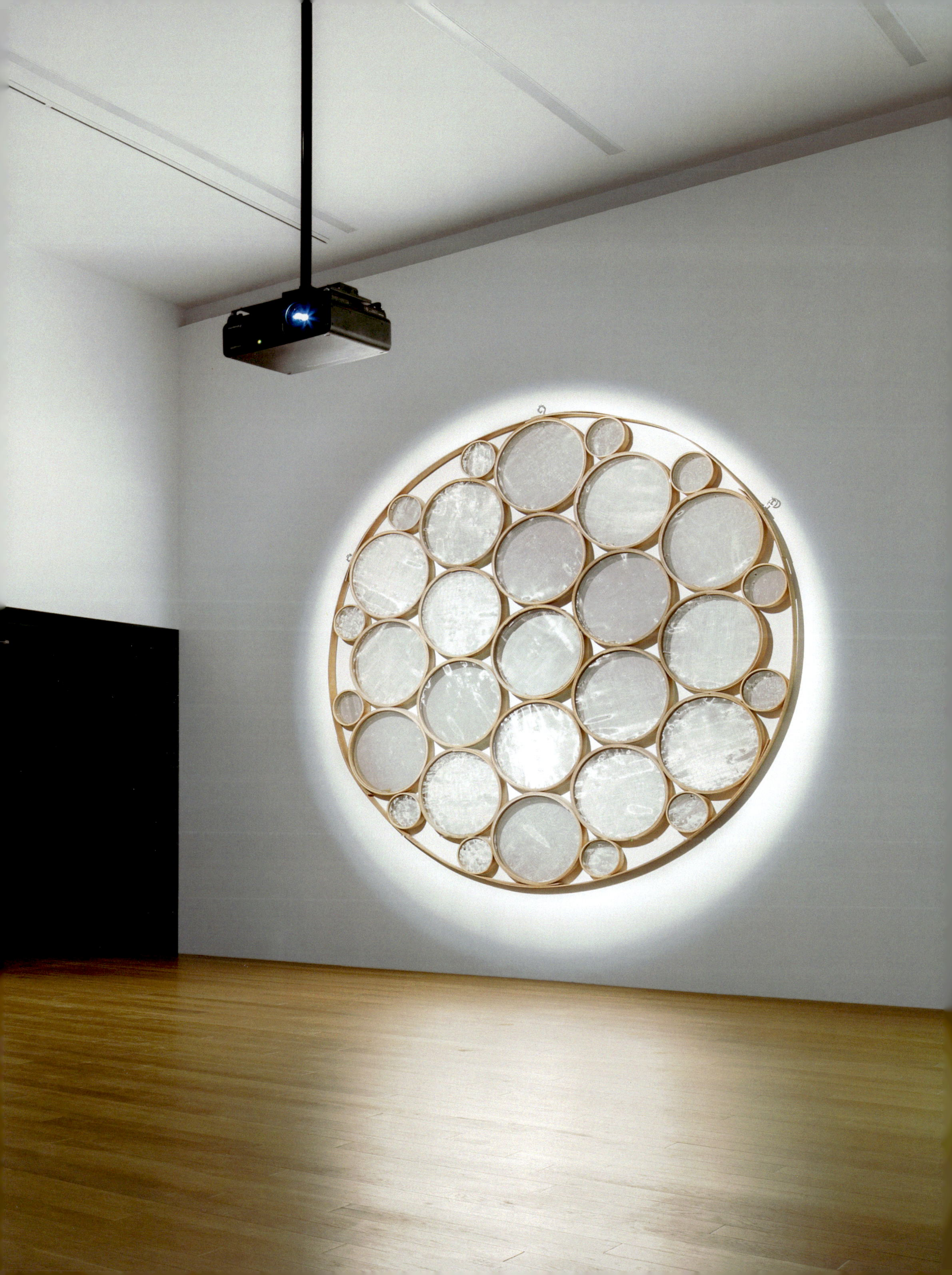

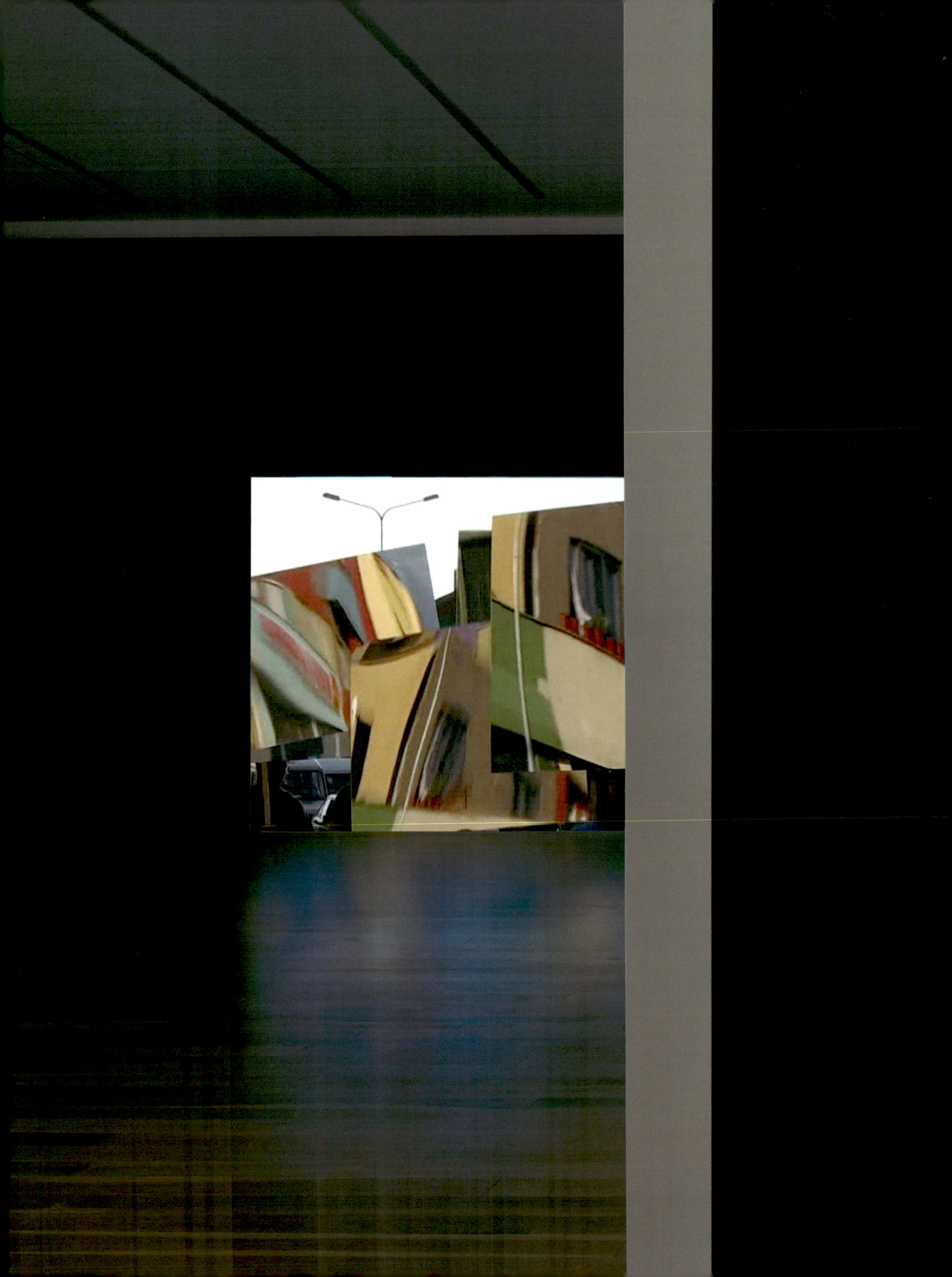

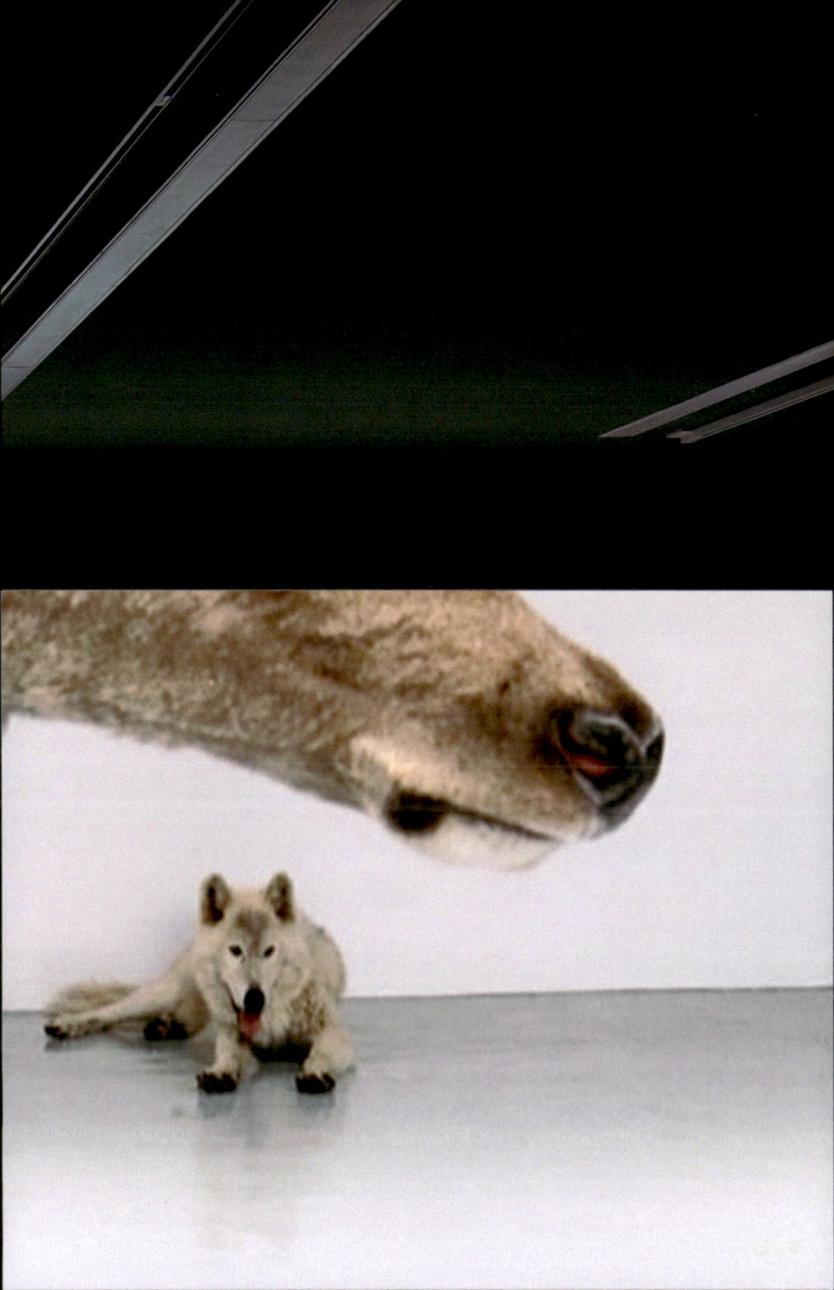

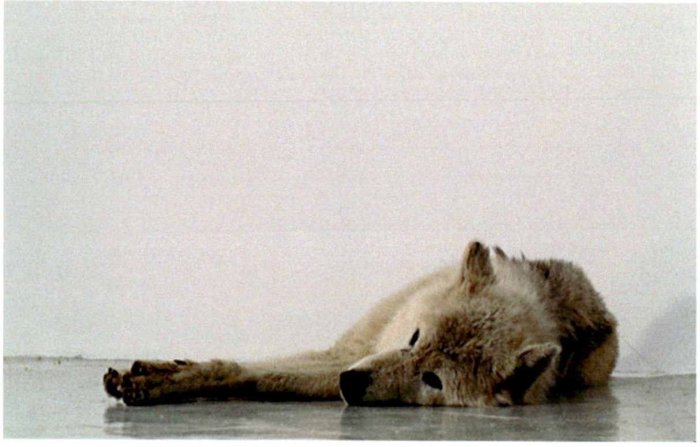
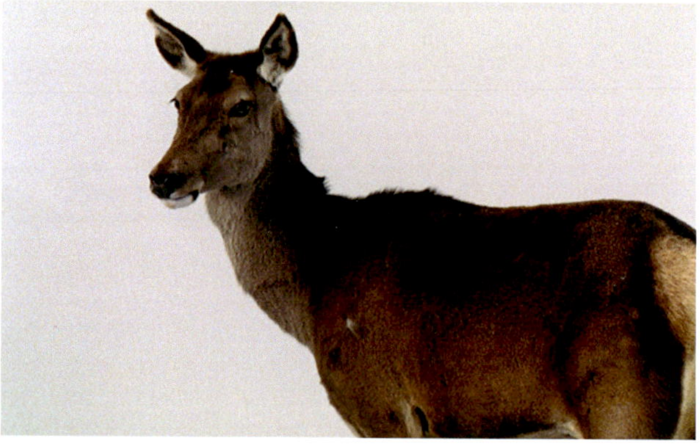
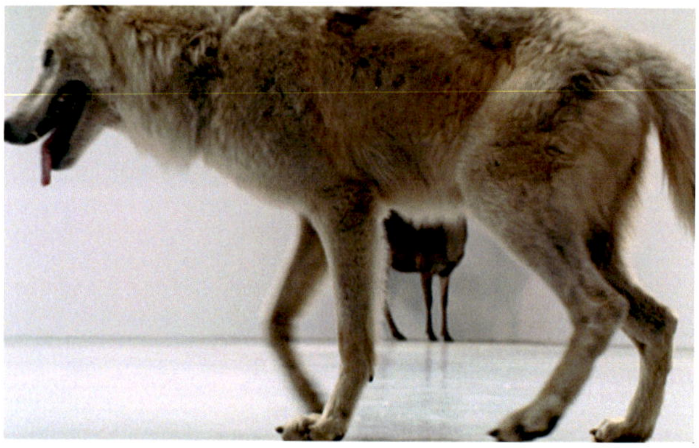
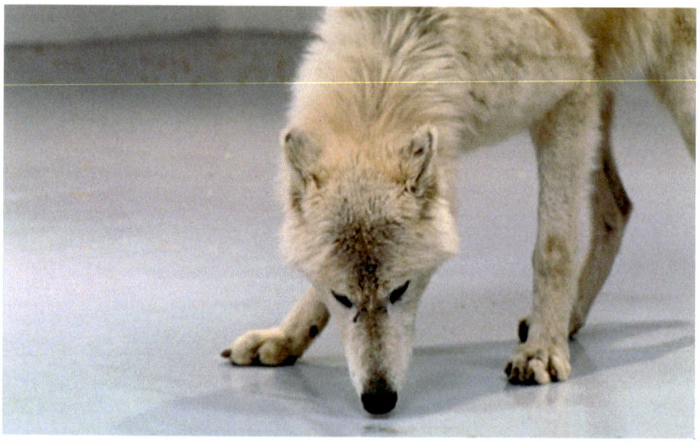
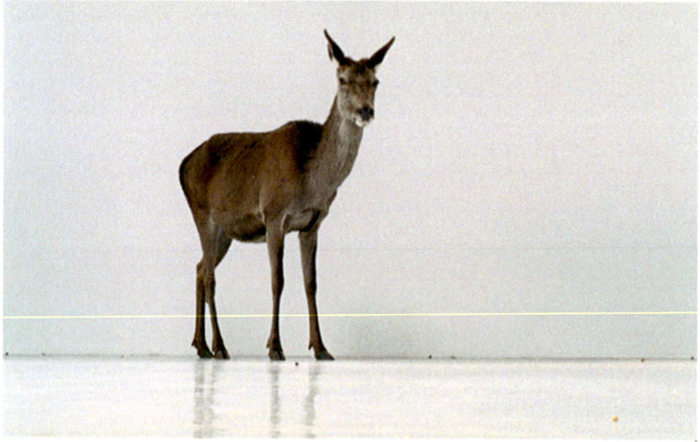
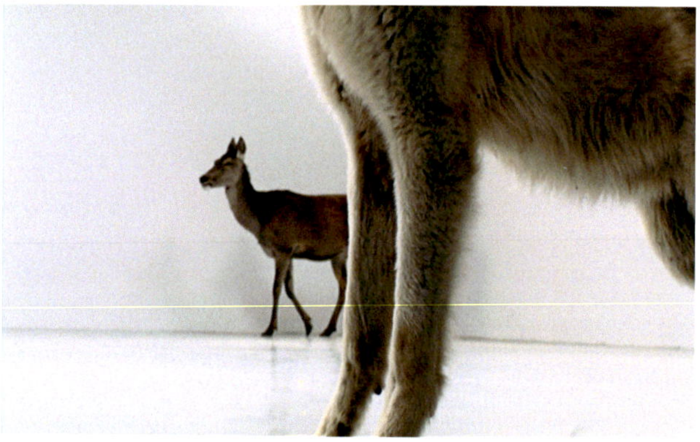
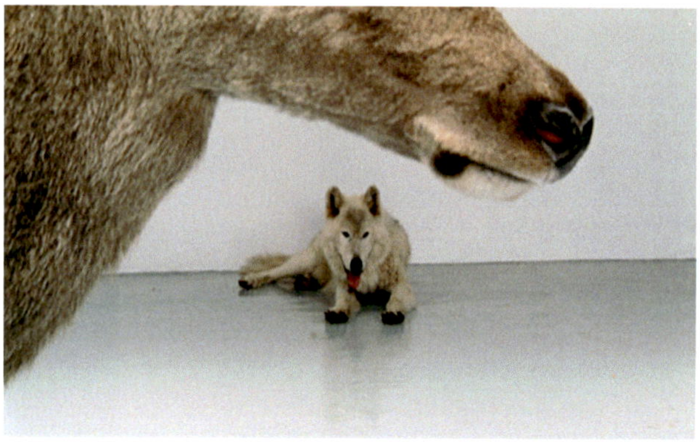
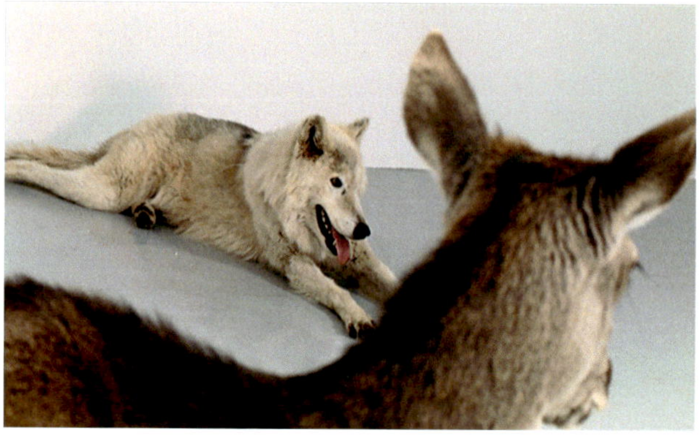

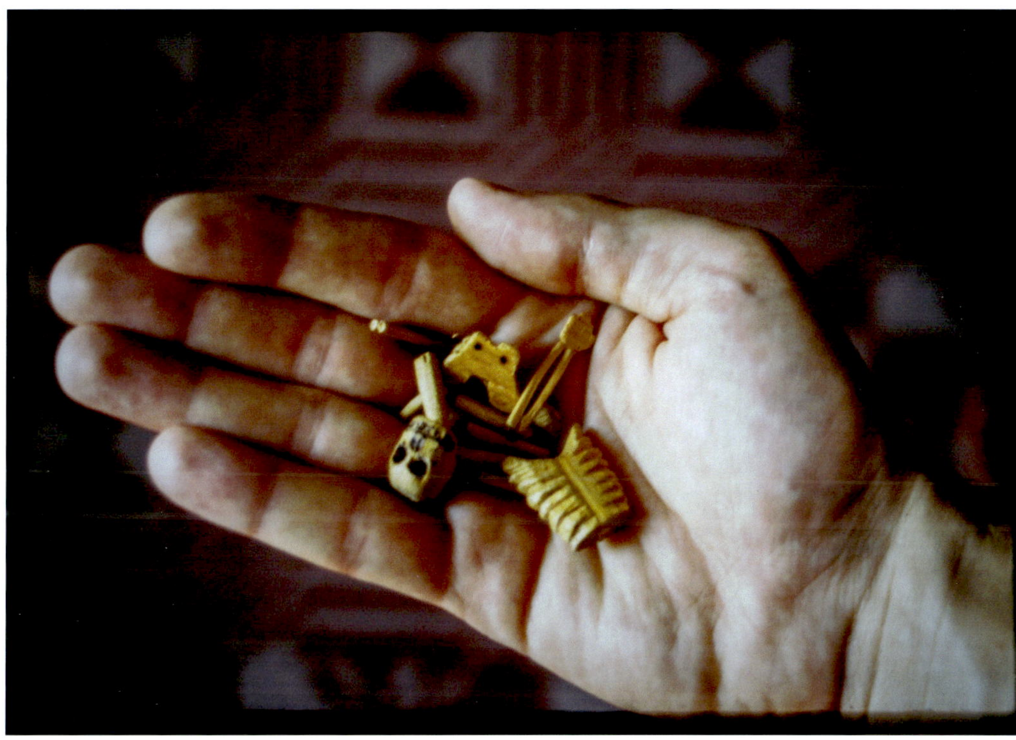

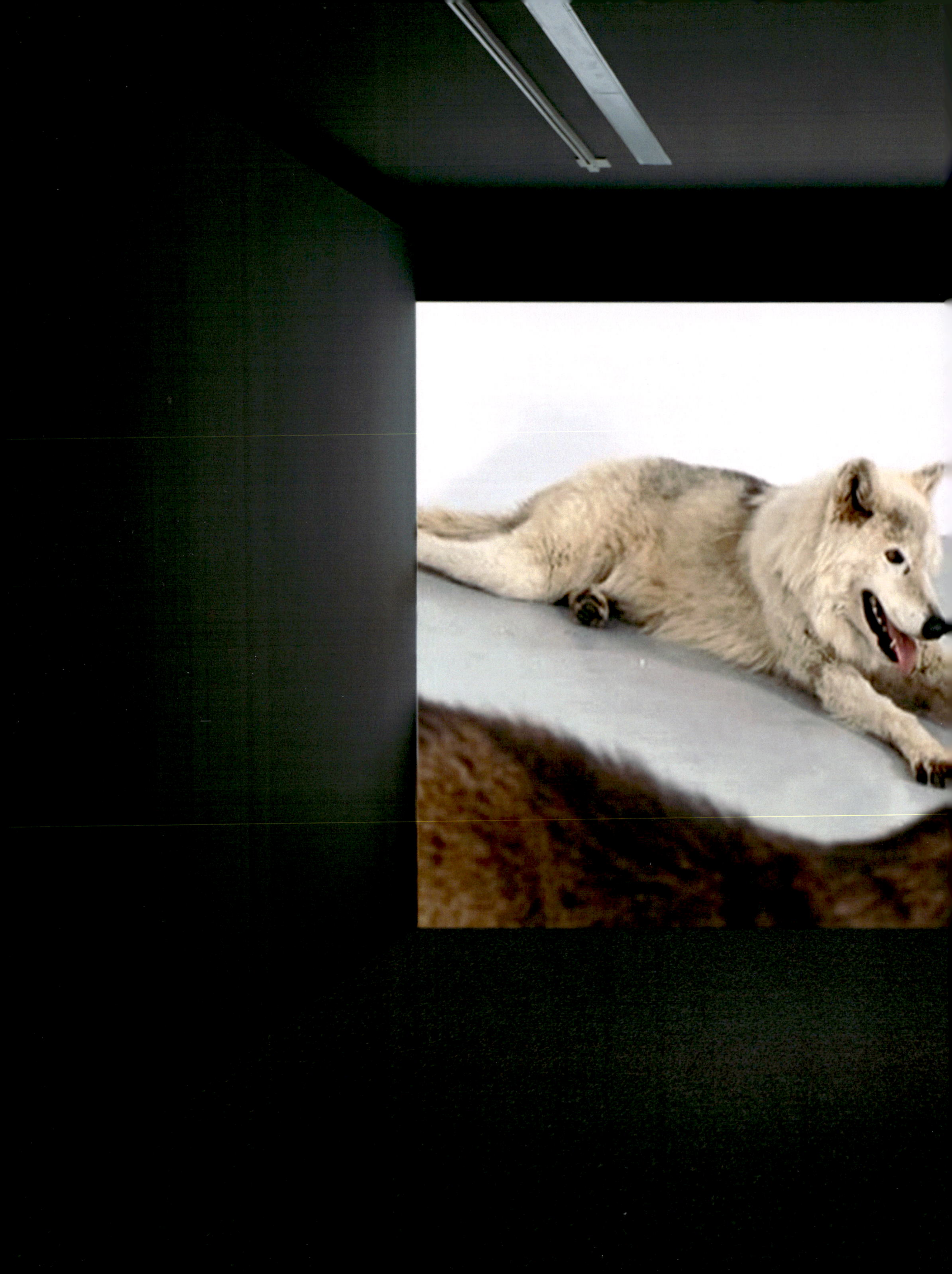

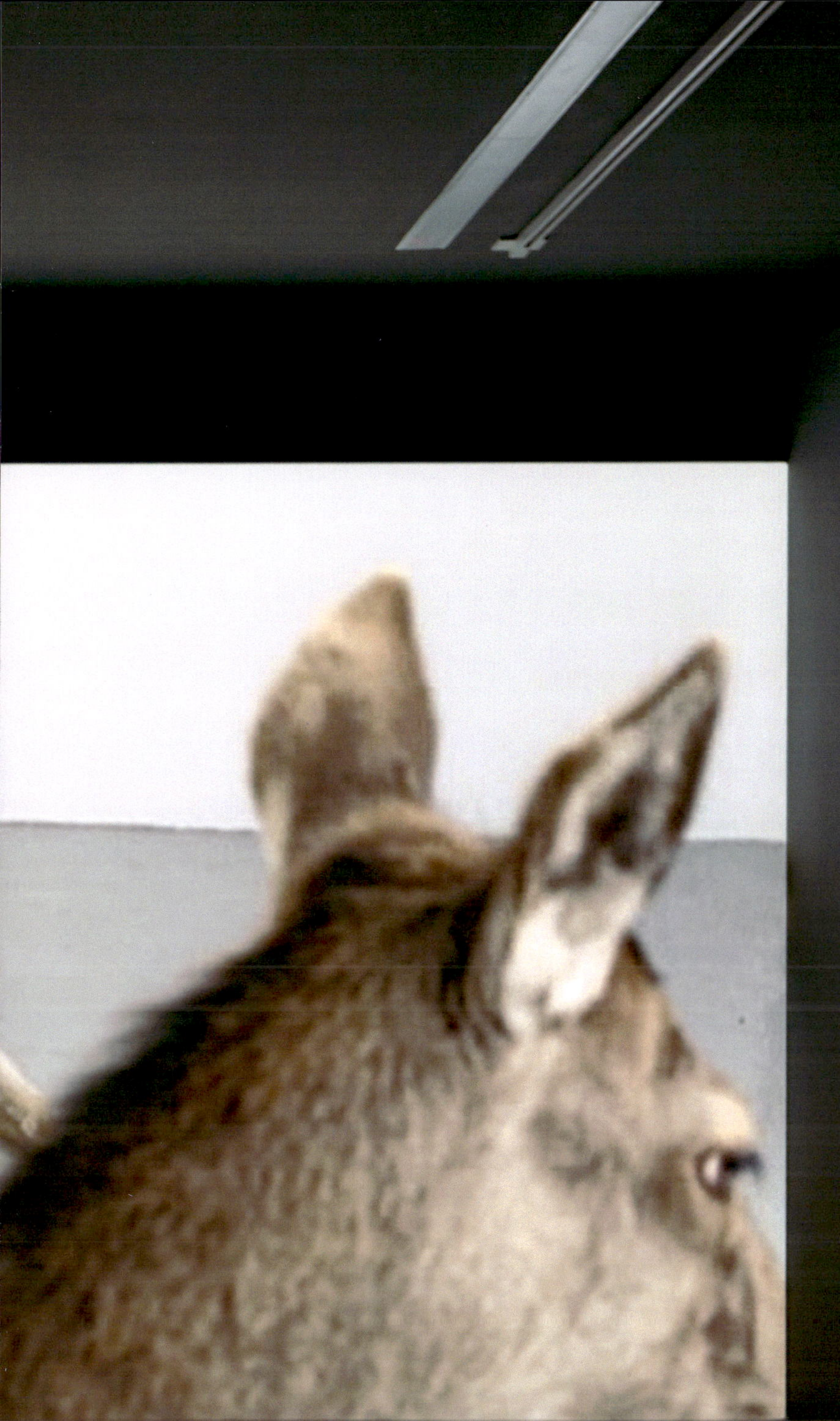

COLLECTED WORKS

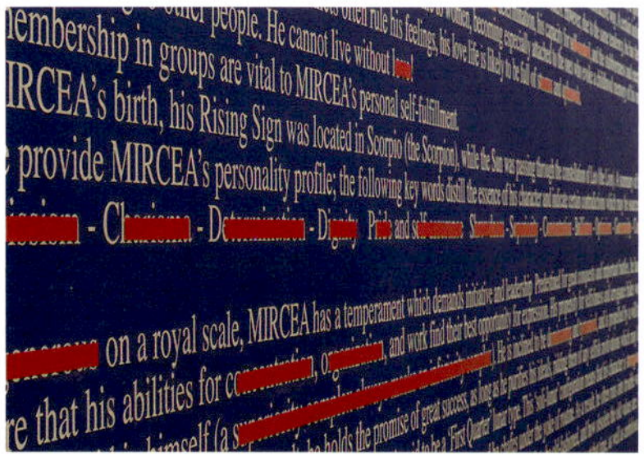

A fost odata . . . (Once upon a time . . .), 2002
vinyl text on painted blue wall
dimensions variable

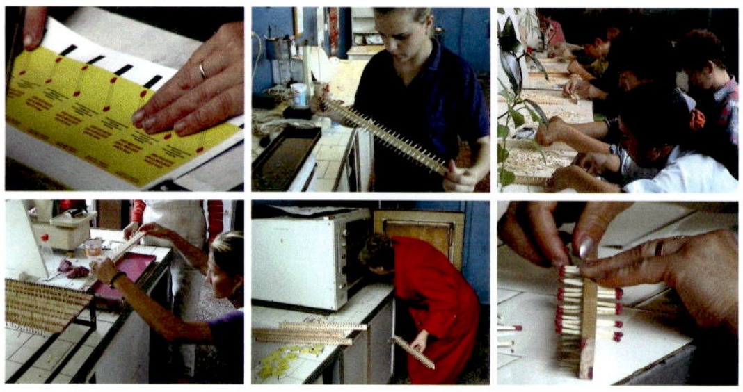

Double Heads Matches, 2002–2003
DVD, master mini DV, colour, sound, 4:3
duration: 17:17
Edition of 5

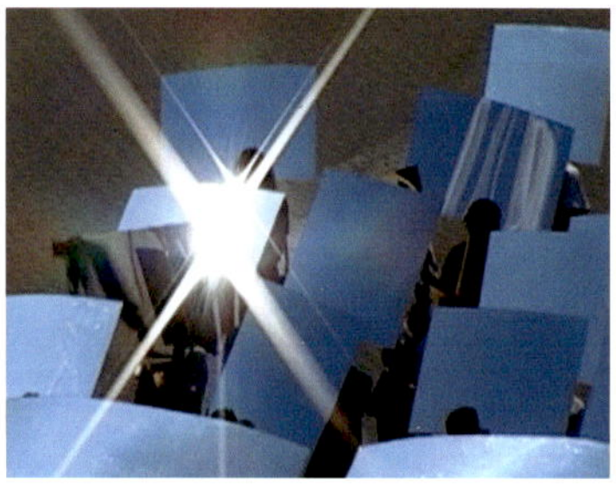

The Landscape Is Changing, 2003
digital Betacam, DVD, colour, sound, 4:3
duration: 22:07
Edition of 5

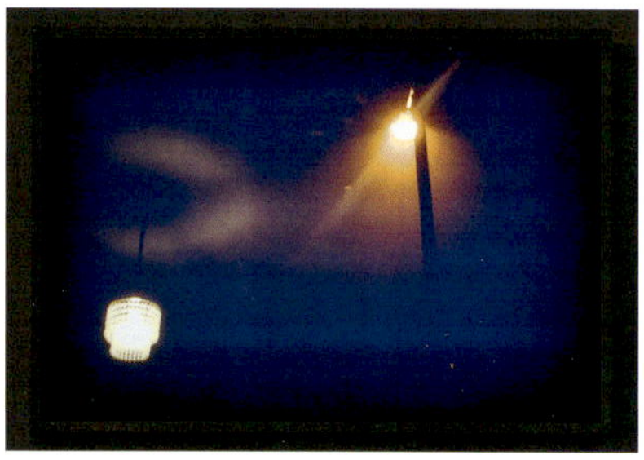

(Never)Mind Game, 2003
light box
$25\frac{3}{8} \times 37\frac{3}{8} \times 2\frac{3}{4}$ inches
(64.5 × 95 × 7 cm)

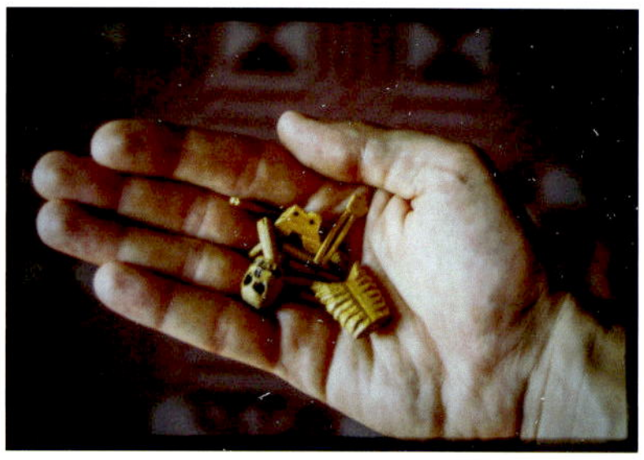

0 - ∞, 2004
light box
$6\frac{5}{16} \times 9\frac{1}{4} \times 3\frac{1}{8}$ inches
(16 × 23.5 × 8 cm)
Edition of 3

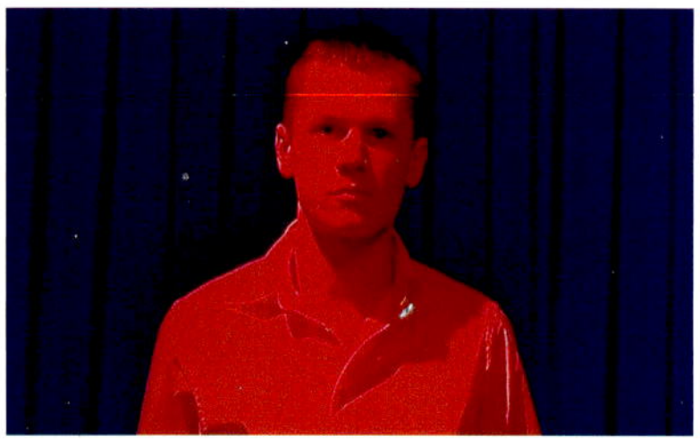

The right man at the right place I and II, 2002
video installation in two parts
digital Betacam, DVD, colour, sound, 16:9 and 4:3
duration: 03:58 each
Edition of 5

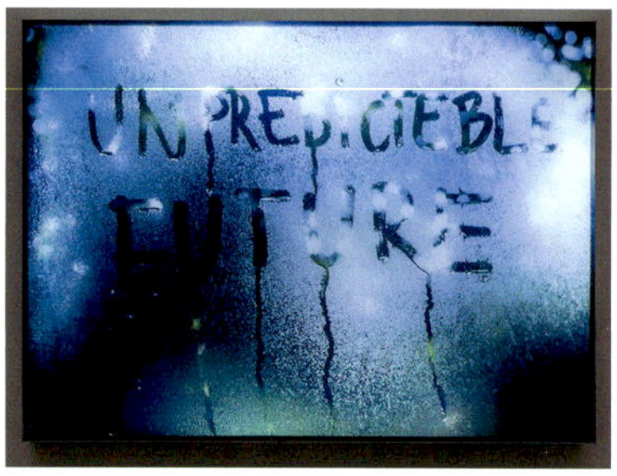

No title, 2004
light box
$22\frac{7}{16} \times 31\frac{1}{2} \times 3\frac{1}{8}$ inches
(57 × 80 × 8 cm)
Edition of 3

2012, 2005
light box
26 × 120 × 5 inches
(66 × 304.8 × 12.7 cm)
Edition of 3

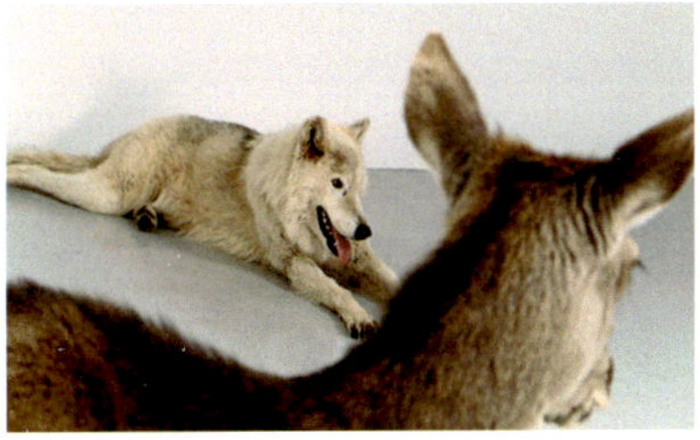

Deeparture, 2005
16 mm film transferred on DVD, colour, silent
duration: 02:43
Edition of 5

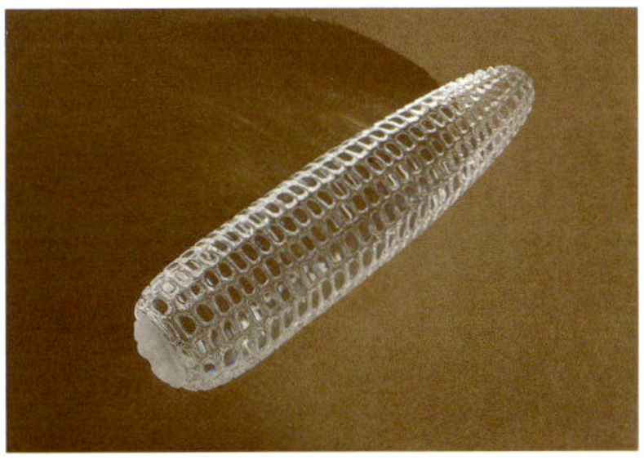

Diamond Corn, 2005
cast crystal, cardboard box
corn: 2¾ × 9¾ × 2¾ inches (7 × 25 × 7 cm)
overall: $42\frac{1}{8}$ × 19¾ × 19¾ inches (107 × 50 × 50 cm)
Edition of 20

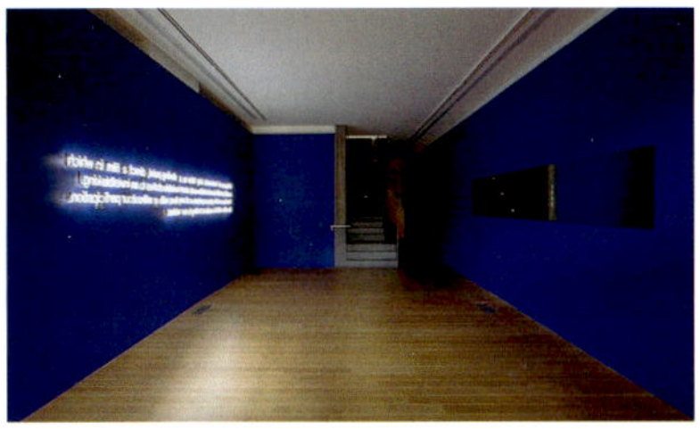

Untitled film, 2005
two parts: white neon, mirrors
$25\frac{9}{16}$ × $224\frac{7}{16}$ × $2\frac{3}{16}$ inches each
(65 × 570 × 5.5 cm)
Edition of 3

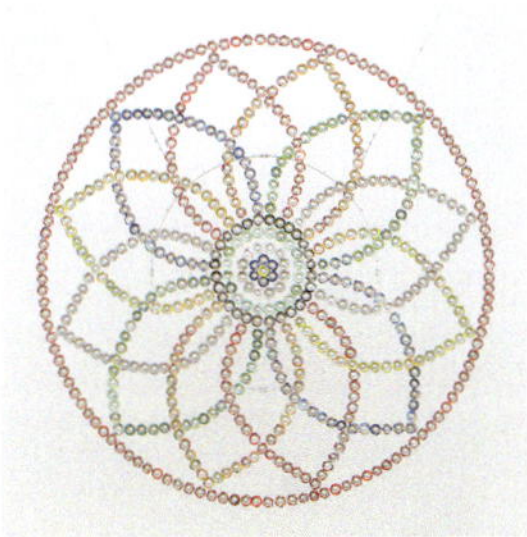

Rosace, 2007
plexiglas, soda cans
157½ inches (400 cm) diam. × ¾ inches (2 cm)

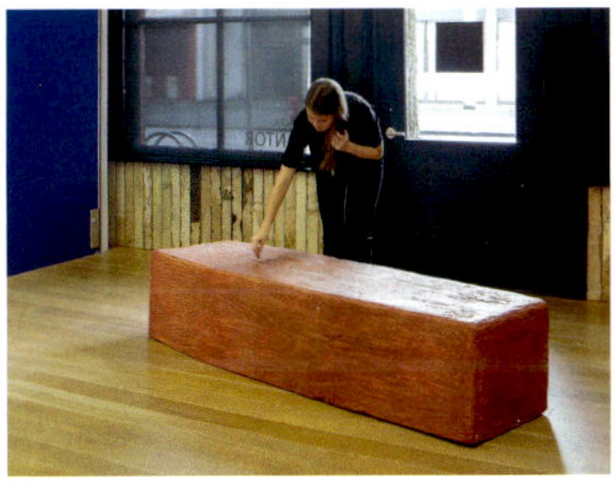

With a Free Smile, 2007
terra cotta
$76\frac{3}{8}$ × 23½ × 16½ inches
(194 × 59.7 × 42 cm)
Edition of 3

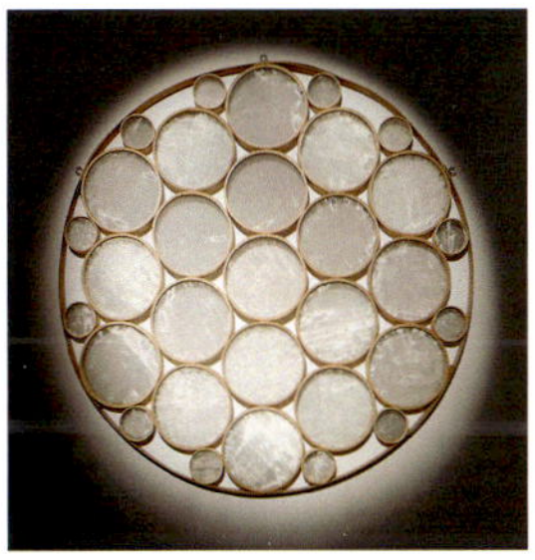

Don't Judge, Filter, Shoot, 2012
sieves, golden bullets, concrete bullets
$137\frac{13}{16}$ inches (350 cm) diam. × $3\frac{15}{16}$ inches (10 cm)

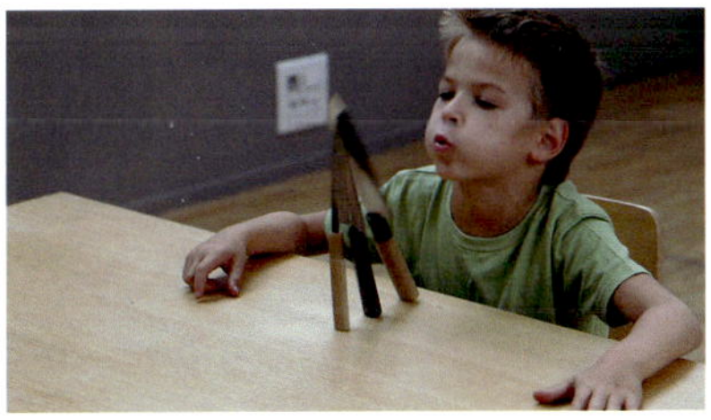

Wind Orchestra, 2012
HD video, colour, sound
duration: 13 sec, looped
Edition of 7

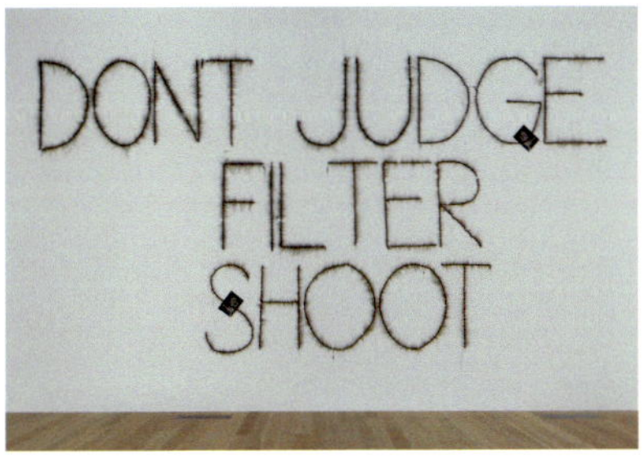

Untitled, 2012–2014
Quickmatch, clear tape
$135\frac{11}{16}$ × $334\frac{5}{8}$ inches
(344.6 × 850 cm)

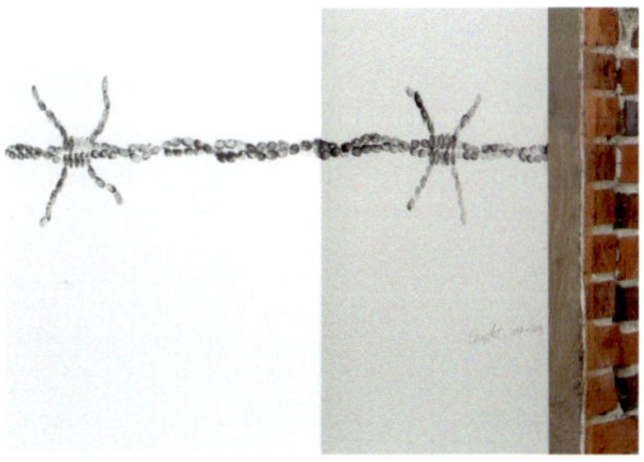

Chaplet, 2007–2014
oil-based ink
installation dimensions variable

SELECT BIOGRAPHY

Born 1977 Romania
Lives and works on Earth

2003 DNAP, Ecole Régionale des Beaux-Arts, Nantes

2000 Post Graduate, Ecole Régionale des Beaux-Arts, Nantes
Corso Superiore di Arti Visive Fondazione Antonio Ratti, Como

1999 University of Art and Design, Cluj-Napoca, Romania

Solo Exhibitions

2018 *Adjective to Your Presence*, Fondation d'enterprise Hermès, Tokyo
Mircea Cantor, Centro de Arte Contemporáneo de Málaga, Spain

2017 *Your Ruins Are My Flag*, Fondazione Giuliani, Rome

2016 *La partie invisible de l'infini*, L'atelier Brancusi (Centre Pompidou), Paris
5775 (Part II) by Mircea Cantor, Dvir Gallery, Tel Aviv
SOLO SHOW – Part III, Fondation Francès, Senlis, France
SOLO SHOW – Part II, Fondation Francès, Senlis
SOLO SHOW – Part I, Fondation Francès, Senlis

2015 *ART UNLIMITED – Special Project*, Art Basel, Basel
Mircea Cantor – 5775 (Part I), Dvir Gallery, Tel Aviv

2014 *Mircea Cantor: Collected Works*, Rennie Museum, Vancouver
Ti do la mia giovinezza, Magazzino d'Arte Moderna, Rome

2013 *Mircea Cantor: Q.E.D,* National Museum of Contemporary Art, Bucharest

2012 *Mircea Cantor: Prix Marcel Duchamp 2011,* Centre Pompidou, Paris
Special screenings at TIFF, Transylvania International Film Festival, Cluj-Napoca, Romania
Sic Transit Gloria Mundi, MACRO – Museo d'Arte Contemporanea Roma, Rome
RESTLESS: Films and Other Works, Museum of the Moving Image, New York City

2011 *Phishing,* Salzburger Kunstverein, Salzburg
More Cheeks Than Slaps, Le Crédac, Ivry-sur-Seine, France

2010 *Heilige Blumen (Holy Flowers)*, Kunsthalle Nürnberg, Nuremberg
Solo Screening of Vertical Attempt, KW Institute for Contemporary Art, Berlin
Shooting, Dvir Gallery, Tel Aviv
Klug wie die Schlangen und einfältig wie die Tauben / Wise As Serpents and Innocent As Doves, Museum Abteiberg, Mönchengladbach, Germany
Deeparture, Musée Rodin, Paris

2009 *Which Light Kills You,* The Common Guild, Glasgow
Tracking Happiness, Kunsthaus Zürich
Preventative Kiss for Suspicious War, Johnen Galerie, Berlin
White Sugar for Black Days, Galerie Yvon Lambert, Paris
The Need for Uncertainty, Camden Arts Centre, London

2008 *Future Gifts,* Mucsarnok/Kunsthalle, Budapest
The Need for Uncertainty, Arnolfini, Bristol
The Need for Uncertainty, Modern Art Oxford, Oxford

2007 *Mircea Cantor,* Magazzino d'Arte Moderna, Rome
A Free Smile, Yvon Lambert Gallery, New York City
Deeparture at Black Box, Hirshhorn Museum, Washington, D.C.
The Landscape Is Changing, Milton Keynes Gallery, Milton Keynes, UK
Ciel variable, FRAC Champagne-Ardenne, Reims, France
Deeparture, Museo Tamayo, Mexico City

2006 *The Title Is the Last Thing*, Philadelphia Museum of Art
Burn to Be Burnt, GAMeC – Galleria d'Arte Moderna e Contemporanea di Bergamo, Italy
Solo Screening of The Landscape Is Changing, Tel Aviv Museum of Art
Jucarii pentru copii (Toys for Children), Protokoll Studio, Cluj-Napoca, Romania

2005 *Mircea Cantor*, Dvir Gallery, Tel Aviv
Deeparture, Yvon Lambert Gallery, New York City
Mircea Cantor, Prix Ricard S.A., Centre Pompidou, Paris
Si tu marche plus vite, il pleut moins fort, Calouste Gulbenkian Museum, Lisbon

2004 *Preview*, Magazzino d'Arte Moderna, Rome

2003 *In Front of My Eyes*, TRANS>Area, New York City
Corporate Identity, FRAC des Pays de la Loire, Carquefou, France
Mircea Cantor, Galerie Yvon Lambert, Paris

2002 *The Right Man at the Right Place*, Galerie Yvon Lambert, Paris
Ping Pang Pong, Entre-deux Association, Nantes

1999 *Headlines*, GAD Photo-Gallery, Bucharest

Group Exhibitions

2018 *Line of Sight*, MUDAC, Musée de Design et d'Arts Appliqués Contemporains, Lausanne, Switzerland
Table Manners, Genia Schreiber University Art Gallery, University of Tel Aviv, Israel
Art Safari, Bucharest
Double Heads Matches, New Budapest Gallery

2017 *The Noise of Time*, Dvir Gallery, Tel Aviv
Bivouacs / The Walks Academy, Le Magasin CNAC, Grenoble
KIZART, Palazzo delle Esposizioni, Rome
The Electric Comma, V-A-C Foundation, Palazzo delle Zattere, Venice
Chicago, Ibiza, etc, Galerie nächst St. Stephan Rosemarie Schwarzwälder, Vienna
MOMENTA Biennale de l'image, Montreal
Innocent Materials, Dvir Gallery, Brussels
ARTDOOR, Teleki Castle, Gornesti, Romania
Notes on a Landscape – Art Safari, Kretzulescu Galleries, Bucharest
The Place to Be, Fondazione Maxxi, Rome
Violenti / Confini, Pinacoteca Comunale, Città di Castello, Italy
Placed Someplace with Intent, Dvir Gallery, Tel Aviv
Punto de Partida. Colección Isabel y Augustín Coppel, Sala de Arte Santander, Madrid
Pallaksh (I don't know just where I'm going), Dvir Gallery, Tel Aviv

2016 *Historicode: Scarcity and Supply*, Nanjing International Art Festival, Nanjing
Da Fuga e do Encontro: Inversões do Olhar, Espaço Novo Banco, Lisbon
Paravent, Dvir Gallery, Brussels
Wall to Wall: Carpets by Artists, Museum of Contemporary Art Cleveland, Cleveland
MACBA Collection 31, Museu d'Art Contemporani de Barcelona, Barcelona
Dans un monde magnifique et furieux, Dvir Gallery, Brussels
CHOICES, Palais de Tokyo, Musée d'art contemporain, Paris
DO DISTURB, Palais de Tokyo, Musée d'art contemporain, Paris
A History: Contemporary Art from the Centre Pompidou, Haus der Kunst, Munich

2015 *ArtLine Milano*, Palazzo Reale, Milan

The Nude in the XX & XXI Century, Sotheby's S|2 Gallery, London
An Autumn Afternoon, Dvir Gallery, Tel Aviv
Là où commence le jour, LaM – Lille Métropole Museum of Modern, Contemporary and Outsider Art, Villeneuve-d'Ascq, France
Appearance & Essence, Art Encounters Foundation, Timisoara, Romania
Sequential Strings, Art Encounters Foundation, Timisoara
Com'è viva la città, Villa Olmo, Como
Shibboleth, Dvir Gallery, Tel Aviv
Reflexiones, Colleccion CGAC, Santiago de Compostela
Rastros y vestigios: Indagaciones sobre el presente, Museo Amparo, Puebla, Mexico
#Anthroposynaptic – ART UNLIMITED, Art Basel, Basel
Fire and Forget. On Violence, KW Institute for Contemporary Art, Berlin
Mapping Bucharest: Art, Memory and Revolution 1916–2016, MAK – Museum of Applied Arts, Vienna
VITA VITALE, 56th Biennale di Venezia, Venice
Invitation au voyage – 15 years Marcel Duchamp prize, La Centrale, Brussels
Cluj Connection 3D, Galerie Judin, Berlin
Now, at the latest, Kunsthalle Krems, Krems, Austria

2014
Menagerie, Australian Centre for Contemporary Art, Melbourne
Zero Tolerance, MoMA PS1, New York City
Le Mur, La collection Antoine de Galbert, La Maison Rouge, Paris
La science à l'oeuvre, Centre d'art contemporain de Pontmain, Pontmain, France
Manifest Intention. Drawing in all its forms and languages, Castello di Rivoli, Turin
Me and You in a Living Room: Artists from the Ricard Foundation Award, SongEun ArtSpace, Seoul
Damage Control, Art and Destruction since 1950, Kunsthaus Graz, Graz
Fantome, Dvir Gallery, Tel Aviv
The Red Queen, MONA – Museum of Old and New Art, Hobart, Tasmania
The Disappearance of the Fireflies, Collection Lambert, Avignon
Will Happiness Find Me?, Tokyo Opera City Art Gallery, Tokyo
Les yeux seuls sont encore capables de pousser un cri, Dvir Gallery, Tel Aviv
19th Biennale of Sydney: You Imagine What You Desire, Sydney
A Few Grams of Red, Yellow, Blue. New Romanian Art, Centre for Contemporary Art, Ujazdowski Castle, Warsaw
Ichihara Art × MIX 2014, Ichihara, Japan
Il Piedistallo vuoto. Fantasmi dall'Est Europa, Museo Civico Archeologico di Bologna, Bologna
Une histoire – Art, architecture et design, des années 80 à aujourd'hui, Centre Pompidou, Paris

2013
Neuromast: Certain Uncertainty and Contemporary Art, Franklin Street Works, Stamford, Connecticut
Oeuvres de la Collection Phillippe Cohen ans d'acquisitions, Passage de Retz, Paris
0 Performance: The Fragile Beauty of Crisis / Special Projects 5th Moscow Biennale of Contemporary Art, Moscow State Exhibition Hall, Moscow
Dinard, L'Amour atomique, Palais des Arts et du Festival, Dinard, France
Together, Dvir Gallery, Tel Aviv
Le Pont, MAC – Musée d'art contemporain, Marseille
Vom Zaudern. Motive des Aufschubs, Übergangs und Abschweifens, Württembergischer Kunstverein, Stuttgart
Capitale(s), Galerie Gourvennec Ogor, Marseille
Makhno's Boys / Isaac Babel, Dvir Gallery, Tel Aviv

2012
FOOD: Reflections on Mother Earth, Agriculture and Nutrition, Musée Ariana, Geneva
Desire Lines, Australian Centre for Contemporary Art, Melbourne
Voices of Images, Palazzo Grassi-Francois Pinault Foundation, Venice
Raüme der Erinnerung, Kunsthalle Düsseldorf, Düsseldorf
TRACK, S.M.A.K., Ghent
European Travellers – Art from Cluj Today, Mucsarnok Kunsthalle, Budapest
I decided not to save the world, Salt, Istanbul
One Sixth of the Earth. Ecologies of Image, Museo de Arte Contemporáneo de Castilla y León, León, Spain

2011
Just Another Brick in the Wall, Barbara Seiler Galerie, Zürich
Big Up 6, Ecuries de Baroja, Anglet, France
I decided not to save the world, Tate Modern, London
Sphères 4, Galleria Continua, Le Moulin, Boissy-le-Châtel, France
My Paris – Collection Antoine de Galbert, me Collectors Room Berlin, Berlin
Nuit Blanche Paris, International Visual Theatre, Paris
Spin Off, Koffler Centre of the Arts, Toronto
Our Magic Hour, Yokohama Triennale, Yokohama
Rebus, Simon Lee Gallery, London

Prix Marcel Duchamp, LaM – Lille Métropole Museum of Modern, Contemporary and Outsider Art, Villeneuve d'Ascq
Characters in Search of an Exit, MOT International, London
Big Brother: Artists and Tyrants, Palais des Arts et du Festival, Dinard
The Workers, MASS MoCa, North Adams, Massachusetts
Image to be projected until it vanishes, Museion, Bolzano, Italy
Salonul de mai, Galeria Plan B, Cluj-Napoca, Romania
Alles Kannibalen? / All Cannibals?, me Collectors Room Berlin, Berlin
Communism Never Happened, Galerie CUC – Charim Unger Contemporary, Berlin
Curated by, Galerie Charim, Vienna
Life: A User's Manual, The Israel Museum, Jerusalem
The Animal Gaze, Sheffield Institute of Arts Gallery, Sheffield, Massachusetts
Investigations of a Dog, Magasin III – Museum & Foundation for Contemporary Art, Stockholm
AT THE GATES OF JERUSALEM, A BLACK SUN IS ALIGHT, Dvir Gallery, Tel Aviv
Bold Tendencies 5, Peckham Space, London
How to disappear, The Luminary Arts Center for the Arts, Saint Louis, Missouri

2010 *I Believe in Miracles*, Collection Lambert, Avignon
Les recherches d'un chien, La Maison Rouge, Paris
Höhepunkte der Kölner KunstFilmBiennal, KW Institute for Contemporary Art, Berlin
Unsichtbare Schatten – Bilder der Verunsicherung, MARTa Herford, Herford, UK
A Shot in the Dark, Walker Art Center, Minneapolis
Romances sans paroles, La Kunsthalle Mulhouse, Mulhouse, France
Over the Counter – Economy in Post-Socialist Art, Mucsarnok Kunsthalle, Budapest
Investigations of a dog, Ellipse Foundation, Alcoitão, Portugal
Face your demons, Milliken Gallery, Stockholm
Linguaggi e sperimentazioni. Giovani artisti in una collezione contemporanea, Museo d'Arte Moderna e Contemporanea di Trento e Rovereto, Rovereto, Italy
La Carillon de Big Ben, Centre d'art contemporain d'Ivry: le Crédac, Ivry-sur-Seine
Art for the World, World Expo Shanghai 2010, Shanghai
Trei culori cunosc pe lume / Ich kenne drei Farben auf Erden, Nassauischer Kunstverein, Wiesbaden
Natural History, Justina M Barnicke Gallery, University of Toronto, Toronto

Les Promesses du passé – Une histoire discontinue de l'art dans l'Ex-Europe de l'Est, Centre Pompidou, Paris
Fische hinterlassen keine Spuren, Künstlerhaus Bremen, Bremen
CUE: Artists' Videos, Vancouver Art Gallery, Vancouver
Indefinite Destinations, Depo, Istanbul
Fall Out: Desire and Disengagement in Contemporary Art, Malmö Konsthall, Malmö, Sweden

2009 *All Creatures Great and Small*, Zach ta – National Gallery of Art, Warsaw
Barock, Museo MADRE, Naples
Investigations of a Dog. Works from the FACE Collections, Fondazione Sandretto Re Rebaudengo, Turin
Les Archipels réinventés, Centre Pompidou, Paris
Reflection, PinchukArtCentre, Kiev
GO EAST II – Mudam Collection supported by KBL European Private Bankers, Musée d'Art Moderne Grand-Duc Jean, Luxembourg
El tiempo del arte, Fundación PROA, Buenos Aires
Exposition Fleuves, CNEAI – Centre national de l'estampe et de l'art imprimé, Chatou, France
THE WORLD IS YOURS, Louisiana Museum of Modern Art, Humlebæk, Denmark
Wintry, Magazzino d'Arte Moderna, Rome
Universal Code, The Power Plant, Toronto
Monument to Transformation 1989–2009, City Gallery Prague / Galerie Hlavního Města Prahy, Prague
2nd Thessaloniki Biennale, Thessaloniki
Videos Europa, Le Fresnoy, Lille
La force de l'art 02, Grand Palais, Paris
Transmission Interrupted, Modern Art Oxford, Oxford
Lichtzwang, Dvir Gallery, Tel Aviv
Shifting Identities. (Swiss) Art Now, Contemporary Art Centre, Vilnius
Portraits of the Artists as Young Artists, Galeria Andreiana Mihail, Bucharest
Travail de la rivière, Le Crédac, Ivry-sur-Seine
D'ailleurs – I Won't Play Other to Your Same, Galerie Art & Essai, Rennes
Kunst Film Biennale, Cologne

2008 *Las Líneas de la mano,* Museo Universitario de Arte Contemporáneo, Mexico City
Ricard Foundation Prize – Winzavod, Moscow Contemporary Art Center, Moscow
28th Bienal de São Paulo, São Paulo
Stop. Look. Listen: An Exhibition of Video Works, Haggerty Museum of Art, Marquette University, Milwaukee
Here is Every: Four Decades of Contemporary Art, MoMA – Museum of Modern Art, New York City

Berlin Show #1, Galeria Plan B, Berlin
I am never at home, Johnen Galerie, Berlin
Eurasia, Museo d'arte moderna e contemporanea di Trento e Rovereto, Rovereto
Be a Happy Worker: Work-to-Rule! Galerija Miroslav Kraljevic, Zagreb
Spazi Aperti, Accademia di Romania, Rome
Shifting Identities – (Swiss) Art Now, Kunsthaus Zürich
Paradies und zurück – Sammlung Rheingold Zeitgenössische Kunst, Stiftung Schloss Dyck, Jüchen, Germany
Dada East?, Zacheta National Gallery of Art, Warsaw
God and Goods – Spirituality and mass confusion, Villa Manin Centro d'Arte Contemporanea, Passariano, Italy
Locked In, Casino Luxembourg, Luxembourg
Artes Mundi 3, National Museum Cardiff, Cardiff
Mimetisme, Extra City Kunsthal, Antwerp

2007 *Solo24Ore24Stunden*, Museion, Bolzano
French Kissing in the U.S.A., The Moore Space, Miami
Taking Time, MARCO – Museo de Arte Contemporánea, Vigo, Spain
Stop. Look. Listen: An Exhibition of Video Works, Johnson Museum of Art, Cornell University, Ithaca, New York
An Atlas of Events, Calouste Gulbenkian Museum, Lisbon
Dada East? The Romanians of Cabaret Voltaire, Färgfabriken, Stockholm
House Trip, ART FORUM, Berlin
Art Projects, Galerie Yvon Lambert, Paris
Crimes & Splendors, Galerie Ron Mandos, Amsterdam
Borderline/Moving Images 2007, Borderline, Beijing
Numerica, Palazzo delle Papesse – Centro Arte Contemporanea, Siena
Rouge baiser, FRAC – Pays de la Loire, Carquefou, France
Critical Foreground, New Langton Arts, San Francisco
Love Addiction: pratiche video dal '61 ad oggi, GC.AC – Galleria Comunale d'Arte Contemporanea di Monfalcone, Monfalcone, Italy
Logiques du rêve éveillé, Instants Chavirés, Montreuil
Power Play, Artpace, San Antonio
Airs de Paris, Centre Pompidou, Paris
Brave New Worlds, Walker Art Center, Minneapolis
Fairytale, Tirana Institute of Contemporary Art, Tirana
I want to believe, Galerie Eva Presenhuber, Zürich
Confined Innocence, Art Gallery of Windsor, Ontario
Paranoia, Freud Museum, London
Temporally, The Israeli Center for Digital Art, Holon
Noise, Poëzie Zomer 07, Watou, Belgium
Hay algo de revolucionario en todo esto, Sala Parpalló, Valencia
Human Game – Vincitori e Vinti [Winners and Losers], Stazione Leopolda, Florence

2006 *Contos Dixitais*, CGAC, Santiago de Compostela
Cluj Connection, Haunch of Venison, Zürich
I Bienal de Arquitectura, Arte y Paisaje de Canarias
War is Over, 1945–2005, The Freedom of Art from Picasso to Warhol and Cattelan, Galleria d'Arte Moderna e Contemporanea, Bergamo
October Art Salon, Belgrade
Printemps de septembre, Toulouse
Dada East? The Romanians of Cabaret Voltaire, Cabaret Voltaire, Zürich
Busan Biennale, Busan
Voices of Silence, Herzliya Museum of Art, Herzliya, Israel
Paranoia, Leeds City Art Gallery, Leeds
4th Berlin Biennial for Contemporary Art, Berlin
Periferic 7: Focusing Iasi / Why Children?, Iasi, Romania
La Force de l'art, Grand Palais, Paris
Czeslaw Milosz "To Allen Ginsberg", Dvir Gallery, Tel Aviv
LESS, Strategie alternative dell'abitare, PAC – Padiglione d'Arte Contemporanea, Milan
Message Personnel, Galerie Yvon Lambert, Paris
Notre histoire, Palais de Tokyo, Musée d'art contemporain, Paris
International Biennial of Contemporary Art of Seville, Seville
Marcher, Maison des Arts Georges Pompidou, Cajarc, France
Whitstable Biennale, Whitstable, UK

2005 *Global Tour, Art Travel and Beyond*, W139, Amsterdam
May you live in interesting times, Cardiff Festival of Creative Technology, Cardiff
Modern Times, Museo d'Arte Provincia di Nuoro, Nuoro, Sardinia, Italy
Nach Rokytník, The EVN Collection, Museum Moderner Kunst Stiftung Ludwig, Vienna
On Difference, Württembergischer Kunstverein, Stuttgart
Theorema, une collection privée en Italie, Collection Lambert, Avignon
Generations of Art – 10 years at F.A.R., Fondazione Antonio Ratti, Como
The Need to Document, Kunsthaus Baselland, Basel
e-flux video rental, Project room of KW Institute of Contemporary Art, Berlin
Revolution Is on Hold, Isola Art Center, Milan
Works from the Collection, Magasin 3 Konsthall, Stockholm

Universal Experience: Art, Life, and the Tourist's Eye, Museum of Contemporary Art, Chicago
Irreducible: Contemporary Short Form Video, 1995–2005, CCA Wattis, San Francisco

2004 *Cosmopolis,* State Museum for Contemporary Art, Thessaloniki
Stock Zero (OPERA), MNAC – National Museum of Contemporary Art Bucharest, Bucharest
I'll Be Your Mirror, special project for Frieze Art Fair 2004, City Inn Westminster Hotel, London
Prosismic, Espace Paul Ricard, Paris
Nine Points of the Law, NGBK, Berlin
Cetinje Biennale, Cetinje, Montenegro
Mediterraneo, MACRO – Museo d'Arte Contemporanea di Roma
Plug in, Futura, Prague
Quick-sand, De Appel, Amsterdam
Imagine Limerick, Limerick City Gallery of Art, Limerick
New Video, New Europe: A Survey of Eastern European Video, Renaissance Society, Chicago; Tate Modern, London
The Happy Worker, Center for Curatorial Studies Museum, Bard College, Annandale-on-Hudson, New York
TEXT ground, Display Gallery, Prague
The Works I Told You About, Galerie Yvon Lambert, Paris

2003 *Phalanstère,* Centre d'art contemporain de Brétigny, Brétigny-sur-Orge, France
Tirana Biennale 2, National Gallery of Arts, Tirana
In the Gorges of the Balkans, Kunsthalle Fridericianum, Kassel
Poesis. The Everyday Differently, Kunsthalle/Mucsarnok, Budapest
Displaced, Hammer Museum, UCLA, Los Angeles
Clandestine, 50th Biennale di Venezia, Venice
Unoccupied Territories, K&S gallery, Berlin
International Film Festival, with Smen video, Rotterdam

2002 *ForwArt 2002*, Brussels
Les enfants du paradis, Galerie Yvon Lambert, Paris
Urban Tension, Museum in progress, Brussels, Vienna, Frankfurt, Rome
Boundless Borders, Billboards project in the city, Belgrade, Sarajevo, Bucharest, Thessaloniki, Kassel
Rendez-vous Roumain, Espace en Cours, Paris
A9 Forum Transeuropa, Museum Quartier, Vienna

2001 *Traversées,* ARC – Musée d'Art Moderne de la Ville de Paris, Paris
49th Biennale di Venezia, Romanian Pavillion, Venice
Jean Pierre Magazine, CNEAI – Centre national de l'estampe et de l'art imprimé, Chatou
Heimsuchung, FRAC des Pays de la Loire, Carquefou
Documents 11 young photographers, New Gallery, Bucharest
Art Judgment Show, Moderna Galerija, Ljubliana

2000 *Transitioland*, Muzeul National de Arta, Bucharest
Transferatu, Ifa Gallery, Bonn
Actif-Reactif, C.R.D.C., Nantes
One Night Stand, Klemens Gasser & Tanja Grunert Gallery, New York City
International Boutique > Public, Paris
MK2 Project Café, Paris
Voyages d'affaires (with Gabriela Vanga), ERBAN, Nantes
Say What? Eforie Gallery, Bucharest
Periferic 4, Turkish Bath, Iasi
Transferatu, Ifa Gallery, Berlin
Argos Project 2000, Vevey, Switzerland

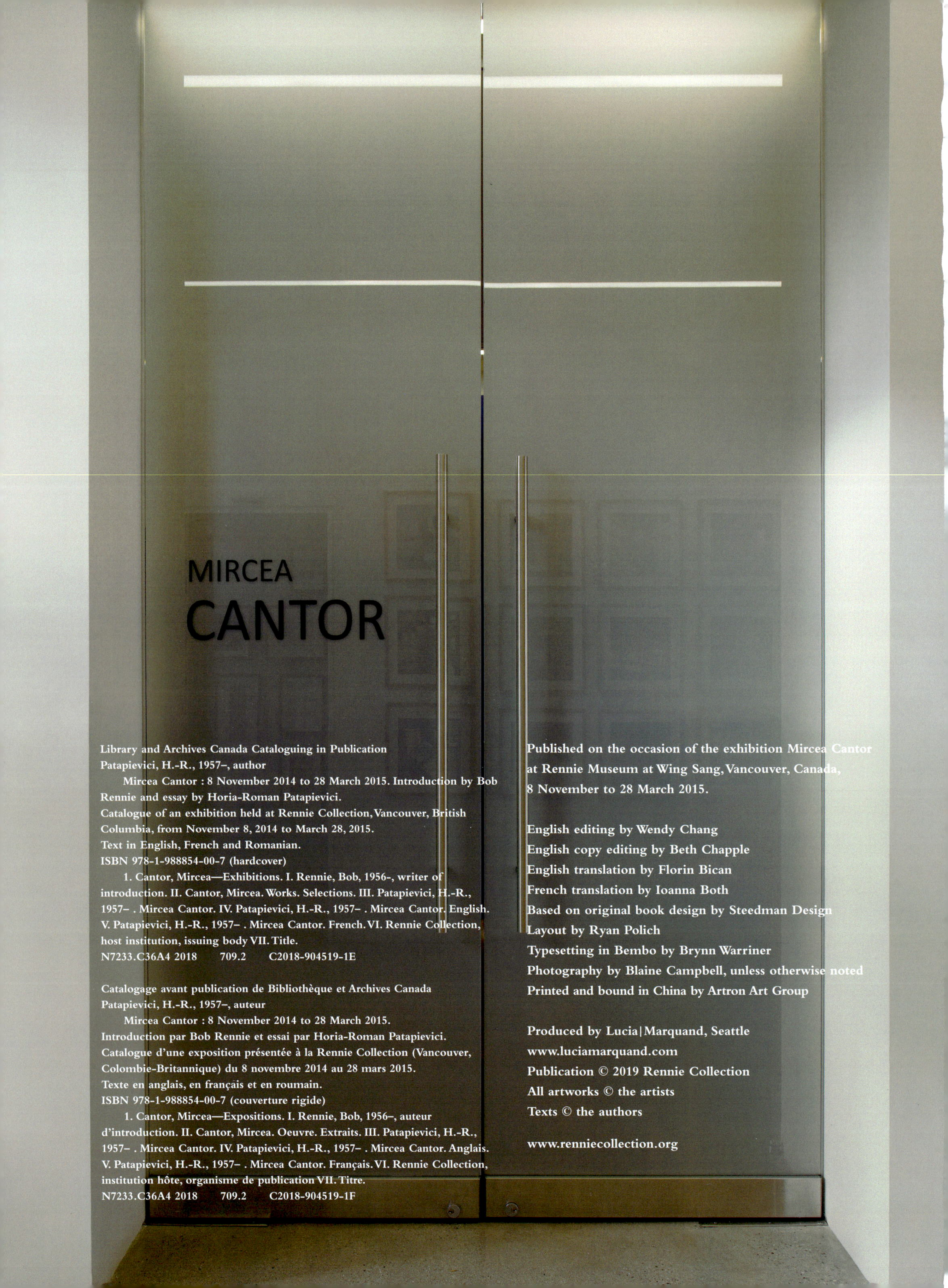

Library and Archives Canada Cataloguing in Publication
Patapievici, H.-R., 1957–, author
Mircea Cantor : 8 November 2014 to 28 March 2015. Introduction by Bob Rennie and essay by Horia-Roman Patapievici.
Catalogue of an exhibition held at Rennie Collection, Vancouver, British Columbia, from November 8, 2014 to March 28, 2015.
Text in English, French and Romanian.
ISBN 978-1-988854-00-7 (hardcover)
1. Cantor, Mircea—Exhibitions. I. Rennie, Bob, 1956–, writer of introduction. II. Cantor, Mircea. Works. Selections. III. Patapievici, H.-R., 1957– . Mircea Cantor. IV. Patapievici, H.-R., 1957– . Mircea Cantor. English. V. Patapievici, H.-R., 1957– . Mircea Cantor. French. VI. Rennie Collection, host institution, issuing body VII. Title.
N7233.C36A4 2018 709.2 C2018-904519-1E

Catalogage avant publication de Bibliothèque et Archives Canada
Patapievici, H.-R., 1957–, auteur
Mircea Cantor : 8 November 2014 to 28 March 2015.
Introduction par Bob Rennie et essai par Horia-Roman Patapievici.
Catalogue d'une exposition présentée à la Rennie Collection (Vancouver, Colombie-Britannique) du 8 novembre 2014 au 28 mars 2015.
Texte en anglais, en français et en roumain.
ISBN 978-1-988854-00-7 (couverture rigide)
1. Cantor, Mircea—Expositions. I. Rennie, Bob, 1956–, auteur d'introduction. II. Cantor, Mircea. Oeuvre. Extraits. III. Patapievici, H.-R., 1957– . Mircea Cantor. IV. Patapievici, H.-R., 1957– . Mircea Cantor. Anglais. V. Patapievici, H.-R., 1957– . Mircea Cantor. Français. VI. Rennie Collection, institution hôte, organisme de publication VII. Titre.
N7233.C36A4 2018 709.2 C2018-904519-1F

Published on the occasion of the exhibition Mircea Cantor at Rennie Museum at Wing Sang, Vancouver, Canada, 8 November to 28 March 2015.

English editing by Wendy Chang
English copy editing by Beth Chapple
English translation by Florin Bican
French translation by Ioanna Both
Based on original book design by Steedman Design
Layout by Ryan Polich
Typesetting in Bembo by Brynn Warriner
Photography by Blaine Campbell, unless otherwise noted
Printed and bound in China by Artron Art Group

Produced by Lucia|Marquand, Seattle
www.luciamarquand.com

www.renniecollection.org

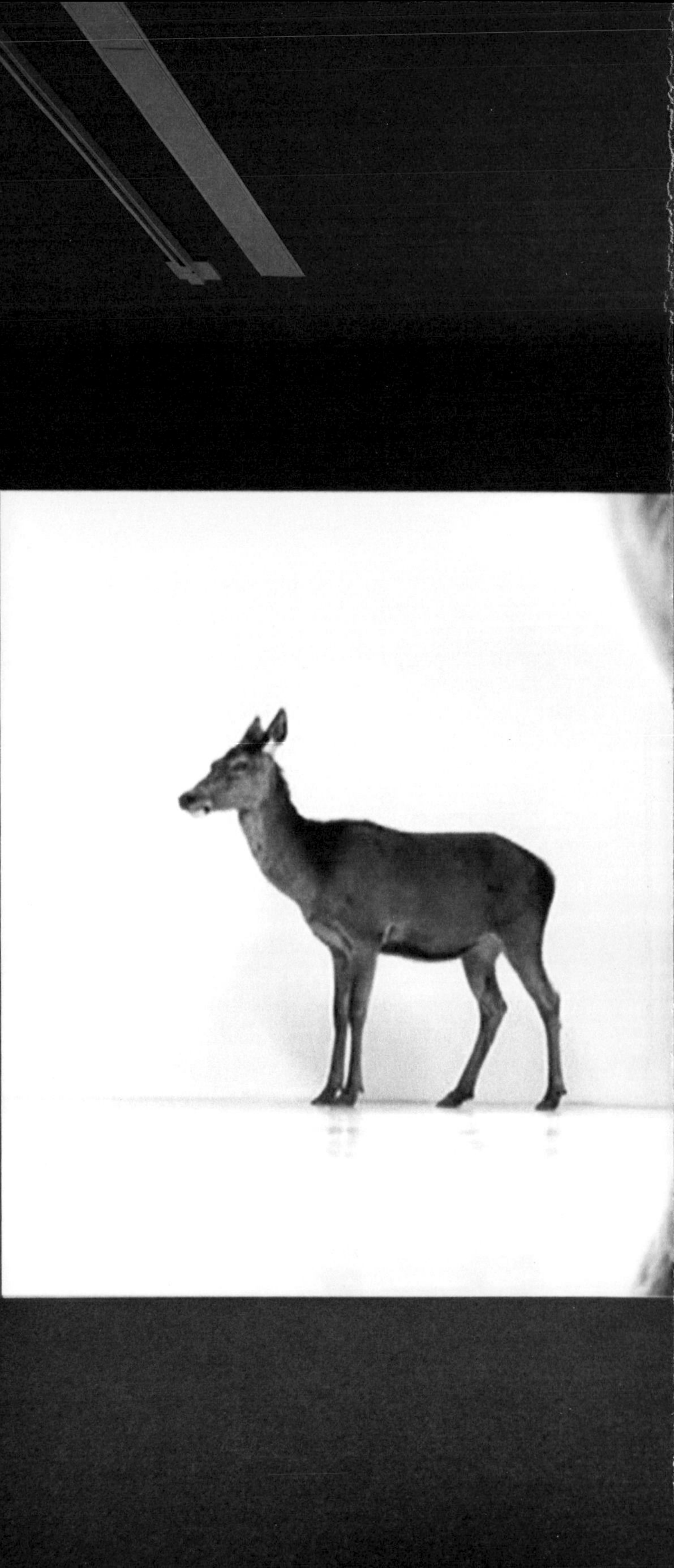